Integrating Service Learning and Multicultural Education in Colleges and Universities

Integrating Service Learning and Multicultural Education in Colleges and Universities

Edited by

Carolyn R. O'Grady
Gustavus Adolphus College

 LAWRENCE ERLBAUM ASSOCIATES, PUBLISHERS
2000   Mahwah, New Jersey   London

Lawrence Erlbaum Associates, Inc., Publishers
10 Industrial Avenue
Mahwah, NJ 07430

Cover design by Kathryn Houghtaling Lacey

Library of Congress Cataloging-in-Publication Data

Integrating service learning and multicultural education in colleges and universities / edited by Carolyn R.
O'Grady
   p. cm.
Includes bibliographical references and index.
ISBN 0-8058-3344-7 (cloth : alk. paper) — ISBN
0-8058-3345-5 (pbk. : alk. paper)
Student service—United States. 2. Multicultural education—United States. 3. Community and college—United States. I. O'Grady, Carolyn R.
   LC220.5 .I58 2000
378'.017'0973—dc21
                              99-087306
                                  CIP

Books published by Lawrence Erlbaum Associates are printed
on acid-free paper, and their bindings are chosen for strength and
durability.

Printed in the United States of America
10 9 8 7 6 5 4 3 2 1

Contents

Foreword   ix
Sonia Nieto

Preface   **xiii**
Carolyn R. O'Grady

1   Integrating Service Learning and Multicultural   **1**
Education: An Overview
Carolyn R. O'Grady

Part I: Theoretical Frameworks   **21**

2   Beyond Empathy: Developing Critical Consciousness   **23**
Through Service Learning
Cynthia Rosenberger

3   Service Learning and Multicultural Education: **45**
Suspect or Transformative?
Kathleen Densmore

4   Service-Learning: Does It Promote or Reduce   **59**
Prejudice?
Joseph A. Erickson and Susan E. O'Connor

5   Reconciling Service Learning and the Moral   **71**
Obligations of the Professor
Kip Téllez

6   From a Distance: Service-Learning and Social   **93**
Justice
Rahima C. Wade

Part II: Reports From the Field   113

7 Developing a Critical Pedagogy of Service Learning: 115
Preparing Self-Reflective, Culturally Aware,
and Responsive Community Participants
Kathleen Rice and Seth Pollack

8 Social Justice, Service Learning,   135
and Multiculturalism as Inseparable Companions
Herbert L. Martin, Jr. and Terri A. Wheeler

9 We Made the Road by Talking: Teaching Education   153
310, "Service-Learning With Multicultural Elders"
at the University of Michigan
Stella Raudenbush and Joe Galura

10 Teaching Diversity Through Service-Learning   169
Immigrant Assistance
Robert E. Koulish

11 Service-Learning and Social Reconstructionism: 189
A Critical Opportunity for Leadership
Verna Cornelia Simmons and Wokie Roberts-Weah

12 The Construction of Meaning: Learning From   209
Service Learning
Marilynne Boyle-Baise with Patricia Efiom

13 The Empowering Role of Service Learning in the   227
Preparation of Teachers
Irma Guadarrama

**Part III: Integrating Service Learning   245
and Multicultural Education in Higher Education:
Promises and Possibilities**

14 Maximizing Impact, Minimizing Harm: **247**
     Why Service-Learning Must More Fully Integrate
     Multicultural Education
     Mark Langseth

15 Strengthening Multicultural Education With   **263**
     Community-Based Service Learning
     Christine E. Sleeter

     Afterword   **277**
     Carolyn R. O'Grady

     Author Index   **281**

     Subject Index   **287**

     About the Contributors   **297**

Foreword

Sonia Nieto
University of Massachusetts, Amherst

Years ago, our younger daughter, Marisa, then about 11 years old, was taking part in an organized walk to raise money for an organization that brings young men from urban areas to attend our local high school. I remember someone saying to me, "Oh, it's great that she's learning to do charity work so young."

At first taken aback by the term, I realized that in a particular frame of reference, "charity work" was exactly what Marisa was doing. But I had not thought of it in this way. The term *charity* has always bothered me because it implies a detached beneficence that comes from privilege. Civic obligation is missing in charity work. Similarly, there is no sense of civic responsibility in some conceptions of community service learning.

Community service: the very phrase conjures up images of doing good deeds in impoverished, disadvantaged (primarily Black and Brown) communities by those (mostly White people) who are wealthier and more privileged. The parenthetical terms are seldom expressly mentioned in community service because they make some professors and students uncomfortable, exposing the inequalities around them too explicitly. There is a feeling of noblesse oblige in community service, of doing something to feel righteous, to "do my part." This book challenges the perception of community service as charity, replacing it with the notion of civic responsibility in a pluralistic but unequal society.

What exactly is community service learning? What is its place in colleges and universities, particularly those in or near communities in need? At the heart of these questions is the issue of difference. One cannot help but notice, for instance, that the primary recipients of community service are those who society has deemed disadvantaged in some way, be it through their social class, race, ethnicity, ability, or any combination of these. Those who do community service at colleges and universities, on the other hand, are generally young people who have more advantages than those they are serving. This being the case, concerns about racism and other biases, injustice, oppression, and unearned privilege should figure prominently in discussions of community service. Yet, a framework of social justice is missing in much of the work that has up to now been done in community service learning.

I have been waiting for a book like this for a long time. As a multicultural educator, I have been skeptical of service learning for some of the reasons I have already mentioned. For years I have incorporated some aspect of service learning in my courses, and I was one of the first faculty members at my campus to develop a semester-long community service learning course. But I have not fully embraced it because, despite my best efforts, I have found it difficult to dislodge the perception that community service is missionary work. This book has given me a framework with which to approach this predicament, and I know it will do the same for other educators interested in using community service learning with a critical multicultural lens.

The editor and chapter authors of this book have taken on an immense challenge: to integrate community service learning with multicultural education so that together they inform and redefine one another. It is an awesome task. It means diving headlong into turbulent ideological waters concerning such issues as difference, meritocracy, unequal access to power, and the very purpose of education. By embedding community service learning within the discourse of democracy, social justice, and equality, they have dared our society to live up to its lofty but unfulfilled promises.

The learning in community service is taken seriously by the authors in this book. The editor does an admirable job of framing community service learning and multicultural education as potentially transformative processes and philosophical positions. The chapter authors provide numerous poignant examples of their failures and successes, and of the inherent problems in attempting to affect both the academy and their students through community service learning. Not simply content with immersing students in service for its own sake, they are committed as well to upsetting students' taken-for-granted assumptions about society and about the people with whom they interact in their community service experiences. They ask students to identify cultural and political problems that develop during their service experience, and to ponder why this might be so. They force students to think deeply about what it means to live in a democratic society, and about the links among race, class, gender, and poverty in the United States. The authors in this book help their students—mostly White and economically privileged—to move beyond their stereotypical notions of difference to an understanding of the structural and deep-seated inequities in our society. In doing so, they also move community service learning from a human relations approach to a more transformative model of civic conscience. It is this stance that helps shift community service learning from an individual feel-good experience to a social responsibility.

Caring cannot be taught. This is especially true in courses that focus solely on the head, removing social issues to the sphere of intellectual problems. But caring can be modeled, and community service learning is one of the few places in the academy where this is most likely to happen. Unfortunately, even in community service learning courses, the notion of caring is often perceived only as an individual concern for the "unfortunate" and "underprivileged," and this perception does little to confront the institutionalized nature of inequality. But when an ethic of care is modeled within a framework of inquiry about broad-based inequality and oppression, as O'Grady has done in this book, the potential to change hearts as well as heads is enhanced. Given the increasing diversity in our society and the growing economic disparities between the haves and have-nots, this is a particularly important challenge for our nation at the beginning of the 21st century.

Preface

Attention in higher education to the fields of service learning and multicultural education has exploded since the late 1980s, with more colleges and universities requiring graduation requirements focusing on diversity issues, or on community service, or on both. However, little has been done by theorists or practitioners in either field to make explicit connections between the two pedagogies, a surprising lack for two approaches that share so many fundamental perspectives on education and society. This book is an attempt to forge a dialogue among practitioners of service learning and of multicultural education, and points the way toward promising means of integrating the best of each.

The changes in our nation's demographics as well as the ongoing debate about educational reform make a dialogue about service learning and multicultural education especially important at this time. Although there is no panacea for the troubles that beset our society and our schools, the stronger the coalitions that are forged among those working for educational change, the more effective and long-lasting that change will be. This book offers one avenue for creating connections between multicultural education and service learning practitioners who are at the forefront of educational change efforts. Higher education faculty, administrators, or staff who are involved with or interested in service learning, community–school partnerships, multiultural education, and/or diversity initiatives will find this book particularly valuable in providing theoretical underpinnings for the integration of service learning and multicultural education, with practical approaches for this integration.

The impetus for this book stems from my commitment to multicultural education for social justice. This approach is described in more detail in chapter 1 and is marked not only by cognitive learning, but also incorporates an activist component that I believe is best met through service learning. This approach provides not only a better educational experience for all students, but also builds their capacity for active citizenship to change the world for the better.

Academic study alone reveals only a surface understanding of the complexity of another culture (Berry, 1990). However, practical community-based experience alone is also insufficient, allowing for easy dismissal of a culture by those who focus only on perceived weak-

nesses rather than on strengths of diverse communities and who attempt to "fix" a "needy" community. Service learning without a focused
attention to the complexity of racial and cultural difference can reinforce dominant hegemonic cultural ideology, but academic work that
seeks to deconstruct these norms regarding race and culture without
providing a community-based touchstone isolates students and
schools from the realities of the larger communities of which they are a
part. The argument of this book is that academic study in multicultural education must be combined with community-based service experiences that explicitly reinforce this critical approach. This fusion
provides the most compelling learning experiences for students and,
ultimately, the most potential for creating evolutionary social change.

Lest I sound hopelessly naive and optimistic, let me stress that I believe this kind of change happens slowly and incrementally. Often the
seeds that are sown to create change take more than a lifetime to ma-
ture. Welch (1990) pointed out that it is typical of White, middle-class
change agents to expect change to happen quickly. Many of us become
easily discouraged when our vision of how things could be seems far
from actualized. This loss of hope is debilitating and creates a sense of
powerlessness and apolitical apathy. The result is despair, and with-
drawal from any attempt at trying to make a difference. The challenge to
work for social transformation in the face of seemingly insurmountable
suffering and unrelenting social crises means we must sustain hope,
even when there is no convincing guarantee that change will occur.

> Such a situation calls for an ethic of risk, an ethic that begins with the
> recognition that we cannot guarantee decisive changes in the near future
> or even in our lifetime. The ethic of risk is propelled by the equally vital
> recognition that to stop resisting, even when success is unimaginable, is
> to die. (Welch, 1990, p. 20)

This commitment to "making the effort" is what is called for in a
multicultural education approach that is integrated with the activism
of service learning. Such an approach includes enabling all students
(not only those who are "culturally different") to see the world through
a variety of perspectives. The academic rigor of multicultural education in tandem with service learning requires students to examine
taken-for-granted assumptions and to think critically and comprehen-
sively about human issues that are basic to the quality of human life.
The complexity of human existence requires the ability to view the
world from multiple perspectives. Rhoads (1997) points out that
higher education should prepare people for their life's work, but even
more, it should develop people who "are willing to seek understanding

about others within their communities, their country, and around the world" (p. 208).

The chapters that follow provide varied perspectives into the benefits and challenges of integrating multicultural education and service learning. Although each of the authors included in this text approach service learning and multicultural education from slightly different perspectives, they all are committed to a vision of education that synthesizes both action and reflection. Chapter 1 provides an introduction to the fields of service learning and multicultural education and a rationale for their integration in higher education. This chapter introduces several themes with which practitioners of service learning and multicultural education must grapple, including the meaning of "community" within the context of a social justice service learning pedagogy, the politics of service learning and multicultural education, the implications of these approaches in a democratic nation, and the moral imperative of educating for social justice. In chapters 2 through 6, the authors expand on these themes in order to lay the theoretical groundwork for the specific models described in Part II. Chapters 7 through 13 present reports from the field, actual ways in which the integration of service learning and multicultural education has or has not been successful. These chapters provide rich material for considering both the strengths and challenges of multicultural service learning in education. Finally, in Part III, chapters 14 and 15 consider from two perspectives the imperative need for the integration of service learning and multicultural education.

None of the authors in this book pretend to have all the answers for what this integration should look like, nor do they believe that today's social problems are easily ameliorated through education. Rather, these authors share theories, practices, failures, and triumphs in order to further our conversation about the importance of aligning what educators *say* about the world with how we *act* in and on it. These authors share the view that multicultural education is truly transformative for students only when it includes a community action component, and likewise, service learning is truly a catalyst for change only when it is done from a multicultural and socially just perspective. It is our hope that the ideas explored in this book will further the work of those who share a commitment to the integration of action and reflection.

ACKNOWLEDGMENTS

I am indebted to the individuals who contributed to this book, both for engaging in this conversation with me on a public front, and for their commitment to enacting their vision for education against all the odds. Special thanks go to friends and colleagues who encouraged this project and provided a sounding board for many of the ideas in this book, including Mark Langseth, Mike Miller, Christine Sleeter, Candace Thomas, and Rahima Wade. A special tribute goes to Jim Bonilla, my role model for living a life that integrates engaged service with a passion for social justice. The staff at Lawrence Erlbaum Associates, Naomi Silverman, Lori Hawver, and Robin Marks Weisberg provided encouragement and technical support. The final organization of the text was improved considerably by an early review from Kathleen de Marrais at the University of Georgia. Finally, the inspirational view of the Bay offered by Eric Bohr, Ellen Rinehart, and Daisy Rinehart-Bohr is what got this project off the ground.

—Carolyn O'Grady

REFERENCES

Berry, H. A. (1990). Service-learning in international and intercultural settings. In J. C. Kendall & Associates (Eds.), *Combining Service and Learning: A Resource Book for Community and Public Service* (Vol. 1, pp. 311–313). Raleigh, NC: National Society for Internships and Experimental Education.

Rhoads, R. A. (1997). *Community service and higher learning: Explorations of the caring self.* New York: State University of New York Press.

Welch, S. D. (1990). *A feminist ethic of risk.* Minneapolis: Fortress Press.

Integrating Service Learning and Multicultural Education: An Overview

Carolyn O'Grady
Gustavus Adolphus College

I first heard the term *multicultural education* in 1986 when I signed up for a graduate course in what would become the winding road toward a doctorate in that field. By the time I took this course, my understanding of "culture" had expanded considerably beyond where it had been when I grew up in Idaho in the 1950s. I had lived for several years in New York City, and not long before taking the class, I had returned from more than 15 months of travel outside the United States. By 1986, I had learned through experience that there were a lot of different kinds of people in the world, and that my White, middle-class upbringing was not the "norm" for everyone. I had also begun to realize that some of the attitudes I had toward others whom I perceived as different from myself were based on prejudices I had absorbed growing up or had believed without examination (O'Grady, 1999). From the beginning, the theory and practice of multicultural education helped me make sense of the life experiences I had had, and reflect more critically on how my schooling had educated and miseducated me about the world.

In my very first multicultural education class, we participated as a group in an antiapartheid rally. This was the first time I had ever been asked to take my learning outside the classroom and apply it in some community-based context. I have forgotten much of the reading we did in that class, but I will never forget the experiential component. I did not realize it at the time, but my participation in the rally bore similarities to more intentional service learning activities.

1

I first heard the term *service learning* in 1990 when I became friends with a teacher who was very involved in implementing service learning practices in education. Despite my positive reaction to the more experiential component of my multicultural education class, however, I initially dismissed the concept of service learning. Quite frankly, at the time it struck me as a nice way for well-intentioned White people to feel good about "helping" others. I had a hard time at first distinguishing the concept of service learning from that of volunteerism, and I knew nothing of the relevance service has historically had for many cultural groups. When I came to the college where I now teach, I was challenged by our then service learning director to view service learning as a vehicle for social justice. In collaboration with her, I began to research service learning and to implement it in my own classroom teaching. The results were mixed (O'Grady & Chappell, 1999), but the outcome was that I began to see the ways in which service learning and multicultural education had powerful theories and methods to offer each other.

My own experience in integrating service learning and multicultural education has led me to understand some of the challenges involved, but also how imperative it is for each approach to incorporate aspects of the other. To teach about multicultural issues from a theoretical perspective *without* incorporating a service learning component only widens the theory–practice split articulated by Gay (1995). However, this integration is problematic without both an understanding of the fundamental theories in each field and an analysis of the significant issues raised by such an integration. Points of convergence, as well as points of tension, are explored in this chapter as well as in those that follow.

EDUCATION AS CONTESTED TERRITORY

Before continuing, it is necessary to pause and remind ourselves of the contested nature of education. Education has always been "contested territory," with conflicting and divergent interests competing for dominance. The history of public education in the United States is filled with conflicting demands over what should be taught, how, and by whom. Nieto (1996) described schooling as "a dynamic process in which competing interests and values are at work every day in complex and often contradictory ways" (p. 8). A key difference between service learning and multicultural education is that the latter grew out of an explicitly political movement for civil rights and is often accused of having a political agenda. This does not mean, however, that service learning is not political. Too often the term *politics* is believed to have negative connotations, and discussion of political motives in a movement or perspective is discouraged. Yet, as Morgan (1986) pointed out, the fundamental meaning of politics is the manner in which interests, conflict, and power are used to resolve differences among individuals or groups. Consequently, it is an exercise in tunnel vision to believe that decisions about education are politically neutral. Analyzing the interplay of competing interests that produce conflict among participants in an educational setting, and how power is used by those involved to achieve resolution, provides us with a deeper understanding of the ideology that governs behavior. In reality, all educational approaches can be seen as different avenues to resolving competing interests through the use of power (Morgan, 1986).

This relationship between interests, conflict, and power provides a context for the approach this book advocates of combining multicultural education with an activist component. Thus, while the original impetus for multicultural education emerged from a clearly political perspective (and has been unfairly maligned because of this), much of service learning also grew out of a different, but equally definitive, political ideology about the world. This ideology includes assumptions made by those in the field of service learning about the relationship between the individual and society, the role of democracy, the meaning of justice and compassion in alleviating suffering in the world, and about power, conflict, and group interest.

MULTICULTURAL EDUCATION

Christine Sleeter (1996) pointed out that one way to view multicultural education is as "a form of resistance to oppressive social relationships" (p. 10). Emerging from the civil rights movements of the 1960s, multicultural educators who focus on social justice as a goal have increasingly emphasized the role that oppression and social power play in perpetuating inequitable social arrangements. I follow Adams, Bell, and Griffin (1997) and use the term *oppression* rather than discrimination, bias, or prejudice "to emphasize the pervasive nature of social inequality woven throughout social institutions as well as embedded within individual consciousness" (p. 4). Oppression is reinforced by the disempowerment of subordinated or targeted groups by members of dominant or privileged groups. Each of us participates in multiple group memberships based on our race, socioeconomic status, gender, sexual orientation, and so forth, and to that degree, our personal and social power and privilege are relative. Nevertheless, each of us is also a member of a society founded on and perpetuating White male supremacist ideology and, depending on our social identities, some of us have greater access to power and privilege than others. Both the process and the goal of equal participation of all groups in society is the purpose of multicultural education.

Sleeter and Grant's (1987) review of approaches to multicultural education is helpful in identifying the method used by those who claim to be multicultural educators. *Teaching the Culturally Different* focuses on the perceived needs of children of color or others who do not fit the standard cultural norm and emphasizes assimilation as a desirable goal. *Human Relations* emphasizes intergroup dynamics and "getting along" with others while avoiding broader issues of conflict. Often this approach can be identified by language that emphasizes similarities rather than differences. Each of these first two approaches stems from a political perspective based on a unitary view of society (Morgan, 1986). In this view, individuals are united under an umbrella of common interests, conflict is seen as negative and destructive, and the role of power differentials is largely ignored.

The third approach, *Single Group Studies*, teaches about a specific group's history and culture and includes such programs as Black studies, women's studies, and so on, often failing to articulate interconnections among groups. The *Multicultural Education* approach advocates reform of school processes to meet the interests of a pluralistic society but may overlook issues of conflict caused by structural power and oppression. These last two approaches are based on what Morgan (1986) termed "pluralist political views." In this perspective, diversity is regarded as central to understanding individual and group interests, conflict is considered potentially positive, and power is regarded as a crucial variable through which conflicts of interest are alleviated or solved.

Although each of these four approaches to multicultural education can offer valuable strategies and perspectives for creating more equitable educational structures, they do not address underlying causes of social inequity. The fifth approach, *Social Reconstructionist Multicultural Education*, teaches directly about oppression, discrimination, social justice, and how to take action against these inequities. As Banks (1991) noted, "The knowledge that is institutionalized within the schools and the larger society neither enables students to become reflective and critical citizens nor helps them to participate effectively in their society in ways that will make it more democratic and just" (p. 125). Schooling, however, while usually legitimizing the status quo, can also "enlighten and emancipate, working with rather than against . . . efforts for liberation" (Sleeter, 1991, p. 2). This multicultural approach offers a visionary model for constructive change.

As a more explicit political perspective, it emphasizes conflict as inevitable and constructive, and suggests that more radical changes in social structure are necessary to achieve equity for all. This approach to multicultural education goes beyond a focus on curriculum to examining the societal structures that limit the freedom to learn (Montero-Sieburth, 1988; Sleeter & Grant, 1987). These limits may be especially pronounced for those students who do not fit the dominant "norm" reflected through the curriculum and the school structure, which tends to emphasize middle-class, European-American values. But as Nieto (1996) pointed out, multicultural education is important for *all* students, not only those who are perceived as "culturally different." All students need to be able to see the world through a variety of lenses, without cultural blinders, and to be able to critically reflect on and analyze what they are learning and doing.

There is no doubt that education is "contested territory," with conflicting views about what is appropriate to teach and how. This very conflict about how the world can be interpreted, and by whom, should be grist for the mill in our classrooms, regardless of what students ultimately choose to do with that knowledge. When students can learn to analyze, to critically reflect on, and ultimately—if they choose to—to transform oppressive situations through action, they are engaged in a form of political activism inherent in social reconstructionist multicultural education. "Curriculum within this vein will emphasize reflection as leading to action and change (praxis). Curriculum will tend to critique the structures of oppression and ask why things are the way they are and what can be done" (Montero-Sieburth, 1988, p. 9). This approach to education offers the most promise for enabling students and educators to examine oppressive social relations and to identify strategies for creating a more just and equitable world.

However, even multicultural educators who advocate social reconstructionism are often limited by the circumstances in which they teach. Cuts in funding to public education, increasing pressures on schools from politically and socially conservative organizations, and competition for scarce resources among political and cultural groups has made it very challenging for multicultural educators to implement their vision for schools.

A more disturbing challenge has been mounted by teachers and theorists who have adopted multicultural education as a strategy without understanding or embracing the need to examine fundamental issues of social power. As Densmore (1995) described, the reforms associated with multicultural education have been concentrated in the areas of curriculum and instruction with more emphasis given to individual attitudes than to systemic issues of oppression in society. Sleeter (1996) noted that multicultural education in the 1990s has moved far from its radical origins of the 1960s, and in the process, many teachers who currently describe themselves as multicultural educators are, with the best of intentions, doing little more than reproducing social norms that perpetuate oppressive social relations. As a result, multicultural education as a field, while continually fending off attacks from the conservative right, has also become fair game for critiques from the radical left, who see multicultural education as a way to reduce the threat of social conflict caused by racial and cultural tensions (Spring, 1998) and to pacify advocates of change without making any real systemic changes (Sleeter, 1996).

Service learning, when combined with social reconstructionist multicultural education, can potentially serve as the vehicle for creating systemic change. Although research on the value of field experiences has shown mixed results, multicultural field experiences in particular seem to positively influence prospective teachers' attitudes toward individuals of a different cultural group (Grant & Tate, 1995; Powell, Zehn, & Garcia, 1996). Some of the growing research on service learning has indicated that this kind of community involvement reinforces students' cognitive understandings of multicultural issues (Giles & Eyler, 1994; Wade, 1995). Service learning can help bridge the gap between multicultural education theory and practical experience (Michalec, 1994).

SERVICE LEARNING

The term *service learning* was coined in 1969 by members of the Southern Regional Education Board doing work in Oak Ridge, Tennessee, who described it as "the accomplishment of tasks that meet genuine human needs in combination with conscious educational growth" (Stanton, Giles, & Cruz, 1999). However, the tradition of community service reaches back to early U.S. history, and people helping and caring for one another has been a part of American tradition and a practice in all cultural communities in the United States (Giles & Eyler, 1994; Kinsley & McPherson, 1995; O'Connell, 1990; Stanton, Giles, & Cruz, 1999). The notion of national service reaches from Roosevelt's establishment of the Civilian Conservation Corps in 1933 through the Peace Corps and Vista programs begun in the 1960s, to the Youth Conservation Corps of the 1970s. These government-sponsored programs were the forerunners of the service learning programs that began to spread in K–12 schools and higher education in the 1980s (Wade, 1997). Today's educational philosophy of service learning grows out of this heritage, aided by the intellectual work of such educational theorists as John Dewey, Jean Piaget, and David Kolb (Kinsley & McPherson, 1995), with reinforcement from Paolo Freire's pedagogy of the combination of action and reflection to create change (Galura, Howard, Waterhouse, & Ross, 1995). These educators laid the groundwork for integrating learning experiences into the curriculum.

Many terms have been used to describe the experiential nature of service learning: civic awareness, collaborative learning, community-based education, cooperative education, experiential education, field experiences, internships, public service, volunteerism, youth involvement, and youth service (Kendall & Associates, 1990). However, what moves service learning beyond just volunteerism or just community service is an intentional focus on the academic. In a service learning program, individuals engage in community activities in a context of rigorous academic experience. Service learning allows teachers to employ a variety of teaching strategies that emphasize student-centered, interactive, experiential education. As the Alliance for Service-Learning in Education Reform (1993) stated, "Service-learning places curricular concepts in the context of real-life situations and empowers students to analyze, evaluate, and synthesize these concepts through practical problem-solving, often in service to the community" (p. 3).

As a philosophy and a practice, service learning has seen phenomenal growth over the past 20 years, with much of the widespread discussion and support occurring since the late 1980s. In 1990, the Federal National and Community Service Act established a commission to "explore and test innovative ways to renew the ethic of civic responsibility" (Stephens, 1995). The federally legislated National Service Act of 1993 contained the following definition of service learning as a method:

- Under which students learn and develop through active participation in thoughtfully organized service experiences that meet actual community needs and that are coordinated in collaboration with the school and the community;
- That is integrated into the students' academic curriculum or provides structured time for a student to think, talk, or write about what the student did and saw during the actual service activity;
- That provides students with opportunities to use newly acquired skills and knowledge in real-life situations in their own communities; and

- That enhances what is taught in school by extending students' learning beyond the curriculum and into the community and helps to foster the development of a sense of caring for others. (Silcox, 1995, p. 25)

This definition highlights four key themes often mentioned in discussions of service learning: collaboration with the community, the importance of reflection, active learning, and the development of a sense of caring. In addition, service learning practitioners as well as educational theorists offer two additional arguments for including service learning in the formal curriculum: that it will promote a sense of civic responsibility among students, and that it will ameliorate societal problems (Barber, 1991; Boyer, 1981, 1987; Conrad & Hedin, 1991; Delve, Mintz & Stewart, 1990; Hammond, 1994; Smith, 1994; Stanton, 1990; Wade, 1997). The skills service learning attempts to enhance in students include learning how to critically reflect on their experience and how to work collaboratively with others, theoretically resulting in increased motivation for learning and strengthened social awareness and civic responsibility (Kendall & Associates, 1990).

The existing research on the efficacy of service learning in meeting these goals is still limited. Much of it was based on anecdotal evidence and has primarily focused on the experiences of secondary education students. It is traditionally difficult to gather data on an approach that is as much a process as a product and in which growth and development are key factors. Miller's 1994 review of the research concluded that students value the experience of service learning; it enhances students' self-esteem, it improves participants' social attitudes, it increases knowledge in the areas directly related to the service experience, it improves the integration of theory and practice, and it is most effective when combined with opportunities for students to reflect on their experiences. Additional research is helping to provide the kind of information that will enable service learning to establish a record of proven results (Eyler & Giles, 1999; Giles & Eyler, 1994; Waterman, 1997).

Although much of the language describing service learning appears to be politically neutral, it is vital to remember that service learning is as politically laden as any other educational approach. The long-standing relationship between service-type programs and the federal government, the emphasis on citizenship as a goal, the absence in much of the current service learning literature of analysis of issues of power, and in particular the attention in service learning to the concept of democracy, all indicate a particular ideology behind the notion of service in education.

DEMOCRACY AND COMMUNITY

The fields of service learning and multicultural education are frequently cited as avenues for enhancing democracy and for building a sense of community within the classroom and with others outside the classroom. Indeed, each approach offers the opportunity for educators and students to engage in a discussion about the meaning of community in a diverse and democratic nation. Palmer (1990) described community as "a capacity for relatedness within individuals—relatedness not only to people, but to events in history, to nature, to the world of ideas, and yes, to things of the spirit" (p. 106). This capacity for interrelatedness is an antidote to the current unrelenting emphasis on individualism in today's society.

The ability to coexist in community is at the heart of our survival as a democracy. Horton (1990) described democracy as "a philosophical concept meaning that people are really free and empowered to make collectively the decisions that affect their lives" (p. 169). Berman (1997) echoed this, defining democracy as simply "a way for people of divergent perspectives to make collective decisions" (p. 5). Rhoads (1997) pointed out that a sense of connectedness found in community is not necessarily dependent on commonality. He asserted that connectedness is "an essential aspect of the self" (p. 175) because humans are by nature social. As educators, we can contribute to community building by asking students to envision themselves as part of a larger community. Our goal in doing this is to "engage in a joint struggle for social justice and thus form a sense of community around concerns for democracy and caring" (Rhoads, 1997, p. 216).

In reviewing the service learning literature of the last 10 years, it is evident that many practitioners and theorists view service learning as a way to create positive social change through an increase in students' understanding of social responsibility. Frequently this approach to social change is articulated through the belief that service learning enhances students' civic understanding and participation. Although research in the effectiveness of community service on civic education is still limited, much of the research makes it clear that academic coursework alone has little impact on enhancing students' democratic values or civic participation (Berman, 1997). As Berman (1997) noted, students develop political consciousness when they are able to engage in "direct experience in political conflict" (p. 114). His research on social responsibility underscores the importance of making the "practice of citizenship" a component of education both inside the school and outside. Guarasci (1997) believed that through service, students build a "critical experience" in expanded citizenship through having developed "a greater commitment to social interdependence, reciprocity, and a common destiny with all those 'others' who inhabit their immediate social and professional orbits" (p. 22).

Smith (1994), however, noted that although civic responsibility or citizenship are frequently mentioned as key service learning outcomes by policymakers and theorists, students themselves rarely describe them as learnings. She made clear that unless teachers and those she called "institutional influentials" do not articulate citizenship as an outcome of service learning and pursue it concretely in the curriculum, students will continue to fail to see the connection. Indeed, Berman (1997) described as too limited the conception that most teachers and students hold about citizenship in that it "focuses attention primarily on being a good person rather than being actively engaged in the political process, on protecting self-interest rather than promoting the common good, and on the individual as the locus of responsibility rather than institutional, systemic, or structural aspects of our political culture" (p. 174).

Even with this rhetoric of social responsibility in the field of service learning, however, there are few analyses of issues of diversity in the service learning literature and even fewer discussions of racism or issues of social power and oppression. Yet, as Stanton, Eyler, and Cruz (1999) pointed out in their history of the field, the earliest expressions of service learning made specific connections between service in a community and larger social justice issues. One of the earliest service learning programs, the Lisle Fellowship established in the 1930s, had as its goal to engage students in cross-cultural service learning experiences. In this process, students worked in multiracial and intergenerational teams in short and intensive service projects followed by group discussion and reflection on the issues that arose during their work together. These conversations echo what Berman (1997) believed is important in exploring citizenship within a democracy, to ask "how we can change social structures so that our society becomes a better place in which to live" and, further, to ask "how power and wealth should be shared" (p. 182).

A few service learning writers explicitly articulate an antiracist or antioppression approach (Aparicio & Jose-Kampfner, 1995; Cruz, 1990; Fox, 1994; Guarasci, Cornwell, & Associates, 1997; Hall, 1991a, 1991b, 1992, 1995; Kraft & Swadener, 1994; Mintz & Hesser, 1997; Rhoads, 1997; Waldock, 1995). In addition, many in the field of service learning emphasize the importance of mutuality in the school–community relationship (Delve et al., 1990; Galura, Meiland, Ross, Callan, & Smith, 1993; Howard, 1993; Jacoby, 1997; Kendall, 1990; Rhoads, 1997; Roberts-Weah, 1995; Stephens, 1995; Wade,

1997). However, much of the discussion about multicultural issues in service learning sounds like the Human Relations approach to multicultural education in emphasizing reducing prejudice and getting along with others (Sleeter & Grant, 1987). Too many writers in the field of service learning use terms such as "students" or "communities" with the implication that they mean all students or all communities when in fact they are referring to White students and middle-class communities. Like the Human Relations approach, this unitary view of society (Morgan, 1986) emphasizes only common interests and regards conflict and explicit attention to power as subjects to be avoided.

Jacoby (1997), for instance, while affirming that service learning is about social justice, is uncomfortable with service learning being perceived as a political stance and emphasized that it is a philosophy and pedagogy. Her concern was that service learning participants would be unduly influenced by the political values of proponents or practitioners. Yet because education is "contested territory," in which the relations between interest, conflict, and power are perpetually being played out (Morgan, 1986), teachers who do not specifically explicate political positions can neither teach students the multiple meanings of e pluribus unum nor help students understand the political dimensions of civic responsibility. It is imperative that the analysis of structural politics in education be as rigorous as the analysis of any other aspect of education if educators hope to help students identify possibilities for change. As Rhoads (1997) pointed out, "notions of citizenship often are vague and need to be anchored in a clear understanding of what kind of society we desire. There can be no vision of citizens or citizenship without a vision of society" (p. 208).

To a multicultural educator involved in service learning, these distinctions must be central in identifying cultural issues that arise during the service experience. In describing two service learning projects that combined students' research with service in two low-income, minority urban communities, Reardon (1994) noted two central benefits to students in doing this kind of work:

- Firsthand knowledge of the devastating impact that urban poverty and racial discrimination can have on family and community life;
- A deeper understanding of the social, economic and political dynamics that contribute to increasing levels of social inequality in our major cities . . . (p. 52)

He further reminded us that students who do not get adequate opportunity to reflect on their experiences ". . . may end up embracing stereotypic beliefs about the community residents with whom they are working. While such service may enhance the students' feelings of self-worth and moral virtue, it may contribute little to their intellectual and practical understanding of social justice and racial inequality" (p. 53) and may therefore perpetuate stereotypes that students already have.

SERVICE AND SOCIAL JUSTICE

This warning that students' stereotypes might be strengthened rather than diminished has been echoed by a number of service learning theorists (Anderson & Guest, 1994; Berry, 1990; Kretzmann & McKnight, 1993; Levison, 1990; Reardon, 1994; Tellez, Hlebowitsh, Cohen, & Norwood, 1995; Waldock, 1995). McPherson and Kinsley (1995) described five challenges that face the service learning field, and cautioned that service learning: (1) must not reinforce old stereotypes and perpetuate a duality between the server and the recipient, perpetuating paternalism; (2) must address significant issues that are real social justice issues; (3) must not be trivialized through rote or repetition; (4) must involve real collaboration with the community; and (5) that service learning practitioners must be clear about their deeper motivations for utilizing service learning.

Without the theoretical underpinnings provided by multicultural education, service learning can too easily reinforce oppressive outcomes. It can perpetuate racist, sexist, or classist assumptions about others and reinforce a colonialist mentality of superiority. This is a special danger for predominantly White students engaging in service experiences in communities of color given the U.S. history of White domination of people of color. Students engaged in service, particularly White students, often do not understand the social dynamics of poverty and racism and may accept such circumstances as a given. Their ability to visualize and initiate fundamental change is consequently limited. As Sleeter (1996) noted, a multicultural curriculum must "elucidate crucial differences in perspective and experience in a way that supports genuine dialog across borders of race, ethnicity, gender, sexual orientation, and class and that galvanizes organized work toward a shared project of a just community" (p. 95). If reciprocity between the school and the community is the goal in the best service learning programs, then students must understand the larger issues of social justice that can be learned through multicultural education. Without this context, programs may foster an attitude of paternalism on the part of the server and one of dependence on the part of those being served. Responding to individual human needs is important, but if the social policies that create these needs is not also understood and addressed, then the cycle of dependence remains. As Kretzmann and McKnight (1993) said, "If maintenance and survival are the best we can provide, what sense can it make to invest in the future?" (p. 3).

COMPLEMENTARY APPROACHES
TO SOCIAL JUSTICE EDUCATION

Although two distinct approaches to education, service learning and multicultural education have many similarities. Both are motivated by the belief that "business as usual" in schools is failing not only students but society. Both address needed changes in both curriculum and school culture so as to create more authentic and powerful educational environments. Both have a strong reflection–action dialectic, emphasizing praxis as a vehicle for personal growth and social change. Both emphasize the importance of the relationship between the school and the communities of which it is a part and see the building of community as a crucial component in a just and moral education. Both have been attacked by critics as challenges to a traditional approach to education or have been misunderstood as "one more thing to do" in an already busy school day. Both approaches have seen some of their more crucial components diluted by some theorists or practitioners who claim to "do" service learning or multicultural education but who have incomplete understanding of the philosophy that guides the practice. And finally, both approaches believe each one of us can make a difference in creating a more just and equitable democratic nation.

Although similar in so many ways, service learning and multicultural education are not the same, and their differences both add to their importance to each other and highlight the ways in which they might complement each other.

Service learning has received much more visible and institutional support from schools and communities right on up to Congress and the President. As a result, service learning has benefited in the last 15 years from a significant infusion of grant funding that has given the field status and credibility. The recent call by Colin Powell for volunteers to rebuild America and the extensive positive media coverage his summit received are one example of the pervasive belief held by many that service is the answer to social problems. Multicultural education, on the other hand, has struggled practically since its inception with attacks from those who viewed it as too radical or as divisive. The focus in multicultural education on eliminating oppression and particularly on examining and critiquing White racism has made this movement too "political" and it is perceived as a threat to the interests and power of its detractors. Although there has been some funding available for multicultural education research or program development, it has not been as comprehensive as that for service learning and little of it has been focused on systemic change.

As a consequence of this backlash against multicultural education, theorists and practitioners have been more easily isolated and targeted by critics. Until the development of the National Association for Multicultural Education in 1990, there was no national organization focused on multicultural education, whereas service learning (in its various nomenclatures) has been represented by, among others, the Society for Field Experience Education (founded 1971), the National Society for Internships and Experiential Education (1978), National Youth Leadership Council (1983), and Campus Compact (1985).

Nevertheless, the field of multicultural education has a more comprehensive research and academic record than does service learning, perhaps because many of the leaders in multicultural education have been college or university faculty (unlike in service learning where until recently the driving force in the field was K–12 teachers or student services/affairs staff). This has unfortunately led to the pace of multicultural education theory far outstripping that of practice in the last 15 years (Gay, 1995), a situation opposite to that in service learning (Giles & Eyler, 1994).

Perhaps the most important difference between the two approaches is that multicultural education grew out of an explicitly political social change movement that focused particularly on racism. Having its roots in the struggles of people of color and other oppressed groups continues to provide the field with a standard for challenging oppression that is at the heart of its purpose. As already discussed, service learning originated in reform-oriented, government-sponsored programs designed either to help the needy, to contribute to the community, or to channel students' energies into civic participation. Although these are valuable goals, the field of service learning has had to grow over the last 20 years toward a more sophisticated understanding of the power issues and unwitting colonialist mentality behind "helping others" and "doing good" (Kendall & Associates, 1990). Indeed, most of the current leading theorists in the field of service learning are White and, as discussed, too little of the service learning literature specifically interrogates issues of power, racism, oppression, or social injustice.

CONCLUSION

Given their many similarities and their crucial differences, the fields of service learning and multicultural education have much to offer each other. Service learning can bring to multicultural education an experiential component that will help students apply classroom learning and help them feel empowered to create change. Service learning is an important avenue for helping students expand their "emotional comfort zones" (Dahms, 1994, p. 92), particularly in exploring issues of diversity. Densmore (1995), although not using the term "service learning," emphasized that our social and intellectual objectives as educators require that we go outside the classroom with our students. She noted:

> In the absence of vibrant working relationships between schools and communities, it is difficult for students to experience and recognize the applicability of what they learn in school for their life outside of the classroom. This is especially true for low-income and minority students whose life experiences are typically not reflected in school practices. (p. 413)

When teachers and community members work together, we can achieve the goals of a "curriculum for diversity" that confronts and addresses all students' life experiences and the connection of those experiences to underlying social and economic realities (Densmore, 1995). Through its emphasis on school–community relationships, service learning can reconnect multicultural education practitioners and theorists to the communities in which they work.

Service learning can also help multicultural education return to and continue to develop its original mission: "to use schooling as much as possible to help shape a future America that is more equal, democratic and just, and that does not demand conformity to one cultural norm" (Sleeter, 1996, p. 15). And finally, service learning can help multicultural proponents practice what we preach: building interracial and intercultural coalitions, actualizing the challenging dialectic of theory and action, working with conflict in real-life settings, working on long-term change projects that model justice and equity, learning about one's own beliefs as well as those of others who are different, and learning how to critique while simultaneously sharing power and privilege.

For its part, multicultural education can provide a vehicle to connect service learning to an explicitly political stance regarding social justice. It can provide the theory and application of antiracist, antioppression ideology and thus expand the practice of service learning beyond "doing good." Finally, it can help service learning theorists and practitioners critique the emphasis in service learning on democratic participation, examining the issues of rights and responsibilities from an explicitly social reconstructionist multicultural perspective.

REFERENCES

Adams, M., Bell, L. A., & Griffin, P. (Eds.). (1997). *Teaching for diversity and social justice: A sourcebook.* New York: Routledge.

Alliance for Service-Learning in Education Reform. (1993). *Standards of quality for school-based service-learning.* Chester, VT: Author.

Anderson, J. B., & Guest, K. (1994). Service learning in teacher education at Seattle University. In R. J. Kraft & M. Swadener (Eds.), *Building community: Service learning in the academic disciplines* (pp. 141–150). Denver, CO: Colorado Campus Compact.

Aparicio, F. R., & Jose-Kampfner, C. (1995, Fall). Language, culture, and violence in the education crisis of U.S. Latino/as: Two courses for intervention. *Michigan Journal of Community Service Learning, 2,* 95–105.

Banks, J. A. (1991). *Teaching strategies for ethnic studies* (5th ed.). Boston: Allyn & Bacon.

Barber, B. (1991). Civic education and the university. *Public leadership education: Practicing citizenship.* Dayton, OH: Kettering Foundation.

Berman, S. (1997). *Children's social consciousness and the development of social responsibility.* New York: State University of New York Press.

Berry, H. A. (1990). Service-learning in international and intercultural settings. In J. C. Kendall & Associates (Eds.), *Combining service and learning: A resource book for community and public service* (Vol. 1, pp. 311–313). Raleigh, NC: National Society for Internships and Experiential Education.

Boyer, E. (1981). *Higher education in the nation's service.* Washington, DC: Carnegie Foundation for the Advancement of Teaching.

Boyer, E. (1987). *College: The undergraduate experience in America.* New York: Harper & Row.

Conrad, D., & Hedin, D. (1991). School-based community service: What we know from research and theory. *Phi Delta Kappan, 71,* 754–755.

Cruz, N. (1990). A challenge to the notion of service. In J. C. Kendall & Associates (Eds.), *Combining service and learning: A resource book for community and public service* (Vol. 1, pp. 321–323). Raleigh, NC: National Society for Internships and Experiential Education.

Dahms, A. M. (1994). Multicultural service learning and psychology. In R. J. Kraft & M. Swadener (Eds.), *Building community: service learning in the academic disciplines* (pp. 91–103). Denver, CO: Colorado Campus Compact.

Delve, C., Mintz, S., & Stewart, G. (1990). *Community service as values education* [New Directions for Student Services No. 50]. San Francisco: Jossey-Bass.

Densmore, K. (1995). An interpretation of multicultural education and its implications for school–community relationships. In C. A. Grant (Ed.), *Education for diversity: An anthology of multicultural voices* (pp. 405–418). Boston: Allyn & Bacon.

Eyler, J., & Giles, D. E., Jr. (1999). *Where's the learning in service learning?* San Francisco, CA: Jossey-Bass.

Fox, H. (1994, Fall). Teaching empowerment. *Michigan Journal of Community Service Learning, 2,* 55–61.

Galura, J., Howard, J., Waterhouse, D., & Ross, R. (Eds.). (1995). *Praxis III: Voices in dialogue.* Ann Arbor, MI: University of Michigan Office of Community Service Learning Press.

Galura, J., Meiland, R., Ross, R., Callan M. J., & Smith, R. (Eds.). (1993). *Praxis II: Service-learning resources for university students, staff and faculty.* Ann Arbor, MI: University of Michigan Office of Community Service Learning Press.

Gay, G. (1995, Fall). Bridging multicultural theory and practice. *Multicultural Education, 3*(1), 4–9.

Giles, D. E., Jr., & Eyler, J. (1994, Fall). The theoretical roots of service-learning in John Dewey: Toward a theory of service-learning. *Michigan Journal of Community Service Learning, 1,* 77–85.

Grant, C. A., & Tate, W. F. (1995). Multicultural education through the lens of the multicultural education research literature. In J. A. Banks & C. A. McGee Banks (Eds.), *Handbook of research on multicultural education* (pp. 145–166). New York: Macmillan.

Guarasci, R. (1997). Community-based learning and intercultural citizenship. In R. Guarasci, G. H. Cornwell, & Associates (Eds.), *Democratic education in an age of difference: Redefining citizenship in higher education* (pp. 17–49). San Francisco: Jossey-Bass.

Guarasci, R., Cornwell, G. H., & Associates. (1997). *Democratic education in an age of difference: Redefining citizenship in higher education.* San Francisco: Jossey-Bass.

Hall, M. (1991a). *". . . something shining, like gold—but better." The National Indian Youth Leadership model: A manual for program leaders.* Gallup, NM: National Indian Youth Leadership Project.

Hall, M. (1991b, June). Gadugi: A model of service-learning for Native American communities. *Phi Delta Kappan,* 754–757.

Hall, M. (1992, November). In our own words: Service learning in Native communities. *The Journal of Experiential Education, 15*(3), 38–40.

Hall, M. (1995, Winter). Si-yuu-dze: Service learning in Native schools. *JEB-P,* 34–36.

Hammond, C. (1994, Fall). Integrating service and academic study: Faculty motivation and satisfaction in Michigan higher education. *Michigan Journal of Community Service Learning, 1*(1), 21–28.

Horton, M. (1990). *The long haul.* J. Kohl & H. Kohl. New York: Doubleday.

Howard, J. (Ed.). (1993). *Praxis I: A faculty casebook on community service learning.* Ann Arbor, MI: University of Michigan Office of Community Service Learning Press.

Jacoby, B. (1977). *Service-learning in higher education: Concepts and practices.* San Francisco, CA: Jossey-Bass.

Kendall, J. C., & Associates. (Eds.). (1990). *Combining service and learning: A resource book for community and public service* (Vols. 1, 2). Raleigh, NC: National Society for Internships and Experiential Education.

Kinsley, C. W., & McPherson, K. (Eds.). (1995). *Enriching the curriculum through service learning.* Alexandria, VA: Association for Supervision and Curriculum Development.

Kraft, R. J., & Swadener, M. (Eds.). (1994). *Building community: Service learning in the academic disciplines.* Denver, CO: Colorado Campus Compact.

Kretzmann, J. P., & McKnight, J. L. (1993). *Building communities from the inside out.* Evanston, IL: Northwestern University Center for Urban Affairs and Policy Research.

Levison, L. M. (1990). Choose engagement over exposure. In J. C. Kendall & Associates (Eds.), *Combining service and learning: A resource book for community and public service* (Vol. 1, pp. 68–75). Raleigh, NC: National Society for Internships and Experiential Education.

McPherson, K., & Kinsley, C. W. (1995). Conclusion: Challenges for the future. In C. W. Kinsley & K. McPherson (Eds.), *Enriching the curriculum through service learning* (pp. 115–116). Alexandria, VA: Association for Supervision and Curriculum Development.

Michalec, P. (1994). Service learning and the multicultural education of pre-service teachers. In R. J. Kraft & M. Swadener (Eds.). *Building community: Service learning in the academic disciplines* (pp. 171–178). Denver, CO: Colorado Campus Compact.

Miller, J. (1994, Fall). Linking traditional and service-learning courses: Outcome evaluations utilizing two pedagogically distinct models. *Michigan Journal of Community Service Learning, 1*(1), 29–36.

Mintz, S. E., & Hesser, G. W. (1997). Principles of good practice in service-learning. In B. Jacoby (Ed.), *Service-learning in higher education: Concepts and practices* (pp. 26–51). San Francisco: Jossey-Bass.

Montero-Sieburth, M. (1988, Spring). Conceptualizing multicultural education: From theoretical approaches to classroom practice. *Equity and Choice*, 3–12.

Morgan, G. (1986). *Images of organization.* Newbury Park, CA: Sage.

Nieto, S. (1996). *Affirming diversity: The sociopolitical context of multicultural education.* New York: Longman.

O'Connell, W. R., Jr. (1990). Service-learning in the south: A strategy for innovation in undergraduate teaching. In J. C. Kendall & Associates (Eds.), *Combining service and learning: A resource book for community and public service* (Vol. 1, pp. 593–600). Raleigh, NC: National Society for Internships and Experiential Education.

O'Grady, C. R. (1999). Seeing things as they are. In C. Clark & J. O'Donnell (Eds.), *Becoming and unbecoming White: Owning and disowning a racial identity* (pp. 122–136). Westport, CT: Greenwood.

O'Grady, C. R., & Chappell, B. (1999). With, not for: The politics of service learning in multicultural communities. In C. Ovando & P. McLaren (Eds.), *The politics of multiculturalism: Students and teachers in the crossfire* (pp. 209–224). Boston, MA: McGraw-Hill.

Palmer, P. (1990). Community, conflict and ways of knowing: Ways to deepen our educational agenda. In J. C. Kendall & Associates (Eds.), *Combining service and learning: A resource book for community and public service* (Vol. 1, pp. 105–113). Raleigh, NC: National Society for Internships and Experiential Education.

Powell, R. R., Zehn, S., & Garcia, J.. (1996). *Field experience: Strategies for exploring diversity in schools.* Englewood Cliffs, NJ: Prentice-Hall.

Reardon, K. M. (1994, Fall). Undergraduate research in distressed urban communities: An undervalued form of service-learning. *Michigan Journal of Community Service Learning, 1*, 44–54.

Rhoads, R. A. (1997). *Community service and higher learning: Explorations of the caring self.* Albany, NY: State University of New York Press.

Roberts-Weah, W. (1995). Service learning honors cultural diversity. In C. W. Kinsley & K. McPherson (Eds.), *Enriching the curriculum through service learning* (pp. 159–162). Alexandria, VA: American Society of Curriculum and Development.

Silcox, H. (1995). The need to consider service learning in developing future vocational education programs. In C. W. Kinsley & K. McPherson (Eds.), *Enriching the curriculum through service learning* (pp. 25–28). Alexandria, VA: American Society of Curriculum and Development.

Sleeter, C. (Ed.). (1991). *Empowerment through multicultural education*. Albany, NY: State University of New York Press.

Sleeter, C. (1996). *Multicultural education as social activism*. New York: State University of New York Press.

Sleeter, C., & Grant, C. A. (1987). An analysis of multicultural education in the United States. *Harvard Educational Review, 57*, 421–444.

Smith, M. W. (1994, Fall). Community service learning: Striking the chord of citizenship. *Michigan Journal of Community Service Learning, 1*, 37–43.

Spring, J. (1998). *Conflict of interests: The politics of American education* (3rd ed.). Boston: McGraw-Hill.

Stanton, T. (1990). Service learning: Groping towards a definition. In J. C. Kendall & Associates (Eds.), *Combining service and learning: A resource book for community and public service* (Vol. 1, pp. 65–67). Raleigh, NC: National Society for Internships and Experiential Education.

Stanton, T. K., Giles, D. E., Jr., & Cruz, N. I. (1999). *Service-learning: A movement's pioneers reflect on its origins, practice and future*. San Francisco, CA: Jossey-Bass.

Stephens, L. S. (1995). *The complete guide to learning through community service: Grades K–9*. New York: Allyn & Bacon.

Tellez, K., Hlebowitsh, P. S., Cohen, M., & Norwood, P. (1995). Social service field experiences and teacher education. In J. M. Larkin & C. E. Sleeter (Eds.), *Developing multicultural teacher education curricula* (pp. 65–78). Albany, NY: State University of New York Press.

Wade, R. (1995). Developing active citizens: Community service learning in social studies teacher education. *The Social Studies, 86*(3), 122–128.

Wade, R. (Ed.). (1997). *Community service learning: A guide to including service in the public school curriculum*. New York: State University of New York Press.

Waldock, J. M. (1995, June). *Achieving cross-cultural understanding through service-learning in higher education*. Unpublished paper, Mankato, MN: Minnesota State University.

Waterman, A. S. (Ed.). (1997). *Service-learning: Applications from the research*. Mahwah, NJ: Lawrence Erlbaum Associates.

THEORETICAL
FRAMEWORKS

Beyond Empathy: Developing Critical Consciousness Through Service Learning

Cynthia Rosenberger
University of Massachusetts, Amherst

*Service learning is the closest thing in school that can become a
life experience. You're out there working . . . you're going beyond the walls of the school and helping other people.*
—Tom (interview, 1998)

Tom, a university student who took a service learning course with
me, made this comment during an interview. I was supportive of the
sentiments he expressed, but his comment illustrated concerns I had
about service learning. What are the presuppositions and dynamics
implied in "helping other people"?

In Spring 1997 I taught the course Teaching Social Studies and
Service Learning in the Early Elementary Grades (EDUC 592L) in response to a university-wide initiative to incorporate service learning
into academic work. As one of the assignments, 17 early childhood
and elementary education graduate students engaged in service learning. More than half of the students facilitated an after-school reading
club for second and third graders at a nearby elementary school.
Other students worked with the local Survival Center that provides
clothing, household goods, surplus food, and a hot lunch 4 days a
week to people in the community. One student helped third and
fourth graders in a Homework Club, another provided companion-
ship for an elderly woman, and yet another organized a community
art project in her local community.

Although I believe in experiential learning that serves the community outside the university, teaching this course caused me to question the traditional tenets of service learning and to seek a more critical perspective on what has become a compelling approach in higher education. Recalling Paulo Freire's *Pedagogy of the Oppressed* (1997), I began to question whether service learning is yet another way that those who have power and privilege, even if only by education, name the problems and the solutions for the less privileged. I became concerned that service learning easily carries connotations of "doing good," of the "haves" giving to the "have-nots," of "we" serving "them"— perspectives that reproduce positions of power. For me, the fundamental question became: To what extent does service learning, although intended to meet community needs and promote active citizenship, sustain the hegemony of the elite and perpetuate the status quo of privilege and oppression created by the economic and educational opportunities of class, race, and gender? Stated more positively: To what extent does service learning contribute to the creation of a more just and equitable society?

With these questions in mind, my purpose in this chapter is to explore how a Freirean approach might provide a framework for conceptualizing a critical service learning pedagogy. In bringing a Freirean perspective to service learning, my goals are to deepen the dialogue among theorists and practitioners concerning the dynamics of power and privilege in service learning and to generate a practice that seeks to transcend the status quo and promote justice and equality.

PRESENT DISCOURSES AROUND SERVICE LEARNING

I want to put forth for consideration the constitutive elements in the language of service learning. For source material, I refer to the writing of prominent authors in the field (Jacoby, 1996; Kendall, 1990; Kinsley & McPherson, 1995; Morton, 1995; Rhoads, 1997; Sigmon, 1990; Wade, 1997) as they struggle to define service learning and establish principles of good practice. This is not a comprehensive overview of the service learning literature but rather a window into the ambivalence and struggles in the formation of a service learning philosophy and practice.

Consensus exists in the literature that service learning is action and reflection integrated with academic curriculum to enhance student learning and to meet community needs. Barbara Jacoby (1996) offered the following definition:

Service-learning is a form of experiential education in which students engage in activities that address human and community needs together with structured opportunities intentionally designed to promote student learning and development. Reflection and reciprocity are key concepts of service-learning. (p. 5)

The word service provokes several connotations. Jane Kendall (1990), an early writer among the current authors in service learning literature, observed the strong potential for paternalism that is disguised in the word:

I have tremendous problems with the word "service." It suggests an inequity between the "servers" and "those served." It suggests that the former have resources and that the latter do not. . . . It does not carry the connotation of social justice that is also an essential component of service-learning. . . . And finally, I have heard "service" used many times as a self-righteous, vaguely disguised ticket to salvation for upper and middle class people who feel guilty about their access to resources. (p. 24)

Rahima Wade (1997) offered one of the most nuanced descriptions of service:

Service is more than an action. Service is also an attitude, a relationship, and a way of being in the world. . . . In fact, we may not be truly serving others if we act without compassion, engagement, and a willingness to be "with" rather than just "for" another. (p. 63)

Her definition of service grapples with the importance of being in solidarity and engaged with those being served. Jacoby recognized the dangers in the use of the word service, but concluded "that although the word *service* is problematic, it is the most common and accessible word to use" (1996, p. 8).

A number of authors (Kendall, 1990; Rhoads, 1997; Wade, 1997) have tried to clarify service by distinguishing between charity and service. Wade represented this clarification in the following quote; "charity involves a distance between the server and the served . . . one person is clearly doing something *for* someone else, usually with some feeling of pity" (p. 64). This easily becomes "do-good" action and patronizing, making those who give feel important and those who receive feel indebted. It does not empower. On the other hand, her idea of service was quite different:

With service, compassion should replace pity and separateness should be transformed into community. Instead of doing something one decides is needed for an "other," service involves working alongside people in ways that assist them in defining and helping to fulfill their own needs. . . . Service must be envisioned as empowering individuals to work on their own behalf as much as it is to provide food and shelter. (p. 64)

In this description of service, the concept of working with and empowering others is present. A relational aspect undergirds her understanding of service. Compassion carries a connotation of caring and understanding in a deep sense. Sympathy with, rather than pity for, another is implied.

Keith Morton (1995) posited social change as one of three paradigms for service learning, the other two being charity and social project. For Morton, an understanding of the root causes and the depth of relationships with community members determines the meaningfulness in any of the three paradigms. Robert Rhoads (1997), although using the terminology *community service* rather than *service learning*, spoke of "the challenge that faculty, staff, and student leaders face in structuring community service projects . . . to help students connect individual suffering to larger social problems and to challenge students to consider how they might contribute to social change" (p. 201). He also recognized that "an action/reflection dynamic that contributes to social change is . . . political because it questions how power is distributed and the connection between power and economics" (p. 201). It is rare that social change, power, and economic structures are mentioned within service learning literature.

Most authors have been explicit about the importance of community members determining the need. As early as 1979, Robert Sigmon suggested the following three principles for community service learning:

Principle one: Those being served control the service(s) provided.
Principle two: Those being served become better able to serve and be served by their own actions.
Principle three: Those who serve also are learners. . . . (pp. 9–11)

Jane Kendall (1990) addressed this question with particular clarity. She wrote that in the early years of service learning in the late 1960s and early 1970s, the question of who determines the community needs was overlooked and learned through hard experience. She wrote:

We were learning that without an emphasis on the relationship between the server and "those served" as a reciprocal exchange between equals, that relationship can easily break down. . . . Paternalism, unequal relationships between the parties involved, and a tendency to focus only on charity—"doing for" or "helping" others—rather than on supporting others to meet their own needs all became gaping pitfalls for program after well-intentioned program. (pp. 9–10)

Kendall described how, from these early experiences, some key principles were learned; "the need for critical reflection on experience, reciprocity of learning, [and] a careful balance of power among all parties involved . . ." (p. 11).

Thus, the fourth principle in the Principles of Good Practice in Combining Service and Learning (these principles were drafted at the Wingspread Conference Center in Racine, Wisconsin in May, 1989 and are frequently referred to as the Wingspread principles) states that "an effective and sustained program allows for those with needs to define those needs" (Kendall, 1990). Other current writers (Kinsley & McPherson, 1995; Morton, 1995; Rhoads, 1997; and Wade, 1997) have emphasized the importance of the receiver determining the need. The Standards of Quality for School-Based Service-Learning (1993) from the Alliance for Service-Learning in Education Reform state that "youth are involved in the planning" (p. 3), but a relationship with the community members being served is not mentioned. These standards focus on the benefits to students and the meaningful contribution of service learning to the community but fail to address the role of those receiving the service.

Reciprocity and *mutuality* are frequently occurring words in the literature. Jacoby (1996) named reciprocity as one of two key concepts of service learning in her definition of service-learning (p. 5). Kendall describes reciprocity as:

the exchange of both giving and receiving between the "server" and the person or group "being served." All parties in service learning are learners and help determine what is to be learned. Both the server and those served teach, and both learn. . . . In service learning, those being served control the service provided; the needs of the community determine what the service tasks will be. Building programs on a philosophy of reciprocal learning can thus help to avoid the ever present pitfall of paternalism disguised under the name of service. (1990, p. 22)

Rhoads (1997) used the concept of mutuality to embrace two ideas; that service should be a two-way relationship in that both parties receive benefits; and that both parties should be involved in the development and structuring of the service project (p. 150).

Rhoads went on to craft a concept of critical community service as he called teachers and students to develop a critical consciousness

that transforms their understanding of the social order. He understood this critical consciousness as leading to engagement in the
"larger struggle to improve social conditions" (1997, p. 221). In his
conception of a critical community service paradigm, Rhoads provided a gateway for framing a critical approach to service learning
through a Freirean lens.

LOOKING THROUGH A FREIREAN LENS

The late Paulo Freire, a 20th century educator of monumental stat-
ure, constructed a pedagogy originally intended to promote the liberation of peasants in his native country of Brazil. Since the publication
of *The Pedagogy of the Oppressed* in 1970, his thinking has had a
powerful impact on literacy education and community development
work, particularly in developing countries, but also in Europe and
the United States.

In considering service learning through a Freirean lens, I recognize
that I am transposing Freire's ideas from their original sociopolitical
and cultural context among the peasants and revolutionary leaders of
Brazil to that of the United States. I am casting his ideas onto a different sociopolitical map with certain similarities, to be sure, but with
distinct differences. I am grateful for Henry Giroux's statement in the
introduction to Paulo Freire's *The Politics of Education*; "the object
of his [Freire's] analysis and the language he uses is for the oppressed
everywhere; his concept of the Third World is ideological and political rather than merely geographical" (1985, p. xviii). Giroux added:
"Freire's work . . . is a series of theoretical signposts that need to be
decoded and critically appropriated within the specific contexts in
which they might be useful" (pp. xviii–xix). It is as theoretical signposts that I use Freirean concepts.

The contours of the sociopolitical map in the United States consist
of the very rich and very poor, of comfortable middle and upper-
middle classes, and substantial and growing impoverished classes.
Oppression in the forms of racism, classism, sexism, heterosexism,
ageism, ableism, cultural, ethnic, or language biases, lack of opportunities, and economic inequities is distributed across this map but is
certainly felt more acutely by some groups than by others. The tenets
of our democracy, in principle, assure inalienable rights to all; in reality, the structure of the system offers a position of privilege to the
wealthy and those who are White and denies others the privilege of
sharing equitably in that wealth and status. The context of the United
States, like the context that fostered Freire's ideas, contains the dialectic of oppression and domination.

I also recognize that Freire's ideas grew partly out of Marxist philosophy that assumes political and economic change lies in the collective action of the people. For Freire, such action can occur only through the conscientization of oppressed people who, in becoming conscious of their oppression, become subjects capable of transforming reality. The role of revolutionary leaders is to educate the oppressed to realize their oppression and to empower them to act to liberate themselves.

In contrast, the philosophical basis for change in the United States grows out of the notions of democracy and individualism. The expectation is that change happens through democratic processes and a concern for the common good. An early commentator on United States society, de Tocqueville, noted that social change in the United States arises from the exercise of civic responsibility on the part of educated and morally motivated individuals. He described volunteerism in the form of community service as a unique element in the social fabric of this country. Individuals such as Jane Addams and Dorothy Day, who respectively established the settlement house movement and the Catholic Workers Union, were leaders in creating avenues through which individuals served the poor.

The fact that service learning and Freire's beliefs are rooted in different contexts and philosophies creates both tension and synergy. Freire created a pedagogy that provides a theory and methodology for cultural action, the goal of which is to liberate oppressed people. Service learning has grown out of a long history of community service in which volunteer service to individual people or to the community is perceived as meeting individual needs but not usually as political action intended to transform structural inequalities. Freire's pedagogy is concerned with developing the critical consciousness of the oppressed. Service learning is concerned, in particular, with developing a critical consciousness in those participating in the service, in this case teachers and students. Freire believed that only the oppressed could liberate themselves and that in liberating themselves, they also liberated the oppressors. We in the United States operate on the principle that societal change comes about through citizens and government working together. As a democratic society, ideally we expect that our system of government will enable every human to reach full potential. The contrast, therefore, is between a revolutionary program aimed at bringing down the dominant elite and a service program operating within existing democratic structures. I find these tensions a compelling impetus to explore the synergy between Freire's pedagogy and service learning. Freire's ideas highlight issues that we need to consider if we are to construct a theory and practice of service learning that participates in the creation of a more just and democratic society.

PAULO FREIRE AND A CRITICAL SERVICE
LEARNING PEDAGOGY

Freire wrote, "I consider the fundamental theme of our epoch to be that of domination—which implies its opposite, the theme of liberation, as the objective to be achieved" (1997, p. 84). Precisely because of the connotations that "service" and service learning hold, teachers and students in higher education must think carefully about the dialectic of domination and liberation as they engage with communities in service learning. I remind the reader of my fundamental questions: To what extent does service learning perpetuate the status quo of privilege and nonprivilege? To what extent does service learning contribute to liberating all of us from oppression, recognizing that oppression is experienced in multiple ways? In the following section, I suggest that teachers and students must deal with this dialectic at both a societal and a personal level. At the societal level, responsible citizenship means recognizing the difference between actions that dominate and further oppress people and actions that liberate people. At the personal level, teachers and students must recognize that as they enact service learning, they are, in one or more ways, usually in a privileged position, perhaps merely through education, but often through social status, race, class, or the myriad of other ways that people possess power and privilege. This position carries with it connotations, both real and perceived, for themselves and for others, of power and privilege.

I have chosen four concepts in Paulo Freire's ideology as a critical lens for examining service learning; (1) praxis as cultural action for freedom; (2) the dynamic nature of reality; (3) balance of power; and (4) conscientization. I also find in Freire two pedagogical approaches—dialogue and problem-posing—that contribute to the formation of a critical service learning pedagogy. In the following sections, I discuss the concepts and then the pedagogical approaches, suggesting how they contribute to a critical framing of theory and practice in service learning.

CONCEPTUAL ISSUES

Praxis

Freire defined praxis as "reflection and action upon the world in order to transform it" (1997, p. 33). He was emphatic that the process of creating change that liberates or empowers people must occur through action that is combined with reflection. Action by itself results merely in activism; that is, acting without thinking critically about the consequences is often thoughtless and unmindful of both the process and the results of the action. Reflection and action must go hand in hand so that action, if it is to be thoughtful, is preceded and followed by reflection.

Equally significant for Freire was the transformative nature of praxis. Freire distinguished between praxis as cultural action for domination and praxis as cultural action for freedom. Cultural action for domination is represented by a coup d'état in the political context of Freire's early writing in Brazil. Although a coup d'état constitutes a change in power, it also reinstates a state of domination and a culture of silence. On the other hand, cultural action for freedom assumes characteristics of a cultural revolution; a utopian vision of reality, an unveiling and problematizing of present reality, and an action conceived and enacted with the people (Freire, 1985). For Freire, revolutionary leaders are engaged in cultural action for freedom when they work with oppressed people to help them discover both their own oppression and their power to create a new social order.

A Freirean lens provides a fuller definition of praxis than is usually assumed by those who talk about praxis as practice that combines action and reflection in a reflexive and critical manner. Freire's definition of praxis is "action and reflection upon the world *in order to transform it* [italics added]." This definition perceives transformation of the world as the goal. I suggest this is a different praxis than what is usually meant by community service. For Freire, praxis is cultural action for freedom. This conception of praxis poses a challenge to service learning to become transformative and liberatory in its action and reflection. Such praxis moves beyond the work of taking care of immediate needs to community action that frees people from those needs. Within this fuller view of praxis, we in service learning must search for ways of acting and reflecting that move society toward a more just and equitable reality for all people.

View of Reality

The two cultural action paradigms—cultural action for domination and cultural action for freedom—are based on different views of reality. Three aspects of Freire's discussion of reality are pertinent to our discussion. First, cultural action for domination views reality as rigid and static as opposed to cultural action for freedom that views reality as dynamic and created. In the cultural action for freedom paradigm, "reality is really a process, undergoing constant transformation" (1985, p. 56); the task of humanity is to transform reality. Secondly, cultural action for freedom holds a utopian vision of reality. For Freire, a utopian vision of reality involves the realization of full humanity for all people. Humanization is an historical process that affirms human beings as subjects, not objects, a process of decision making, and one that restores freedom and justice to all people. Embracing a utopian vision and a dynamic view of reality, humans involved in cultural action for freedom demystify present reality. Freire explained:

> The radical, committed to human liberation, does not become the prisoner of a "circle of certainty" within which reality is also imprisoned. On the contrary, the more radical the person is, the more fully he or she enters into reality so that, knowing it better, he/she can better transform it. This individual is not afraid to confront, to listen, to see the world unveiled. (1997, p. 21)

A utopian vision of full humanity for all people calls for the unveiling and problematizing of existing reality. Finally, a third notion in the cultural action for freedom paradigm is that reality rather than oppressed people becomes the object of analysis. That is, it is not people but social structures in the world that become the objects to be transformed. When existing social structures are the object of analysis and transformation, oppressed people are not objects of cultural action but rather subjects who act on reality.

For Freire, then, praxis or cultural action for freedom requires a view of reality that is dynamic, that envisions full humanity for all people, and that understands social structures as the object of analysis. Embedded in the United States Declaration of Independence (1776) is the utopian vision upon which our democracy is based; "that all [people] are created equal . . . and endowed . . . with certain inalienable rights; that among these are life, liberty, and the pursuit of happiness." Service learning is infused by an idealism based on the belief that all citizens are entitled to participate in this vision. But the reality is that all citizens do not enjoy these rights. A Freirean perspective encourages us to ask: Is service learning willing to participate in the unveiling and problematizing of the present reality of our society and to respond to the difficult, complex issues of inequity, oppression, and domination? Is service learning willing to make less-privileged people subjects and not objects?

I propose that unless we who teach and participate in service learning are willing to view reality as dynamic and mutually created and to analyze the structural inequities that create unjust and oppressive conditions, we risk providing what Freire called "false generosity"—acts of service that simply perpetuate the status quo and thus preserve the need for service. Are we willing to risk becoming conscious on a deep level of the structural inequalities in society? Are we willing to analyze the social realities that result from our economic and political policies? Are we willing to act and reflect on the world in a way that questions and transforms the status quo? Answering these questions in the affirmative requires more than acting and reflecting to meet the present needs of a community. Answering in the affirmative requires holding up the vision of humanity that undergirds our democracy and creating a service learning pedagogy that develops the critical consciousness of all people.

Balance of Power

Freire insisted that both the oppressed and the revolutionary leaders must be subjects of revolutionary *praxis* (1997). Cultural action for freedom cannot be revolutionaries thinking and acting for people who are oppressed. "Revolutionary leaders cannot think *without* the people, nor *for* the people, but only *with* the people" (p. 112). He immediately went on to state that the dominant elites, on the other hand, can—and do—think without the people—although they do not permit themselves the luxury of failing to think about the people in order to know them better and thus dominate them more efficiently. Consequently, any apparent dialogue or communication between the elites and the masses is really the depositing of "communiques," whose contents are intended to exercise a domesticating influence (1997, p. 112).

The very existence of oppressed and impoverished people creates a position of power and dominance for the elite. Freire understood the dominant elite's attempts to soften their power by serving the oppressed in their weakness as "false generosity" (1997, p. 26). He described the situation thus:

> In order to have the continued opportunity to express their "generosity," the oppressors must perpetuate injustice as well. An unjust social order is the permanent fount of this "generosity." . . . True generosity consists precisely in fighting to destroy the causes which nourish false charity. False charity constrains the fearful and subdued, the "rejects of life," to extend their trembling hands. True generosity lies in striving so that these hands . . . need be extended less and less in supplication, so that more and more they become human hands which . . . transform the world.

> This lesson and this apprenticeship must come, however, from the oppressed themselves and from those who are truly solidary with them. . . . Who are better prepared than the oppressed to understand the terrible significance of an oppressive society? (pp. 26–27)

For Freire, the oppressed must lead in realizing a new social order that is free of oppression, and those who work with the oppressed must work in solidarity with them. Freire wrote, "only power that springs from the weakness of the oppressed will be sufficiently strong to free both" (p. 26).

We who are privileged and involved in service learning must be watchful lest we assume the characteristics of Freire's "dominant elite" who think without and about people but not with them. Instead, we must be mindful of assuming the characteristics of those that Freire called revolutionary leaders or "truly humanistic educator(s)" (1997, p. 75) who "cannot think *without* the people, nor *for* the people, but only *with* the people" (p. 112). Solidarity with people may require that we give up power and relinquish control. It demands that we listen and hear what other people are saying. Are we willing to allow the voices of the oppressed to shape our praxis? A Freirean perspective calls for true solidarity among service learners and community members and a working together to meet needs and bring about change.

In the service learning literature, the terms reciprocity and mutuality convey the notion that both parties benefit from the interaction, both are teachers and learners, and both are involved in developing and structuring the service project. Although these terms portray a commitment to respectful and mutually beneficial relationships between parties, my concern is that they mask the issue of power. I have referred to the privileged position of many teachers and students in higher education. Privilege and the power that accompanies it, whether real or perceived, need to be recognized and problematized. Praxis that creates a more just society may mean giving up a position of privilege and power. Those in positions of privilege may need to cede their position and become listeners, learners, and followers in order for those with less privilege to become agents of their own change. Only then will the less privileged have space to assume leadership. Only then can the less privileged determine their needs and the solutions.

These are complex issues. I do not intend to portray power and privilege as easily rectified. But I think the development of critical service learning, whose goal is to contribute to the creation of a just and equitable society, demands that we become critically conscious of the issues of power and privilege in service learning relationships. Discussions of these issues will undoubtedly complicate and also clarify the meanings of reciprocity and mutuality.

The dialectic nature of the language used to distinguish the parties in service learning—for example, those who serve and the recipients of the service—contributes to the perception of unequal and unbalanced relationships. While recognizing our need to distinguish the students and teachers involved in service learning from community members, I urge service learning theorists and practitioners to confront this language of duality and to search for metaphors that shape a concept of all of us working and learning together in order to meet community needs that belong to all of us.

What new language conveys the concept that all of us are serving, participating, acting, and reflecting? Might we designate all people who are involved in the service learning relationship as "service learners," "participants," or "stakeholders"? Can we think about new language for "*service* learning"? "Community learning" or "community action learning" are two suggestions I offer. I invite readers to imagine new possibilities that address the connotations in service, servers, and those served.

If, for the present, we must remain within the dialectical boundaries of our language and thinking, I suggest we use the term "service learners" for at least teachers and students who participate in service learning. Service learners implies that those serving are in the process of learning from the community members with whom they are engaged. The connotations of openness and seeking understanding that the term service learners carries may help to clarify the issues of power and privilege. I also use the term "stakeholders" when referring to all the parties involved in service learning activities, for indeed all of us have a stake in the process and outcomes of service learning.

Conscientization

The fourth concept, *conscientization*, was defined by Freire as "the process in which men,[1] not as recipients, but as knowing subjects achieve a deepening awareness both of the sociocultural reality that shapes their lives and of their capacity to transform that reality" (Freire, 1985, footnote 2, p. 93). It is a twofold process of gaining increasingly critical levels of consciousness. It is a process of perceiving, first, one's place in reality and, secondly, one's capability as an agent of change. Freire recognized that people are conditioned by the present reality or social order, so that oppression creates in people a blindness to their own oppression. They must first recognize their

---

[1]In subsequent writings and editions, Freire revised his language to reflect inclusive language practices.

present situation and the obstacles that prevent them from seeing the injustice of their oppressed condition (1985).

After gaining consciousness of their oppressed state, the oppressed can name the oppression and can perceive themselves as change agents for creating a new reality that is more equal and just. This process occurs within praxis in which people work together, not naming the world for each other, but in speaking their word. In a poignant quote, Freire wrote: "To exist, humanly, is to *name* the world, to change it. . . . Human beings are not built in silence, but in word, in work, in action-reflection" (1997, p. 69).

Previously I suggested that teachers and students in higher education are in a relatively privileged position. This privilege may simply be through education, but given the demographics of higher education, it may also be through their socioeconomic status, their gender, or the color of their skin. Therefore, as we look through the lens of Freire and to the "pedagogy of the oppressed," we are, in practice, often envisioning a pedagogy for those in a position of privilege. In stating this, I recognize the multiplicity of identities each of us has and that many of us share in some kinds of oppression and not in other kinds. Both identity and oppression are complex phenomena. But I think it is important for this discussion to recognize the privileged position that many who participate in service learning hold.

Conscientization, then, for those with privilege involves not only seeking to understand the root causes of society's problems but also the willingness to face the personal contradictions that result from that understanding. For those of us with privilege, praxis may mean giving up privileged status because, in quiet, often insidious ways that we choose not to see, our privilege creates oppression for the non-privileged. A critical service learning approach means becoming conscious and reflecting critically on our own positional power and on the dissonance that critical consciousness creates for us personally. Recognizing the underlying causes of inequities may call into question values that we have never questioned. Righting injustices may mean giving up comfortable positions of privilege and power. Similar to the peasants in Brazil, conscientization for the privileged requires reflection outward—on the world, as well as inward—on one's place and agency in the world.

Conscientization in the Freirean sense insists that all stakeholders become conscious of oppression and the underlying causes, and understand themselves as agents of change—as people who have the capacity to effect inequities and unjust practices in society. Conscientization when applied to service learning empowers all stakeholders to think and act on the world in order to transform it. This is work done in solidarity with community members whose oppression is problematized and who, in their positions as subjects, are also conscious of being agents of change.

PEDAGOGICAL APPROACHES

Dialogue

Freire defined dialogue as "the encounter between men, mediated by the world, in order to name the world. . . . Because dialogue is an encounter among men and women who name the world, it must not be a situation where some name on behalf of others" (1997, pp. 69–70). The nonhierarchical nature of dialogue is fundamental to Freire's pedagogy. In a Freirean approach, dialogue occurs between subjects who are open to seeing the world through the eyes of others and who grant others the right of naming the world. The horizontal nature of dialogue generates mutual trust between parties.

As I have noted, much of the service learning literature shares a commitment to building mutual relationships and to letting members of the community identify the need. What is missing, however, is an approach for creating such relationships. Let us examine in more depth what Freire meant by dialogue.

For Freire, dialogue is based on love, humility, and faith in people. Dialogue happens only when there is a "profound love for the world and for people" (1997, p. 70). Freire understood this love as a commitment to the cause of the oppressed that does not manipulate those who are oppressed but rather generates further acts of freedom. Such love is a commitment to others and their plight. I would suggest that love, in the Freirean sense, is different than the "ethic of care" that is mentioned in the service learning literature. Rhoads wrote: "community service is a vehicle for advancing . . . an ethic [of care]" (1997, p. 2). This statement portrays an ethic of care as resulting from participation in community service whereas Freire posits love as a necessary precursor or foundation for dialogue and action. In Freire's pedagogy, love accompanies dialogue.

Humility is required in order to let others name their needs and their own oppression. I share the following quote from Freire about the importance of humility in dialogue and find it particularly pertinent to our discussion.

> How can I dialogue if I always project ignorance onto others and never perceive my own? How can I dialogue if I regard myself as a case apart from others—mere "its" in whom I cannot recognize other "I"s? How

can I dialogue if I consider myself a member of the in-group of "pure" men, the owners of truth and knowledge, for whom all non-members are "these people" or "the great unwashed"? How can I dialogue if I start from the premise that naming the world is the task of an elite and that the presence of the people in history is a sign of deterioration, thus to be avoided? How can I dialogue if I am afraid of being displaced, the mere possibility causing me torment and weakness? Self-sufficiency is incompatible with dialogue. Men and women who lack humility (or have lost it) cannot come to the people, cannot be their partners in naming the world. . . . At the point of encounter . . . there are only people who are attempting together, to learn more than they now know. (1997, p. 71)

Are we able to build this stance of humility into the principles of service learning so as to create service learning practices that are encounters of learning and acting together in love and humility? We who perceive ourselves as educated have difficulty at times listening to and learning from others who do not share a similar academic education. We easily assume we are enlightened or possess more knowledge than others and therefore feel entitled to express our ideas rather than listening and learning from those with different experiences. We must all be attentive to thinking we have the solutions and the ability to name the world for others. Humility is the opposite of arrogance. Humility is necessary if we are to join with people in learning and acting together.

Finally, Freire wrote:

Dialogue . . . requires an intense *faith in humankind* [italics added], faith in their power to make and remake, to create and re-create, faith in their vocation to be more fully human (which is not the privilege of an elite, but the birthright of all). (p. 71)

As service learners we must demonstrate the belief that others are capable of thinking, understanding, and acting. We must trust community members to know what it is they need and to name the process and the solutions.

Problem-Posing Education

Freire defined problem-posing education as a process through which students and teachers investigate universal themes. Freire called them "generative themes" (1997, p. 83), for they in turn lead to new themes and tasks. The themes, however, are hidden by "limit-situations" or mental constructs that prevent people (the oppressed and the oppressors) from seeing reality clearly and critically (p. 83). These constructs act as blinders not only to current reality but also to new possibilities. They prevent a critical understanding of reality. For critical dialogue to occur, the limit-situations must be recognized, deconstructed, and overcome.

Problem-posing education is compelling for strengthening the process of conscientization in service learners, for it "is constituted and organized by the students' view of the world" (1997, p. 90). Freire stated that "the task of the . . . teacher is to 're-present' that universe [that the students present] . . . not as a lecture, but as a problem" (1997, p. 90). Freire encouraged dramatizations and photographs related to people's firsthand experience as ways of posing problems. Role playing, dramatizing situations, and asking questions, for example, "What is wrong with this picture?" are strategies that heighten the relief of what we perceive. Problem-posing education that exposes and questions presuppositions affords students a critical lens through which to view the world and thereby aids in developing heightened consciousness.

Before leaving our discussion of Freire, I want to note that at the heart of Freire's work is an insistence on equalizing power. Creating nonhierarchical relationships, whether between oppressed people and oppressors, leaders and the oppressed, or teachers and students, emerges as a central challenge throughout Freire's ideology. In problem-posing education, Freire suggested new categories of teacher–student and students–teachers, thus forging the concept of co-learners and co-investigators.

I submit that dialogue and problem-posing education offer important approaches for teaching and learning in the service learning arena. Dialogue based on love, humility, and faith in people insists on the breaking down of traditional dichotomies of power. It compels us toward collaborative reflection and action. Problem-posing education provides a framework for unveiling reality and building critical consciousness around universal themes. If service learning is to be transformative, it must generate a thoughtful and critical consciousness in all stakeholders as they collaborate in creating a more just and humane society.

The Freirean concepts and pedagogical approaches that I have discussed afford service learning practitioners and theorists a lens and tools for framing a critical service learning pedagogy. This framework must foster a service learning praxis that strives through action and reflection to bring about full humanity for all people as it helps students uncover the systemic issues underlying social, political, and economic inequities.

PEDAGOGICAL IMPLICATIONS

For service learning to be a critical learning experience, I suggest that
students need the opportunity

- to choose needs or issues in the community that connect to the
  course content;
- to dialogue with stakeholders in framing and defining the problem and action;
- to engage in problem-posing education around the social, political, and economic issues that arise in the service learning experience, so as to be involved in a process of conscientization.

One of the greatest challenges in incorporating these aspects into
the service learning experience of university students is the limited
number of weeks in a semester. How in the time frame of a semester
do we give students the opportunity to construct service learning experiences that are relevant to course content, to dialogue with stakeholders in a way that honors the principle that those being served define the need, and to engage in problem-posing education that leads
to conscientization? What are alternatives to consider so that these
processes can occur in an authentic, meaningful manner?

I now discuss salient aspects of critical service learning.

Choice

Students benefit from choosing the service learning experience. By
grappling with the decision about the type of service learning activity,
students have the opportunity to think about the connections to
course content, the implications of different projects, how needs and
action might be defined, and the inherent dynamics of power and
privilege. In the act of choosing, they develop a sense of ownership.

Dialogue and Agency

Students need the opportunity to dialogue with stakeholders to define the need and determine the action. Yet, when teachers and students work with social agencies, it is difficult to implement the principle that those being served should define the need. The agency
usually defines the need and a response. The experience of interacting directly with those receiving the service in order to determine the
need is frequently absent. The need and nature of the service is pre-

determined. Students miss the opportunity of dialoguing with the people being served to define the problem and the process.

This lack of involvement in the early stages of the process contributes to students feeling a lack of power to effect change in an already established structure. Rather than feeling they are agents of change, they feel obliged to participate in the status quo. Again, this frustration is common when working with a service agency whose programs are in place.

I suggest that teachers create service learning or community action projects in which students engage in face-to-face dialogue with the stakeholders involved. I am aware of how complicated this can be. But, in doing so, students have the opportunity to participate in a fundamental principle of service learning—that community members define the need and the process—and, within that encounter, students have the opportunity to practice the skills and attitudes of dialogue. Creating service learning experiences in which this dialogue can occur is one of the challenges for service learning practitioners.

Problem-Posing and Conscientization

Problem-posing and conscientization are closely related. Service learners need the opportunity to problem-pose if they are to become critically conscious, and problem-posing requires a preliminary awareness of possible questions. I remind us that problem-posing is not problem solving. Problem-posing is the process of unveiling and problematizing reality for the purpose of searching for more humane and just ways of living.

Problem-posing breaks open the mental constructs we bring to a service learning situation and allows us to see what we previously had not seen. We develop new consciousness and imagine new possibilities for action and reflection. As teachers, we can pose a variety of questions with our students that generate themes and new tasks to pursue.

Can a familiar school setting promote significant conscientization for preservice teachers? I believe it can. The unveiling of the familiar and often unquestioned leads to "a-ha!" learning experiences. Schools are microcosms of society and mirror the issues of power, privilege, and inequity that exist in the larger society. It is often more difficult, and thus more important for the purpose of conscientization, to look at that which is familiar.

Combining a problem-posing approach of education with service learning opens the possibility of unveiling the structural inequalities that create injustice. Problem-posing education has the potential to help students construct knowledge about economic and social complexities and with this knowledge, to begin to entertain alternatives to present reality.

A CRITICAL PERSPECTIVE: BEYOND
"HELPING OTHERS" AND EMPATHY

As educators, we need to create service learning experiences that extend beyond empathy and "helping others." Important as these are, service learning must be an avenue of education that enlarges students' critical consciousness and contributes to the transformation of society. Such transformation must be toward a fuller humanity for all of us.

I have suggested that the concepts and pedagogical approaches that Paulo Freire offered are important considerations for framing a critical service learning pedagogy. Engagement in a service learning praxis that seeks to transform requires that we perceive reality as dynamic and recognize social structures as objects for analysis. Confronting issues of privilege and power must accompany praxis that strives to correct inequalities and injustices in society. Freire's ideas challenge us to create service learning relationships that are nonhierarchical, collaborative, and empowering of all stakeholders.

As we serve and learn in community-action work, a Freirean approach calls us to appropriate the pedagogical approaches of dialogue and problem-posing education. Only as we assume the stance of listening to and learning from others, allowing them to name the need and determine the action, will we be co-workers with people in righting injustices and correcting inequality. Love, humility, and faith in people must serve as the basis for this dialogue. Posing situations as problems—allowing the structural realities that do not contribute to full humanity for all people to emerge and be discussed—leads to deeper levels of consciousness and new commitments for action and reflection.

Paulo Freire's ideas alert us to the challenges that service learning poses. As service learning educators, we must constantly seek to understand the implications of our praxis and the responsibilities we have to all stakeholders. We must pursue a critical framing of service learning through an examination of the presuppositions underlying our discourse. We must strive to enact service learning that positions people as subjects and fosters growing critical consciousness in all stakeholders. Creating a more just and equitable society must be our goal.

REFERENCES

Alliance for Service-Learning in Education Reform. (1993). *Standards of quality for school-based service-learning.* Chester, VT: Author.

Freire, P. (1985). *The politics of education.* New York: Bergin & Garvey.

Freire, P. (1997). *Pedagogy of the oppressed.* New York: Continuum Publishing. (Original work published 1970)

Jacoby, B., & Associates. (1996). *Service-learning in higher education: Concepts and practices.* San Francisco: Jossey-Bass.

Kendall, J. (1990). *Combining service and learning: A resource book for community and public service.* Raleigh, NC: National Society for Internships and Experiential Education.

Kinsley, C., & McPherson, K. (1995). Changing perceptions to integrate community service learning into education. In C. Kinsley & K. McPherson (Eds.), *Enriching the curriculum through service learning* (pp. 1–9). Alexandria, VA: Association for Supervision and Curriculum Development.

Morton, K. (1995, Fall). The irony of service: Charity, project and social change in service-learning. *Michigan Journal of Community Service Learning,* 19–32.

Rhoads, R. A. (1997). *Community service and higher learning: Explorations of the caring self.* Albany, NY: State University of New York Press.

Sigmon, R. L. (1979, Spring). Service-learning: Three principles, *Synergist,* National Center for Service Learning, *ACTION, 8*(1), 9–11.

Wade, R. C. (1997). *Community service-learning: A guide to including service in the public school curriculum.* Albany, NY: State University of New York Press.

3

Service Learning and Multicultural Education: Suspect or Transformative?

Kathleen Densmore
San Jose State

One of John Dewey's more valuable insights is commonly overlooked. Many years ago, Dewey argued that in addition to facilitating the personal growth of individual students, education should also help to rectify inequalities of income and social position and to integrate young people into society, in part by transmitting the dominant culture and the norms of appropriate behavior. For Dewey, when society is democratic, these functions do not conflict; democracy is a precondition for a sound educational system. For Dewey, democracy is not simply government by majority rule. Rather, it is a set of social relations in which people treat one another as equals, in ways that promote the full development of each person's capacities.

Following Dewey, if we want students to be free of elitism, racism, and sexism, we need to construct a society that eliminates the basis for these injustices. It is, therefore, in the interests of educators to work toward creating a just and democratic society. Yet, as LaBelle and Ward (1994) remarked,

> When discussing education and change in the United States, it is uncommon to hear of proposals for making more than minor adjustments to the ongoing educational and social system . . . it is uncommon to think of schooling and education as part of the larger society within which the control of knowledge is associated with economic and political power, exploitation, privilege, and cultural hegemony. (p. 152)

This observation typically holds true for both service learning and multicultural education, as I argue in this chapter. This perspective

45

persists despite the wealth of scholarship showing how schools promote the dominant political, cultural, social, and economic interests of the society in which they exist. The idea that education does not exist in a vacuum, that it both influences and is influenced by society, is not new. Since the beginnings of public schooling, various groups of people have attempted to use formal education to promote a particular kind of society. Multicultural education and service learning programs represent such attempts today. Yet, only the progressive advocates of these programs recognize that although schools help some individuals enhance their status and power, schooling is most likely to reinforce social inequality by encouraging students to accept a society that showers its largesse on a privileged elite.

The 21st century calls for a profoundly different course for both schools and society if we want schools to educate our young to help construct a society that no longer requires extreme divisions by social class, gender, race, and ethnicity. In this chapter, I make some suggestions for this course, pointing to directions in which I think our schools should be heading. I argue that in conceiving of a course for our educational system, we must keep in mind that without simultaneously altering the political and economic systems in which our schools are enmeshed, schooling is likely to continue to perpetuate a society where the poor, and especially oppressed nationalities, remain relatively impoverished and disenfranchised.

In this chapter, I examine service learning and multicultural education as two educational reforms that presumably contribute to positive social change. I argue that the extent to which these reforms would enable teachers and students to improve the quality of democracy in our society will be partially determined by how educators design the kind of "involvement" students have. I argue that advocates of these two initiatives must carefully select what they teach, to include the multifaceted dimensions, causes, and realities of social injustice. Equally important, educators and students must learn about the conditions under which social change occurs. For example, how do particular economic and demographic contexts influence specific social movements? I try to suggest the benefits for teachers of working with students and community members on a wide range of social as well as educational issues.

SERVICE LEARNING

In the past 10 years, service learning programs and requirements for community service for graduation have mushroomed in the United States. With the encouragement of high-level national efforts, a great deal of experimentation in the field of service learning is evident at the grassroots level. Concern for civic responsibility, heightened by a realization that government alone cannot solve current social problems, a commitment to learning by doing on the part of educators, and efforts to forge stronger links between schools and their surrounding communities help explain the reasons behind the recent profusion of service initiatives in educational institutions. Intended outcomes of service learning for students typically include enhanced self-worth, improved ability to think critically, greater capacity to effect social change, and greater commitment to being socially responsible in a pluralistic democratic society (Barber, 1992; Billingsley, 1994; Eads, 1994). Although to date there is a general lack of solid evidence on the effects of service learning programs, it is likely that they will continue as a key educational innovation for the foreseeable future.

Social Assumptions of Service Learning

One way to understand service learning is to view it in the context of contemporary exhortations to draw on our uniquely American heritage of assisting others less fortunate than ourselves, along with the complementary assertion that volunteerism can transcend selfishness and materialistic values (Etzioni, 1993). Since the mid-1980s, we have witnessed calls for returning to some form of American volunteerism in order to maintain humane values and to restore our communities so that they promote greater individual and general well-being.

Calls for a revival of volunteerism invoke such historical figures as Jane Addams, who founded Hull House in the late 19th century, as well as such historic efforts as mutual aid societies, soup kitchens, barn raising, and the farmers' movements of the south and midwest in the late 1880s and 1890s, when farmers sought to break up monopoly wealth and redirect resources to serve local communities. Many service learning advocates argue that examples such as these represent a kind of "sharing" that has long formed part of what it means to be an American. Tocqueville is typically invoked for his observations on Americans' unique propensity to form volunteer organizations. John F. Kennedy is invoked for his famous injunction, ". . . ask not what your country can do for you; ask what you can do for your country." Former President George Bush is cited for his proposed Thousand Points of Light. Why is it, we might ask, that policymakers, legislators, and educators from across the political spectrum are promoting service initiatives at the local, state, and national levels at this particular time?

Observers of contemporary society have written extensively on the rise of such social problems as homeless children, urban violence, prejudice, and substance abuse and complacency among high school and college students toward these social problems. It has been argued that Americans, especially the young, have become consumer-oriented, self-indulgent, cynical, and alienated from both school and work (e.g., West, 1993). These values have been developing within a larger social context marked by a sharp decline in inflation-adjusted wages of working Americans since 1973; an increased competition for jobs among the skilled, the semiskilled, and the new immigrants; a preponderance of low-wage earners being pushed out of work because of the introduction of cost-saving technology; an unprecedented private and public debt; an ever greater imbalance in resources in favor of the wealthy, regressive taxation (after 1981); and cutbacks or elimination of social programs.

How can we respond? Rifkin (1994) argued that the private and public sectors of the economy are now even less capable of providing access to basic needs such as food, clothing, shelter, education, employment, and health care for individuals. According to Rifkin, the lives of working people over the coming decades will be affected in two ways: The unemployed and underemployed may turn to theft, drug dealing, prostitution, or bartering, or, the employed, having more free time, will take advantage of opportunities to engage in volunteer work. Declaring that volunteerism is the essence of the American spirit, Rifkin argued that the talents and energy of men and women, young and old, could be redirected toward rebuilding thousands of local communities, delivering basic social services.

Many service learning advocates along with advocates of volunteer efforts like Rifkin, have argued that if we act now on our historical tendency to enter into voluntary associations for the benefit of ourselves and others, we can combat the cultural, economic, and spiritual disintegration that so many people are experiencing (Bellah, Madsen, Sullivan, Swidler, & Tipton, 1985; Boyte, 1984; Etzioni, 1993). The notion that reaching out to others can transform both those doing the reaching, and the social conditions that give rise to the need for such outreach, also informs the pedagogical foundations of service learning.

Pedagogical Assumptions of Service Learning

The work of John Dewey is central to the pedagogy of service learning; in broad terms, it focused on the relationship between self and society. His ideas on how learning takes place, and for what purpose, informs many of the arguments and concrete proposals for service learning. In *Democracy and Education* (1916) Dewey theorized the importance of intellectual development in relation to social development, including the value of service to, and engagement with, others. Dewey stressed the importance of requiring students to engage in real problems, with the aim of making learning meaningful. Service learning is attractive to many educators because it is a way to involve students in active learning, something akin to the "project method," advocated by Kilpatrick (1918), a follower of Dewey and leader of the Progressive Movement. Kilpatrick argued that education should engage students in meeting real community needs. The assumption behind this approach is that learning by "serving" will lead to a more democratic society because students will have exercised (i.e., *experienced*) such democratic skills and attitudes as problem-solving skills and commitment to building pluralistic communities (Barber, 1992; Seigel & Rockwood, 1993). The quality of democracy will be enhanced because individual students will assume a measure of social responsibility. Service learning is, therefore, a method of civic education.

Critique of Assumptions

As a result of economic and social distress from joblessness and a shift of the tax burden from the wealthy to the majority of the population, many neighborhoods, civic associations, and labor unions have been deteriorating. There has been a polarization of racial and ethnic attitudes between working families, hard pressed to make ends meet. Those bearing the burden of these problems are disproportionately people of color. Given this context, it is not surprising to find high levels of poverty, drug abuse, violence, homelessness, and discrimination in poor areas.

Even though one of the functions of governments is to provide basic services, it too has laid off employees and cut programs, just as the private sector has, in order to function within its budget. Given that our economic system is driven by the logic of profitable production, it is understandable that necessary services, social in character, will be inadequately addressed. Historically, as well as today, our economy has often failed to meet the minimum needs of large sectors of Americans.

Perhaps, then, we should not be surprised that many of the projects taken up by community service efforts and service learning programs respond to various malfunctionings of our political and economic system. Thus, rather than being guided primarily by altruism, as is typically implied in the enthusiastic support for service learning, volunteerism is often driven by the imperative to ease social crises. This is not to say that altruistic motives are (or were) absent among the people involved in volunteer work. Rather, volunteer efforts have also served as a stop-gap measure to bail out impoverished sectors of society. Volunteerism is often one more attempt to deliver social services with minimum cost to government. Further, the type of social services that students typically perform in service learning programs (e.g., registering the homeless for shelter; accompanying seniors on errands) does not develop sophisticated analytical skills or a solid knowledge base. The assumption is that active citizenship is to be morally, but not necessarily intellectually, rewarding.

As an alternative to government programs, volunteerism also tends to alleviate social tensions that might otherwise erupt. This attempt to mitigate social distress was true historically, often in the form of church-based charities, such as the Salvation Army, or private charities, such as Jane Addams Hull House. Significantly, Serow and Biting (1995) traced the antecedents of the National Community Service Trust Act to the Depression and two of its programs, in particular, for employing young adults; the Civilian Conservation Corps (CCC) and the National Youth Administration (NYA). "Both programs had been created as part of the Roosevelt administration's attempt to reinvigorate the national economy and *control the social tensions arising from joblessness* [italics added]" (1995, p. 87). Sharp population growth, increased life expectancy, drastic reductions in employment, and global economic depression greatly increased the numbers of impoverished people that overwhelmed the efforts of private and church-based volunteer groups to address these needs. In response, massive government programs (e.g., social security, unemployment benefits) had to be developed. With the present decline of employment in the military sector, however, compounded by corporate and government downsizing, it seems unlikely that volunteers will be able to address current demands for social services.

It also seems doubtful that there is something unique about the American character that inclines us toward voluntary work. First, people all over the world engage in work for the benefit of others; mutual aid societies, for example, have been formed in many cultures. It is plausible that Tocqueville was struck more by the absence of feudal institutions in 19th-century America, which allowed Americans to form voluntary associations, than by our ancestors unique know-how in forming such groups. Second, this kind of giving has often been carried out by the privileged, who have enjoyed the resources to help others, rather than by Americans in general. Additional issues that receive scant attention in the literature on community service are the facts that many of the people who were "volunteered" during the Depression, for example CCC and WPA workers, performed work that no one else was doing, or, sometimes embarked on entirely new jobs. CCC workers did not replace other employees as is occurring today with some volunteers replacing public sector workers. Moreover, historically, volunteer associations have varied in composition and in aim. The original American colonies and commonwealths were akin to self-help "communities," often mutually hostile and segregated by race, religion, and incompatible economies that inevitably clashed in a bloody civil war.

Volunteerism is often associated with the idea that people on the local level can solve their own problems. This was probably true in the era of the open frontier when many working families could support themselves by homesteading. As part of the ideology of self-help, this idea still appeals to many Americans, suggesting boundless possibilities and reinforcing the notion that public support for social services can be greatly reduced. The ideology of self-help calls to mind America's "rugged individualism" identified with freedom (and slavery); liberty (and the genocide of Manifest Destiny). Yet, this ideology ignores the reality that we now live in an interdependent "global village," where nearly all of the products we rely on for our existence come from a multitude of producers living outside our "community." It also suggests that people can solve their own problems without addressing institutionalized economic injustices (low wages, poverty). The idea of people providing for themselves is also commonly linked to the belief that volunteerism automatically promotes participatory democracy. Yet, contemporary volunteer organizations such as Operation Rescue and the "Freemen" remind us that volunteerism can also be authoritarian and divisive, pitting a self-seeking minority against the majority, providing for themselves at the expense of others.

Kahne and Westheimer (1996) discussed contrasting rationales for service learning programs. Arguing that the means and ends of service learning receive insufficient attention from program proponents, these scholars distinguished the moral, political, and intellectual goals that motivate service learning advocates. They did this by asking whether a service learning program stresses charity and altruism, or change and critical analysis of the causes of social problems. Noting that the most commonly supported goal for service learning programs today is a stress on the importance of charity, Kahne and Westheimer argued that this does not accurately reflect the notion of "experiential education" held by past reformers such as Dewey (1916), Kilpatrick (1918), or Counts (1932). Instead, these curriculum theorists and education reformers conceived of service as a way to effect social reform by combining inquiry with action. Kahne and Westheimer (1996) warned against service learning initiatives serving a conservative political agenda, for example, by denying a role for government social programs. "While requiring students to 'serve America' (the rhetoric of the federal legislation) might produce George Bush's 'thousand points of light,' it might also promote a thousand points of the status quo" (1996, p. 596).

MULTICULTURAL EDUCATION

One starting point for understanding multicultural education is the various educational conditions encountered by Native Americans, Puerto Ricans, African Americans, Asian Americans, and Mexican Americans in the late 18th, 19th, and early 20th centuries. These conditions were shaped, in large part, by the colonialist ideology that English Colonists brought to North America (Spring, 1997). These values supported slavery, segregation, and involved concerted attempts to strip away different groups' cultures and replace them with Anglo-American Protestant culture (Spring, 1997; Takaki, 1993; Tyack, 1974). Reflecting their mission to colonize the "New World" and destroy indigenous cultures, the "founding fathers" advocated a uniform society and culture—unified around Protestant Anglo-American culture. For example, in 1790, Congress approved the Naturalization Act, which excluded from citizenship all non-Whites including Indians. This law was used to deny immigrants (e.g., Asians) the right to own property.

According to Spring (1997), the common school movement of the 1830s and 1840s was, in part, an attempt to halt the recognition of a multicultural society. Most of the common school reformers were native-born Anglo-American Protestants with a notion of common schooling that revolved more around imposing Protestant and capitalist values than access to schooling for *all* youth (Kaestle, 1983; Katznelson & Weir, 1985).

During the 19th century, schools increasingly became the institution to assimilate the young, prepare them for citizenship, and socialize future workers in the habits and attitudes needed for an industrial economy (Lazerson, 1977). Groups such as Catholics and Irish immigrants, were maligned for possessing inferior cultural values. Dominant group educators taught attitudes, behaviors, and language that were necessary for assimilation and economic advancement. A classical conservative notion of democracy was influential with its premise that America's capitalist system of social relations needed a class of highly educated leaders to administer and govern. This notion, together with profound changes in the nature of work, helped usher in vocational education and ability tracks in public schools. Children of workers and immigrants were prepared for particular occupations, whereas the children of managers and professionals were prepared for higher status, higher paying positions (Carnoy & Levin, 1985; Spring, 1972 ; Tyack, 1974). Later, in the late 1910s and early 1920s, Nativist sentiment rejected notions of cultural diversity in the United States; in particular, events such as World War I and the ensuing Depression of the 1930s made ethnic identity suspect and reinforced Nativist and xenophobic intolerance.

During the booming economy of the 1960s, however, minority ethnic and racial groups organized and insisted on having more influence on such issues as: Which race or ethnicity may teach in public schools; Which group decides what counts as knowledge and, Which group decides what is taught in school? This pressure increased the political possibilities for expanding democracy for those groups that had been excluded from public life. As La Belle and Ward (1994) explained, during this period, four factors came together, contributing to the rise of multicultural education; the civil rights movement, a rise in ethnic consciousness, a more critical analysis of textbooks, and a discrediting of theories of cultural deprivation (pp. 9–27). The crucial role that the civil rights movement and diverse activist organizations played in the rise of multicultural education, with its recognition of structural inequalities in access to intellectual and economic resources, particularly in relation to demographic trends, is critical for understanding the relationship between social and educational change and the hope for multicultural education to break down these barriers (Banks, 1988; Gay, 1983).

Conflicting Definitions of Multicultural Education

One key reason why multicultural education continues to mean different things to different people is that its meaning depends largely on underlying assumptions about the nature of power relations in our society. For example, those educators who view multicultural education as simply teaching about ethnic customs and traditions often fail to examine institutionalized racism (McCarthy, 1990). Similarly, those approaches to multicultural education that intend to reduce discrimination by changing individual attitudes and by tolerating lifestyles of peoples of color often fail to take into account the systemic nature of racism in U.S. society (Sleeter & Grant, 1987).

The popular emphasis on cultural pluralism (usually defined as cultural *diversity*) and mutual tolerance does not really change the reality of particular groups of people living under inferior conditions of wealth without access to power. These conditions necessarily prevent us from living together in social harmony. Tolerance alone does little to increase the influence or life chances of people of color in our political and economic public life (May, 1994, pp. 37–38). Multicultural education is an advance beyond the ethnocentrism of previous assimilationist educational policies. However, there remains a need for us, as educators, to examine the various explanations for contemporary and historical inequities. Having our students analyze and discuss which among competing explanations are the most powerful for understanding asymmetrical power relations can and should replace what sometimes is interpreted as educators imposing their own ideology.

DISCUSSION

Service Learning and Multicultural Education for Democracy

Historically, community service has been aimed more at easing social tensions than at analyzing or eliminating the underlying causes of social antagonisms. Today, many service learning programs are oriented toward helping individuals and groups accommodate themselves to current economic and political realities, rather than toward designing and constructing new possibilities for social progress. Conceived in these terms, service learning tends to reinforce basic inequalities and, at best, to postpone explosive social conflict.

Multicultural education, on the other hand, was initiated as a way to challenge the existing social institutions that imposed the values of the dominant culture on all groups typically barred from equal access to the economic and political resources of society. Curriculum theorists and educational reformers, from both past and present, however, are mindful of the possibility for this initiative, like service learning, to focus on adapting students to an unjust society rather than focusing on digging out the roots of injustice.

Both community service and multicultural education explicitly posit social reforms as an aim of active citizenship, which is a basic tenet of their philosophy. Those advocates of community service and multicultural education who believe in both the necessity and the viability of working toward fundamental socioeconomic change need to ask what a full democracy specifically means. American society continues to be sharply divided along social class, racial or ethnic, or gender lines. The opportunities for people to fully participate in society depend in large part on where we are born and where we go to school. A complete democracy, in contrast, would give everyone concerned the right to participate in making collective decisions affecting their lives. In order for this to genuinely maximize the social knowledge and the varied perspectives that come together in institutionalized decision making, everyone would have the right to learn as much as their temperament and talent would allow. This would challenge the premise of our current educational system that enables only a few students to achieve significant academic success.

For Gundara (1982), the important issue was "how to educate a society that no longer requires a disadvantaged class of people" (p. 113). Viewed from this perspective, our job is not to "help" the hungry but to remove the obstacles that lie in the way of excluded and underrepresented groups of people to live satisfying and productive lives. Similarly, we cannot assume that the "celebration" of diverse peoples in itself implies a "democratic" setting. Marginalized groups must be acknowledged and assured effective representation.

Multicultural education and service learning therefore require that many of us change not just how we teach but also what we teach. We must teach students about the systemic nature of social inequality, including its sources, history, and contemporary manifestations. Teachers need to incorporate into their teaching a conceptual framework that analyzes the relationship between dominant and subordinate groups. Together, teachers and students can consider proposals for redressing current forms of injustices.

These two reforms must also be part of a larger strategy to address not only the education of the individual student, but the relationship our schools have to their communities, especially the quality of life in poor communities, and in the larger society. We can no longer discuss educational reform without considering the issues that surround ethnic and racial minorities. Advocates of these two reforms, therefore, must demonstrate to their students how social disadvantage is directly linked to educational disadvantage and must challenge the myth that inequities primarily result from individual capabilities and efforts. Educators must take active interest in such issues as housing desegregation and health care as well as issues that are more strictly educational. If we believe that our schools can better contribute to civic responsibility in a pluralistic society, then we must explore ways that the public school system can participate in progressive social reforms. By participating in these social and educational activities, we deepen the potential for taking real steps toward educational and social change. Further, through these actions we model our perspective that education is a community responsibility; that the democratization of society entails the democratization of education.

In addressing these concerns, our concepts of "community" and "culture" need to incorporate a critical understanding of social relations that assumes equality among diverse social groups. Service learning, with its emphasis on community can, in effect, deny or ignore social difference, including class stratification. Appeals to community typically imply a model of the good society as one composed of decentralized, face-to-face, small towns. For many, these small communities are, ideally, composed of people with the same values and same lifestyle. This model, however, is not relevant to today's landscape of diverse, often segregated and sharply stratified communities where the vast majority of people live and work. This ideal must be questioned therefore from the standpoint of inclusion, diversity, and social justice.

Equality does not mean sameness any more than different means deviant. Learning to contribute to social betterment in the coming century, a century in which the traditional majority will become the minority in densely populated states, means that we have to recognize and accept differences among individuals and within and between groups. Group differences entail some common problems and common interests but they also project vitality in public spaces. Social groups do not have to be based on mutual identification; they can overlap and intermingle, allowing distinct peoples the freedom to identify with diverse groups. Diverse groups could experience themselves as working, worshipping, doing business in and belonging to the same institutions, for instance, but without being subsumed by a homogeneous culture. In these institutions, each group would have a voice in decision making across an expanded range of issues. The important issue here would be the nature of social interactions among diverse groups. Individuals integrate best into society, Dewey reminded us, to the extent that they can control their lives and can effectively interact with others, while preventing the power of a select few to curb the opportunities of others.

Social groups, relating to one another in the above manner, represent an ideal of public life. Ideals, like education, are necessary for determining what needs changing, why it must change, and what alternatives exist for change. Ideals guide our concerted efforts to bring about social progress, progress that occurs when our ideals that reflect today's realities are properly carried out. A fundamental weakness of contemporary work in both service learning and multicultural education is the tendency to overlook the collective roles of teachers, parents, community representatives, and others with a stake in education, in making progress toward equity in education. Our practice is outstripping our understanding of what constitutes effective practice. As we know from the work of Freire, education, in and of itself, cannot be liberating and empowering. Possibilities increase, however, once educational projects are embarked upon in harmony with progressive social movements. Learning about, while participating in, social change is beneficial to both teachers and students. Such involvement helps; (1) clarify the reality of institutional inequities; (2) discern the interconnectedness between various forms of oppression and, (3) advance a notion of "citizenship" that centers on collective action instead of individual charity to serve in the voluntary sector. The historical precedents of multicultural education represent a notion of struggle around equity and justice to improve both the content and processes of schooling as well as the quality of democracy in our society. This lesson should not be forgotten.

As advocates of service learning and multicultural education programs, we must reassess our educational priorities as educators and as equal citizens. As part of this reassessment, we must ask ourselves to what extent are we willing to work toward advancing real social and economic change to meet the human needs underlying the problems our service learning and multicultural programs attempt to address?

REFERENCES

Banks, J. (1988). *Multiethnic education: Theory and practice* (2nd ed.). Boston: Allyn & Bacon.

Barber, B. (1992). *An aristocracy of everyone.* New York: Ballantine.

Bellah, R., Madsen, R., Sullivan, W., Swidler, A., & Tipton, S. (1985). *Habits of the heart.* Berkeley: University of California Press.

Billingsley, R. (1994). Leadership training and service learning. In R. J. Kraft & M. Swadener (Eds.), *Building community: Service learning in the academic disciplines* (pp. 23–33). Denver, CO: Colorado Campus Compact.

Boyte, H. C. (1984). *Community is possible: Repairing America's roots.* New York: Harper & Row.

Carnoy, M., & Levin, H. M. (1985). *Schooling and work in the democratic state.* Stanford, CA: Stanford University Press.

Counts, G. (1932). *Dare the schools build a new social order?* New York: Scribner.

Dewey, J. (1916). *Democracy and education.* New York: Macmillan.

Eads, S. E. (1994). The value of service learning in higher education. In R. J. Kraft & M. Swadener (Eds.), *Building community: Service learning in the academic disciplines* (pp. 35–40). Denver, CO: Colorado Campus Compact.

Etzioni, A. (1993). *The spirit of community: The reinvention of American society.* New York: Simon & Schuster.

Gay, G. (1983, April). Multiethnic education: Historical developments and future prospects. *Phi Delta Kappan, 64,* 560–563.

Gundara, J. (1982). Approaches to multicultural education. In J. Tierny (Ed.), *Race, migration and schooling* (pp. 108–118). London: Holt, Rinehart, and Winston.

Kaestle, C. F. (1983). *Pillars of the republic: Common schools and American society, 1780–1860.* New York: Hill and Wang.

Katznelson, I., & Weir, M. (1985). *Schooling for all: Class, race, and the decline of the democratic ideal.* New York: Basic Books.

Kahne, J., & Westheimer, J. (1996). In service of what? The politics of service learning. *Phi Delta Kappan, 77*(9), 592–599.

Kilpatrick, W. H. (1918). The project method. *Teachers College Record, 19,* 319–335.

La Belle, T. J., & Ward, C. (1994). *Multiculturalism and education, diversity and its impact on schools and society.* Albany, NY: State University of New York Press.

Lazerson, M. (1977). Consensus and conflict in American education: Historical perspectives. In J. S. Coleman (Ed.), *Parents, teachers, and children: Prospects for choice in American education* (pp. 15–36). San Francisco: Institute for Contemporary Studies.

McCarthy, C. (1990). *Race and Curriculum: Social Inequality and the Theories and Politics of Difference in Contemporary Research On Schooling.* Lewes, UK: Falmer Press.

May, S. (1994). *Making multicultural education work.* Clevedon, UK: Multilingual Matters Ltd.

Rifkin, J. (1994). *The end of work: The decline of the global labor force and the dawn of the post-market era.* New York: Putnam.

Seigel, S., & Rockwood, V. (1993). Democratic education, student empowerment, and community service: Theory and practice. *Equity and Excellence in Education, 26*(2), 65–70.

Serow R. C., & Biting, P. F. (1995, Winter). National service as educational reform: A survey of student attitudes. *Journal of Research and Development in Education, 28*(2), 86–90.

Sleeter, C., & Grant, C. A. (1987). An analysis of multicultural education in the United States. *Harvard Educational Review, 57,* 421–444.

Spring, J. (1972). *Education and the rise of the corporate state.* Boston, MA: Beacon.

Spring, J. (1997). *Deculturalization and the struggle for equality: A brief history of the education of dominated cultures in the United States* (2nd ed.). New York: McGraw-Hill.

Takaki, R. (1993). *A different mirror: A history of multicultural America.* Boston: Little, Brown.

Tyack, D. (1974). *The one best system: A history of American urban education.* Cambridge, MA: Harvard University Press.

West, C. (1993). *Prophetic thought in postmodern times: Beyond Eurocentrism and multiculturalism* (Vol. 1). Monroe, ME: Common Courage Press.

Service-Learning: Does It Promote or Reduce Prejudice?

Joseph A. Erickson
Susan E. O'Connor
Augsburg College

Among the many claims made for engaging in service-learning has been the assertion that service-learning is a pedagogy that can change values and attitudes, including attitudes such as prejudice. These claims come from practitioners and participants who have observed attitude change among service-learning participants toward former outgroup members. What is known about attitude change and service-learning? Are service-learning "best practices" in alignment with what is known about attitude change and prejudice reduction? Do we know anything about the optimal conditions under which antiprejudice service-learning should be conducted? In this chapter, we investigate these questions and attempt to promote a framework from which future practice of service-learning as an antiprejudice tool might be shaped.

SERVICE-LEARNING THEORY AND PRACTICE: CAN SERVICE-LEARNING BE AN ATTITUDE CHANGE TOOL?

One may trace the theoretical basis for claims of service-learning's efficacy as an antiprejudice tool all the way back to Dewey (1938). Dewey's theory of experience has formed the foundation for experiential education's claim that learning through experience is superior to passive or rote learning. Others extended Dewey's thinking to the practice of service-learning (e.g., Giles, 1991). Kolb's experiential learning cycle plotted a path for engaging learners in an active reflection process that he demonstrated has positive outcomes for learning and retention (1975, 1984). The standard practice of service-learning has been shaped by these pioneers' formulations. These theories also form the basis for evaluating what is appropriate service-learning practice. What are the significant elements that create what is considered to be "good" service-learning?

Key to answering this question are 10 principles that were developed through consultation with over 70 organizations in 1989 known as the Wingspread principles or ASLER (Honnet & Poulsen, 1989). These principles helped to clarify the role of service-learning and its acceptance within educational institutions (Mintz & Hesser, 1996). Based on these principles, and the experiences of students participating in community service, the Campus Outreach Opportunity League (COOL) developed the critical elements of thoughtful community service, which include community voice, orientation and training, meaningful action, reflection, and evaluation. These principles have acted as a guide for many service-learning programs (Mintz & Hesser, 1996).

More recently, others have claimed that the theoretical basis for service-learning is consistent with attitude change theories, including self-perception theory, cognitive consistency, and social judgment (Covey, 1994). Many standard texts in which service-learning practice is discussed feature claims of service-learning's effectiveness in changing negative social attitudes toward outgroups (i.e., target groups of people about which one has a stereotypic, biased, or prejudiced set of attitudes and/or beliefs). For example, Delve, Mintz, and Stewart (1990) drew on frequent examples illustrating ways in which service-learning creates the necessary conditions for positive attitude and value change.

Another set of important service-learning principles are those developed by Robert Sigmon. He suggested three principles:

Principle one: Those being served control the service(s) provided.

Principle two: Those being served become better able to serve and be served by their own actions.

Principle three: Those who serve also are learners and have significant control over what is expected to be learned (Sigmon, 1990, p. 57).

In describing these principles, Sigmon also suggested the critical need for reciprocity. Through reciprocity, all parties are learners and all influence what is learned. Giles and Eyler (1994) validated this as well. They contended that the difference in distinguishing good from bad service-learning is related to the nature of the social exchange between the service learner and those who are being served. They asserted that the exchange is influenced by the values of the person doing the service, as well as by the institutional and social context within which the service-learning occurs (Stanton, 1990).

Another perspective on service-learning and attitude change focuses on the issue of exposure versus engagement (Levinson, 1990). Although exposure is one element of service-learning and what most students experience, it appears to be the minimum that can be gained from the experience. A step beyond exposure is engagement. Engagement, according to Levinson, is a level of intensity of service that requires not only student engagement both physically and intellectually, but also the engagement of the sponsoring institution. An institution committed to service requires that students engage in the broader issues faced by the people with whom they are interacting. He also suggested that engagement occurs when both parties are fully engaged, thus leading to a deeper understanding of the issues and the societal forces that affect people—such as discussions of underlying causes of poverty as they relate to broader cultural constructs (Levison, 1990). Reflection and information are also important elements of engagement. Students may be asked to journal or conduct further research on a topic related to the service experience. Programs that engage students require more than students feeling badly for the people with whom they are involved. Rather, Levinson argued, engagement requires students to reflect on the experience as well. He contended that service without reflection and understanding of underlying causes leads to a lack of engagement that prepares students to make things "less bad" but fails to help make the connections that will lead to change (Levinson, 1990). Engagement then requires an ongoing exchange or dialogue as well as the sponsoring institution's being responsible to provide more in-depth material and ongoing feedback or dialogue with the students. This focus on engagement (rather than purely on the service outcome) engages students both cognitively and affectively. An emphasis on engagement also requires that service-learning programs provide clear and comprehensive objectives versus broad or vague ones. Engagement programs try to push students beyond "feeling badly" and toward understanding issues related to the imbalance of power.

Additional principles for good practice and suggested principles for continuous improvement have been proposed by Mintz and Hesser (1996). Termed metaprinciples, they include collaboration (among institutions, the student, and the community), reciprocity (every member is teacher and learner), and diversity (multiple voices engaged in dialogue). Their contention was that these three principles bring into focus insights and dilemmas occurring within the ongoing and changing relationships. They also asserted that principles and practice of service-learning are interdependent and must be continually reassessed. They described metaprinciples as a kaleidoscope that should be accomplished in partnership with the college (institution), students, and community. This validates that each entity brings their own perspective and interpretations to the dialogue and experience (Mintz & Hesser, 1996).

Whereas principles set guidelines, the underlying theme of what makes good service-learning is that it demands responsibility for one's actions (Kendall & Associates, 1990). Many service-learning experiences provide opportunities for service, but opportunity alone does not guarantee attitude change. According to Kendall, it is the structure within which the service occurs that provides the most effective opportunity for change. How the principles discussed are carried out becomes the key to effective service-learning. For example, ASLER Principle # 8, which states that an effective program includes training, supervision, monitoring, support, recognition, and evaluation to meet service goals, also specifies that these are a reciprocal responsibility requiring open communication between the recipients and the providers of service. Effective service-learning may occur if this principle is actually carried out and if it raises significant questions as to the outcomes of the service experience.

Kendall and Associates (1990) suggested that programs can do more harm than good if they are too short or are given too little attention by participants. When ASLER principle #10 (effective programming is committed to participation with diverse populations) is met, students report that their stereotypes break down and they learn to appreciate cultural differences when they engage in culturally integrated activities. In addition, Milton (as cited in Kendall & Associates, 1990) noted that mutual respect between the givers and the receivers of service is also essential. She contended that although it is time consuming to develop mutual respect, it must be an essential element of the service-learning partnership for the experience to be good for all.

The authors and resources cited here provide hints and clues regarding the conditions under which authentic attitude change might occur during service-learning activities, but to more completely understand this issue, we propose that a more precise and relevant social theoretical framework needs to be applied to this challenge.

CONTACT THEORY: MINIMUM CONDITIONS
TO REDUCE PREJUDICE

Contact theory (CT), also called the contact hypothesis, was introduced and developed by social psychologists to examine and evaluate the various conditions under which face-to-face contact would promote greater personal and social understanding between members of different ethnic and racial groups (Allport, 1954; Amir, 1969; Cook, 1985). In this chapter, we use CT to provide a theoretical framework from which we can evaluate the potential effectiveness of service-learning as an antiprejudice tool. CT traces the minimum necessary conditions through which favorable experiences with individual members of an outgroup may be transmitted or generalized to one's group-related attitudes (Pettigrew, 1988; Rothbart, 1996). Although several important limitations and clarifications to CT have been proposed over the years—primarily concerns regarding the context(s) in which varied social identities are aroused (e.g., Brewer & Miller, 1984; Pettigrew, 1988)—the elements of CT can continue to be characterized as the minimum, but not sufficient conditions under which positive attitude change is likely to occur.

According to CT, the necessary conditions under which contact inhibits or reduces prejudice are:

1. Pursuit of common goals
2. Equal status contact
3. Contact that contradicts stereotypes
4. Long-term contact
5. Social norms (cultural "zeitgeist") favor contact (Cook, 1985)

We discuss what each of these conditions might mean in the context of commonly practiced service-learning pedagogy (i.e., those practices promoted as "best practices").

Pursuit of Common Goals

Contact theory posits that the activity in which persons engage should be in the pursuit of common goals. In a service-learning teaching situation, one might look at this from two perspectives—the outgroup member might be a service recipient, or he or she might be a colearner. In either case, are the learning activities that bring learners in contact with outgroup members done in pursuit of common goals?

In the case of the service recipient, the answer is maybe. Take for example tutoring as a service activity. To the extent that a tutor builds some authentic empathy for the learning outcomes of their "student," then the service provider and service recipient are working toward common superordinate goals (e.g., "we both want you to pass your citizenship exam").

In contrast, perhaps many students' objectives when they engage in course-embedded service-learning tutoring is simply to fulfill the service-learning assignment (accumulate a certain number of hours of service, produce acceptable reflection documents, etc.). If service providers do not develop some authentic contact and regard for their recipients (which could be difficult if a tutor does not work consistently with one student, e.g., when tutoring programs employ a drop-in model), then it may be unlikely for common goals to be achieved.

In the case of the colearner, the answer is again maybe. Our experience with service-learning usually assumes that all learners in a particular academic course are engaged in achieving equivalent learner outcomes. But although all learners may be in pursuit of the same set of teacher or learner-derived objectives, this does not mean the objectives are common, in the sense that they are interrelated, interdependent, or cooperative (see Johnson & Johnson, 1987 for a discussion of the contrasting goal structures available in teaching/learning settings). Students are very likely to be pursuing independent goals in which the outcomes of one's colearners are irrelevant or nearly irrelevant to any other learner's goals. If this scenario is the case (i.e., an independent goal structure), then one would suggest colearners are not in pursuit of common goals.

If, on the other hand, learner objectives in a service-learning course are interdependent in the manner described by Johnson and Johnson (1987; "I swim, you swim, I sink, you sink") then student-to-student interaction might be characterized by mutual interdependence ("my goals and your goals are intrinsically tied to one another"). In this case, a common goal structure would be achievable.

Equal Status Contact

Equal status contact is achieved when the perceived status of ingroup and outgroup members is more or less equal in the context of the particular face-to-face activity (of course, one would assume status is quite context specific, a point raised by Brewer & Miller, 1984).

Is the contact between learner and service recipient (or learner and colearners) of equal status in most service-learning activities? This is difficult to generalize, in part because of the above-mentioned context issues, and also because there is no single type of service-learning pedagogy.

Several advocates of service-learning have attempted to highlight the issue of status differences between learner and service recipient (and between the schools engaged in service-learning and agencies receiving service-learning assistance) by discussing these issues in terms of the need for authentic collaboration within the service-learning relationship (Mintz & Hesser, 1996; Sigmon, 1990). They have suggested that the type, duration, and logistics of a service interaction needs to be consciously negotiated with the full and equal participation of the service recipients. To not do so may lead to a "missionary mentality." This advice is similar to the need for equal status contact. To the extent that the service-learning relationship heeds this advice, then the contact may be of equal status.

Contact That Contradicts Stereotypes

A central component of CT states that the contact between individuals and members of outgroups must not conform to the standard stereotypes prevalent in the culture. Presumably, if the contact with outgroup members was in concert with the prevailing stereotypes, reinforcement of those stereotypes would occur.

One of the early and persistent criticisms of CT was the extent to which people persist in their stereotypes despite personal evidence to the contrary (Hovland, 1959). The basic mechanism of CT proposes that when faced with contradictory personal evidence, people will change their preexisting biases. Much research has demonstrated that this is not likely (e.g., Amir, 1976; Cook, 1984). This cognitive "refencing" [to "functionally isolate" or cognitively separate disconfirming exemplars (Rothbart, 1996)] is one of many defensive actions used by the ego to preserve preexisting ways of thinking. One approach to understanding this tendency is discussed in greater detail below.

The totalitarian ego is a theory of the self (or ego—i.e., the "totality of the answers to the question, 'Who am I?,' " Shaver, 1985, p. 242) in which the inherent tendency of individuals to preserve their current knowledge organizations is likened to the characteristics of totalitarian political systems (Greenwald, 1980). Greenwald used the metaphor of totalitarian information-control strategies to highlight the nature of the self and the intractability of preexisting ego formulations. His theory is not an attempt to describe the thinking patterns of fascists and bigots; we *all* engage in these strategies.

Greenwald's theory proposes that the self is "characterized by cognitive biases strikingly analogous to totalitarian information-control strategies" (1980, p. 603). These "totalitarian-ego biases" function to maintain knowledge of self and others in current cognitive schemes. Individuals distort information about self and others in predictable ways. Greenwald highlighted three major factors (which he calls cognitive biases) in this process: "Egocentricity (self as the focus of knowledge), Beneffectance (perception of responsibility for desired, but not undesired outcomes) and Cognitive conservatism (resistance to cognitive change)" (1980, p. 603). Together, these three biases or routines form the foundation of the totalitarian ego. These habituated information-control strategies preserve our sense of who we are and how we fit with others. They also help us to identify our standing in the many different social situations in which we find ourselves. The totalitarian ego is not a bad thing—it is a part of normal mental health and is crucial to the support of our sense of who we are in a complex social environment.

Although these findings are important, they only serve to highlight the inherent difficulty of attitude change and the cumulative nature of CT—just having one or two of the five necessary elements is not enough. At least these five elements (and maybe more) are necessary to achieve a reduction in prejudice. Interactions possessing fewer elements are most likely ineffective—maybe even counterproductive.

These issues aside, do the interactions in which learners engage during service-learning activities contradict prevailing cultural stereotypes? Once again, the answer is maybe. Although many service-learning practitioners consciously select service-learning placement sites in which counterstereotypic contact is likely, many service-learning placements take place in social service agencies, schools, and so forth in which economically disadvantaged members of outgroups would almost certainly be overrepresented. Likewise, those seeking assistance from social agencies (whether or not they are poor) are easily categorized by their salient deficits or addictions (e.g., the mentally ill do not possess "normal" behavior, addicts take too many chemicals, etc.). Although contact with these people may "put a face" on otherwise faceless statistics, the contact may have the boomerang effect of confirming and hardening preexisting biases and prejudices, even though the educational objective was just the opposite.

Long-Term Contact

CT suggests that interaction between learners and outgroup members must occur over an extended time period. Definitions of what exactly constitutes "long-term" vary in part because of the mix of both experimentally manipulated and natural interactions examined in the literature. How long should service-learning contact be to reduce prejudice?

To answer this question, service-learning practitioners might reflect on the multiple objectives being placed on any one service-learning activity. For example, whereas a learner might adequately understand how a city ordinance is passed by lobbying his or her city council over a 3-week period, issues such as prejudice and bias are probably unlikely to be substantially impacted in such a time frame unless the interactions are quite dramatic and salient for the learner. Perhaps service-learning practitioners might be better advised to develop antiprejudice learning encounters that accumulate over much longer periods of time, perhaps across several semesters or school years, and with the assistance of several instructors.

Social Norms (Cultural "Zeitgeist") Favor Contact

For positive attitude change to occur and for this change to be sustained over relatively long time periods, CT proposes that the social norms of one's community and culture need to favor contact with outgroup members and reexamination of old outgroup-specific stereotypes. It might be said that this point is the bleakest one of all. How can a service-learning practitioner change the social norms of his or her community if the community does not favor contact with a particular social group?

Of course, the short answer is that they cannot. We cannot expect to easily change attitudes in the larger community, but salient social norms occur within many disparate but concentric levels—the classroom culture, the team esprit de corps, school–community attitudes, neighborhood values, regional ideals, and so forth. Although not guaranteed by any means, service-learning is a pedagogical structure in which critical reflection on social norms and potential change in these values may be addressed in ways that have some hope of making a positive impact.

This also raises another troubling issue for many service-learning practitioners—the degree to which service-learning is still a revolutionary and isolated activity in some school communities. The cultural norms in many communities not only do not favor contact with outgroups, but also may not favor community-based service-learning. Some service-learning practitioners must function as "subversives" in their own communities in order to engage in service-learning. Although we hope this sort of difficulty will become less frequent in the future, it remains a potent roadblock for some service-learning practitioners to initiate effective antiprejudice service-learning.

CONCLUSION

The theory of the totalitarian ego helps to highlight the complex nature of attitude change. Changing prejudice or other deeply held beliefs is a very difficult enterprise that is linked to factors necessary to our recognition and maintenance of our sense of self. Changing prejudice involves no less than a change in a person's recognition and organization of their ego. No wonder prejudice is so difficult to change!

Taken together with the cautions suggested by contact theory, we get a more complete picture of the challenges facing those who would engage in service-learning as an antiprejudice pedagogy. Contact theory proposes a set of minimum conditions in which attitude change may occur (i.e., pursuit of common goals, equal status contact, contact that contradicts stereotypes, long-term contact, and social norms favoring contact). Fulfilling fewer than the minimum conditions may actually *increase* prejudice as individuals engage in more and more frequent ego-defensive strategies (the cognitive equivalent of digging in one's heels). Making sure that all five conditions are present raises the probability that the inherent defensiveness of the self might be eased and authentic prejudice reduction will take place.

ACKNOWLEDGMENTS

This research was supported in part by a grant from the Corporation for National Service, as a subgrant of the Service-Learning and Teacher Education (SLATE) project of the American Association of Colleges of Teacher Education—Joost Yff, National Project Director.

REFERENCES

Allport, G. (1954). *The nature of prejudice.* Cambridge, MA: Addison-Wesley.
Amir, Y. (1969). Contact hypothesis in ethnic relations. *Psychological Bulletin, 106,* 74–106.
Amir, Y. (1976) The role of intergroup contact in change of prejudice and ethnic relations. In P. Katz (Ed.), *Toward the elimination of racism* (pp. 245–308). New York: Pergamon.
Brewer, M., & Miller, N. (1984). Beyond the contact hypothesis: Theoretical perspectives on desegregation. In N. Miller & M. B. Brewer (Eds.), *Groups in contact: The psychology of desegregation* (pp. 281–302). New York: Academic Press.

Cook, S. (1984). Cooperative interaction in multiethnic contexts. In N. Miller & M. B. Brewer (Eds.), *Groups in contact: The psychology of desegregation* (pp. 155–185). New York: Academic Press.

Cook, S. (1985). Experimenting on social issues: The case of social desegregation. *American Psychologist, 40,* 452–460.

Covey, M. (1994, August). Values and attitudinal changes associated with experiential service-learning. In J. Erickson (Chair), *Service-learning in the psychology classroom: A theoretical introduction with practical applications.* Symposium conducted at the annual meeting of the American Psychological Association, Los Angeles.

Delve, C., Mintz, S., & Stewart, G. (1990). *Community service as values education.* San Francisco: Jossey-Bass.

Dewey, J. (1938). *Experience as education.* New York: Collier Books.

Giles, D., Jr. (1991, Winter). Dewey's theory of experience: Implications for service learning. *Journal of Cooperative Education, 27*(2), 87–90.

Giles, D., Jr., & Eyler, J. (1994). Impact of a college community service laboratory on student's personal, social and cognitive outcomes. *Journal of Adolescence, 17,* 327–339.

Greenwald, A. (1980). The totalitarian ego: Fabrication and revision of personal history. *American Psychologist, 35,* 603–618.

Honnet, E., & Poulsen, S. (1989). *Principles of good practice for combining service and learning* [Wingspread Special Report]. Racine, WI: Johnson Foundation, Inc.

Hovland, C. (1959). Reconciling conflicting results derived from experimental and survey studies of attitude change. *American Psychologist, 14,* 8–17.

Johnson, D., & Johnson, R. (1987). *Learning together and alone* (2nd ed.). Englewood Cliffs, NJ: Prentice-Hall.

Kendall, J., & Associates. (Eds.). (1990). *Combining service and learning: A resource book for community and public service.* Raleigh, NC: National Society for Internships and Experiential Education.

Kolb, D. (1975). Toward an applied theory of experiential learning. In C. Cooper (Ed.), *Theories of group processes* (pp. 33–57). New York: Wiley.

Kolb, D. (1984). *Experiential learning: Experience as the source of learning and development.* Englewood Cliffs, NJ: Prentice-Hall.

Levison, L. M. (1990). Choose engagement over exposure. In J. C. Kendall & Associates (Eds.), *Combining service and learning: A resource book for community and public service* (Vol. 1, pp. 68–75). Raleigh, NC: National Society for Internships and Experiential Education.

Mintz, S. D., & Hesser, G. W. (1996). Principles of good service learning. In B. Jacoby & Associates (Eds.), *Service-learning in higher education: Concepts and practices* (pp. 26–52). San Francisco: Jossey-Bass.

Pettigrew, T. (1988). The intergroup contact hypothesis reconsidered. In M. Hewstone & R. Brown (Eds.), *Contact and conflict in intergroup encounters* (pp. 169–195). Oxford, England: Basil Blackwell.

Rothbart, M. (1996). Category-exemplar dynamics and stereotype change. *International Journal of Intercultural Relations, 20*(3/4), 305–321.

Shaver, K. (1985). *Principles of social psychology* (2nd ed.). Hillsdale, NJ: Lawrence Erlbaum Associates.

Sigmon, R. L. (1990). Service-learning: Three principles. In J. Kendall & Associates (Eds.), *Combining service and learning: A resource book for community and public service* (pp. 56–64). Raleigh, NC: National Society for Internships and Experiential Education.

Stanton T. K. (1990). Service-learning and leadership development: Learning to be effective while learning what to be effective about. In J. Kendall & Associates (Eds.), *Combining service and learning: A resource book for community and public service* (pp. 336–351). Raleigh, NC: National Society for Internships and Experiential Education.

5

Reconciling Service Learning and the Moral Obligations of the Professor

Kip Téllez
University of Houston

> *We cannot afford to be ungenerous to the city in which we live . . .*
> —Jane Addams (1909/1972, p. 14)

I began my interest in service learning as a professor in education several years ago by incorporating a service learning component into an introduction to teaching course at the University of Houston. I have a firm belief in the importance of what is often called "prior knowledge," that teachers cannot teach well unless they know what their students already know. By knowing more about the lived experiences of their students, teachers can develop lessons that connect the children's everyday knowledge of the world to the academic knowledge of the classroom. By including a service learning component in my course, I had the general goal of helping teacher education students to understand the lives of students outside of schools. A corollary goal was to enlarge my students' vision of what transformative teaching could be. In the tradition of Jane Addams and the progressives, I hoped that they would see themselves as defenders of the poor.

My colleagues and I have had some success with service learning among our teacher education students, and our experience has been documented elsewhere (e.g., Téllez & Cohen, 1996; Téllez, Hlebowitsh, Cohen, & Norwood, 1995). In spite of claiming some service learning success with preservice teachers, lingering doubts have cautioned me against continuing its use in all my courses. In particular, I have been faced with dozens of professional and ethical dilemmas that would never have arisen without a service learning requirement. Furthermore, I am concerned about the widespread emergence of service learning in universities and colleges[1] and the direction it is taking. I have found a general and uncritical acceptance of this pedagogical tool and a disturbing inclination to consider a service learning requirement the mark of a university's devotion to the poor and oppressed in the community. I am also concerned about the wide goals and indeterminate purposes to which service learning is often put. The quick emergence and varying directions of service learning suggest that it is gaining ground as an answer to many pedagogical and even policy "problems" in the university, but some of these "answers," in my view, have preceded important questions. This chapter focuses on four particular questions, which I believe must be addressed if service learning is to be a viable tool for students and professors.

1. Is service learning's usefulness generalizeable across contexts and communities? And, does "place" matter?
2. How do we weigh for students the opportunity costs of service learning? If students say that they do not have time to engage in service learning, what is the professor to do?
3. Must the professor engage in service learning along with the students? If so, can service learning survive within a tenure and merit system that values only service utilizing the professor's specialized content knowledge?
4. Can professors recast established features of professional training, such as student teaching, to address the moral dilemmas found in requiring service learning?

Undergirding this analysis is the most important question of all, which concerns the moral dimensions of service learning. Teaching always confronts morality; therefore, what new moral issues are presented for professors who ask university students to engage in service learning? Because I am a teacher educator, many of the examples I use come from the teacher education context. However, I hope that I have been general enough in my thinking to allow professors in other disciplines to find applications to their own work.

---

[1] I use the term *university* to refer to all postsecondary universities, colleges, and schools.

DEFINING SERVICE, SERVICE LEARNING, AND THE CONTEXT OF SERVICE LEARNING

This section's title oversells its content. In fact, service learning cannot be reasonably defined because what is service to one is obligation to another. For instance, a student taking a class on exceptional children who volunteers in a classroom for children with severe developmental disabilities is ostensibly performing service. Yet, another student who must devote time to her sister who is affected by a similar disability is obligated to "serve." Let us assume that both are learning equal amounts about developmental disabilities in their service. Therefore, having equated the "learning" element in the two situations, are both serving equally? Is the definition of service learning broad enough to include both experiences? Certainly the latter of these situations has not yet been included in the current, and perhaps limited, definitions of service. As professors in education, we have the moral obligation to define service learning in a way that recognizes the service in a range of activities. We should not endorse each and every service activity, but we should also not limit what is considered service based only on traditional views of service.

And other questions remain. Service learning often takes the form of university students assisting with tasks that may be obviously service, but that likely involve little learning. For instance, many university students have taken part in Habitat for Humanity, helping to build houses for low-income families. If such students are architecture or engineering majors who have gained insights from their courses and have connected home building to their course work, then serving Habitat for Humanity should be considered service learning. However, if liberal arts majors spend a few days hammering nails into roofing shingles, we might certainly count this activity as service, but was anything learned? Or is it enough to consider moral learning, what Aristotle called phronesis, the goal of service learning?

By contrast, service learning can be short on service but long on learning, sometimes in order to be a means to an end. For instance, in our program at the University of Houston, we wanted preservice teachers to understand more about the lives of low-income, African-American families, in particular, helping them to know something about what African-American families in poverty must do to survive in modern U.S. culture. With that pedagogical goal in mind, we offered a homeless shelter for families as a service learning site where many of the residents were African American. In the papers they wrote about their experience, they found out a great many things by talking to the families, including the fact that many of the children at the shelter received excellent grades in school, but we wondered if they had helped the shelter at all. The director seemed not to mind that they were there, but it was clear that they were not often asked to provide any direct contribution. Perhaps our students' just being there had a positive effect on everyone, but we nevertheless had doubts. In this instance, the placement was identified for the sake of the learning the university students would gain, but it was not necessarily service.

When we invite university students to engage in service learning, we believe that we have our students' growth in knowledge and attitude in mind. However, if the university has a goal of becoming a better "citizen" of the community (and what university does not have that goal?), then perhaps students are pressed into service in the interests of the institution. Universities have a penchant for featuring stories about service learning in the community; therefore, it is possible that service learning may really be more about "university advancement" than about student growth. The promotion of the university may be a praiseworthy goal, but not necessarily one of service learning.

The Importance of Context in Defining Service

Teaching is often considered a service profession. Low salaries, at least relative to other professions requiring a bachelor's degree, contribute to a public regard for teaching as a helping profession, or least one in which one's education, experience, and responsibility are not financially rewarded. Preservice teachers often report that they have chosen teaching because they want to contribute something to society, "to make a difference." But several recent interesting examples have suggested that teaching might be considered service for some and a job for others. These examples further confuse the meaning of service and suggest that service in the interests of children in school depends greatly, if not entirely, on who is serving and who is being served.

Of the contemporary issues in teacher education, few have inspired as much discussion as the initiative known as Teach for America.[2] Teach for America is a privately funded project designed to encourage students from selective liberal arts colleges to teach in rural

---

[2]More broadly, Darling-Hammond (1994) railed against Teach for America, arguing that it disparages teachers who have spent their professional lives serving low-income students of color. She also found it less than genuine when Teach for America suggested that its "recruits" are engaging in bitterly difficult work that no one else will or can do when many, many teachers have successfully taught in the nation's inner cities for their entire careers.

and urban regions where there exists an undersupply of teachers. One cannot argue against the goals of Teach for America, and I will make no such case here. In fact, as a doctoral student, I served as my university's Teach for America advisor.

Teach for America recruits students of any major from liberal arts colleges, initiates them to teaching in a summer-long program, and places them in urban schools for a 2-year commitment. By focusing on the great need for teachers in underserved urban and rural settings and by consistently pointing out the service their recruits are providing, it has received the kind of private support that many schools and colleges of education would envy.[3] What could explain the remarkable attention that Teach for America has received? After all, each year, tens of thousands of traditionally educated and certified teachers enter urban schools as beginning teachers, many of whom will commit their professional lives to teaching. Yet, the approximately 500 yearly Teach for America participants garner much media attention. Naturally, Teach for America participants deserve to be praised for their commitment to the children of poverty. However, Teach for America participants are remunerated with salaries and benefits commensurate with other first-year teachers. Why should Teach for America teachers consider themselves making a huge self-sacrifice whereas other beginning teachers working in poor schools, many who are from working-class backgrounds and often first generation college students, are made to feel that they are engaging in work? Again, without questioning the goals of Teach for America, how can people doing the same work for the same benefit be considered as serving differently? The moral imperative for teacher educators, in my view, is that all teachers, independent of what they could be doing instead of teaching, or why they are teaching, must be considered as serving and working. Some cannot be serving while others are working.

The lesson from Teach for America is that what counts as service depends on who is serving. I would argue that the term service can hold meaning only in a specific context. Therefore, professors who invite students to participate in service learning have an obligation to be realistic about what service the students are actually performing. Service to others, as most of us know, has a morphinelike effect: We feel good when we believe we are giving of ourselves. And like a drug, after

---

[3]Information from Teach for America reports that donations of approximately $500,000 have been received from the John S. and James L. Knight Foundation and the Philip Morris Companies, Inc. With a yearly budget of more than $5 million, Teach for America's annual expenditures exceed those of most colleges of education.

that initial rush of helping, we find ourselves wanting to do more. University students are certainly not immune to this effect. Often eager to define their role in the culture, service learning can become a purposeful, meaningful activity.

Professors must help students understand the limitations of their service while not discouraging them from valuing it. More importantly, they must not allow students to believe that they are somehow serving when others who do "work" are not. For example, university students invited to serve in a care facility for seniors are likely to encounter a staff that may appear as uncaring. In fact, the senior care industry is often troubled by less than honest or uncaring workers. Low pay, unpleasant working conditions, and a general depressive climate makes it hard for that industry to find and keep caring employees, or any employees for that matter. Students, in my view, should not be allowed to disparage staff unless they imagine themselves doing that work for a living. If they are truly upset by conditions, they can choose to work in that industry or work in the interests of better care facilities, but they should not be given license to attack those whose livelihood depends on such work.

The moral dilemma provided in the example just given and in the examination of Teach for America compels us to be clearer on what we mean by service learning. The range of examples found in the literature offer further challenges for those hoping to define service learning. For instance, Schutz and Gere (1998) encouraged one group of students enrolled in an English course to study gender inequality in university athletic programs. The report resulting from their investigation was considered service learning because, as the authors wrote, "although they did not involve caring for specific others outside their own community, they encouraged students to enter their own community, take responsibility for an issue that had relevance in and beyond their own community, and reflect on it" (Schutz & Gere, 1998, p. 140). Of course, professors are free to define service learning as they wish, but I wonder if many teachers would agree that such an activity is service learning?

Some professors have in mind that service learning will help their students see the larger social phenomena contributing to why people are in need in the first place, and will thereby be inspired into social action. Some examples of service learning enlarge students' understanding of political and social realities, but many projects are successful at the local level only. For instance, Herzberg (1994) found that in a literacy tutoring project, his university students easily found compassion for and a deep interest in their adult nonreaders, but very few wondered about the larger social conditions that might be responsible for preliteracy in adults (e.g., racist schools or under-funded literacy programs in poor schools). In the end, Herzberg con-tended, only a few of the students sought to affect adult preliteracy in the political and social arena. We must ask whether a service learning project can be considered service if students see only the immediate challenges and not the more comprehensive issues.

In a paper that focused on the faculty perspective on service learn-ing (Lott, Michelmore, Sullivan-Cosetti, & Wister, 1998), the authors suggested that service learning can be an effective tool for linking the theoretical with the practical, for fomenting self-esteem among uni-versity students, and for encouraging democratic understanding. However, in spite of recognizing the displacing consequences of ser-vice learning, no attention was given to the moral dilemmas faced by professors who require such learning.

Finally, Alexander Astin, who is perhaps the leading writer on the postsecondary student in the United States, argued that service learning holds the potential for nothing less than a cultural recom-mitment to democracy (Astin, 1997). Certainly service learning is an improvement on much of the so-called learning that happens in uni-versities, but can it fairly be asked to save the democracy?

Calling every service experience service learning will guarantee that the term will come to mean nothing at all. University educators and others interested in service learning must agree on a consistent con-text for service learning in which certain conditions are met. We must also consider the possible outcomes of service learning and hold rea-sonable expectations about them.

WHERE WE ARE

Service learning can arguably be done anywhere. Every community has its needy, its oppressed. But clearly some communities have more service learning opportunities, and those communities are typi-cally the urban areas of the nation. Teacher education students can, of course, engage in service learning in rural communities, their work can be valued, and they learn from such experiences. But rural pov-erty has a distinctly different character than urban poverty. And if the goal is to both serve the greatest number and need and prepare teach-ers for the contexts in which they will work, then service learning is most effective in urban areas, where teachers are needed most des-perately. Teachers cannot be given experiences in rural settings and then somehow be expected to understand the complexities of urban schools or vice versa. Teachers must be prepared to teach in schools where they intend to teach. Service learning, I argue, carries the same mandate.

However, surveying the nation's teacher education landscape, few teacher education programs are located in urban areas. Many teacher education institutions, by virtue of their beginnings as normal schools, are located in areas where teachers are not in severe demand. Indeed, the history of the establishment of the normal schools has been called a "mad scramble in trying to draw one of the state institutions as a prize for the legislator's home town or for his constituents" (Humphreys, 1923, p. 21). Most normal schools were founded in small towns whose legislator was able to convince other lawmakers that his district was most deserving. Combine the location of the normal schools with the placement of land-grant universities, whose early and singular mission was to prepare agricultural experts and were located accordingly, the context of teacher education leaves the urban schools and communities underserved.

In order to make service learning worthwhile, students must serve in the communities where service is most likely to result in greater understanding of their teaching context. It may be troubling for teacher education professors to make claims for service learning among their students if those students never see the communities who represent their future students and families. Students must see the relevance of their service learning. Indeed, they may ask why they have been asked to serve in a rural community when they are fully aware that the majority of teaching positions are in urban areas.

WORKING CLASS UNIVERSITY STUDENTS AND THE OPPORTUNITY COST OF SERVICE LEARNING

The foundation of economics is paraphrased, "We do what we can do and want to do with the limited resources available to us." In my experience, I have found that what students can do in their coursework is subject to the same principle, especially when the resource is time. In particular, the principle of opportunity cost is germane to this discussion. First articulated in economic theory, the opportunity cost of a good or service includes the resources lost by choosing to produce that good or provide that service, instead of something else. For instance, a common misunderstanding among the U.S. middle and upper classes is why more poor and working-class young people do not attend public universities and community colleges, which, in many cases, are relatively inexpensive. Although the direct cost of college seems within reach, the opportunity cost of attending school, which includes the cost of not working, makes postsecondary education out of reach for many poor and working-class youth. In order to compute the opportunity cost of postsecondary education, we must add to the typical tuition, books, and fees the total salary potential lost by not entering the work force. When considered in this way, higher education is quite expensive and, since the elimination of strong student financial support in the 1980s, is impossible for many young people.

Service learning, in my own experience, must be analyzed similarly. My own institution, the University of Houston, is among the few public, urban research universities outside the eastern United States. Its urban location and traditional service to local students has gained it the somewhat tarnished image as a "commuter school." However, for many of us who teach at Houston, the unique student body we attract is the very reason we enjoy teaching. Typically older and often the first generation in their family to attend college, many of our students are married with children and nearly all work in full-time or part-time positions off campus, attending school part-time. Many of us find our students' maturity and devotion to their studies very refreshing, especially when colleagues from other institutions share with us their own students' obsession with "partying" or a general lack of worldly experience. Yet, the omission of the full-time university experience has significant drawbacks. For many of our students, the luxury of leisurely attending class, breathing in the life of the university, and having free time is a mystery.[4] In this context, service learning carries with it enormous opportunity costs. In fact, I have been told by several students that in order to complete the service learning project, they would have to quit their jobs, sometimes putting the family's finances seriously at risk. The students who face such difficulties nearly always see the value in service learning and are willing to work hard for their classes, but many did not plan for extra hours outside of class. For many of our students, the opportunity cost of service learning is too high.

When we tally the examples of service learning in universities, it appears that many of those leading the way are smaller, liberal arts universities with a high percentage of full-time students who live on campus. By pointing this out, I am not in any way implying that such universities are feigning care for the community. Nor do I intend to disparage students who do have extra time to devote to service learning. But I am concerned that professors be aware that students may

---

[4]Our university, it should be noted, does have several residential halls designed for undergraduates. About 10% of the university's 30,000 live on campus.

have legitimate reasons for rejecting service learning even when they are committed to social service or even social activism for the poor and oppressed.

As more young people become convinced of the importance of a university education, a broader spectrum of students will enroll in higher education. And it stands to reason that many of the new participants in university education will be poorer. After all, those who have historically been able to afford the university have already taken advantage of higher education. Professors, especially those in education, must understand that the commitment to volunteerism and service involves more than desire alone. University students who cannot take the time to engage in service learning should not be penalized. The dangers of applying service learning requirements indiscriminately can have unwanted effects on individual students, but such effects might be even greater at the institutional level. For instance, if the private liberal arts college in a city requires a service learning component (and makes such a requirement known throughout the community) and the larger public university in the same city cannot ask its students to engage in lengthy service learning, might the community at large question the public university's commitment? It seems that the dangers of applying service learning to individuals is magnified when we consider institutions.

THE INTERSECTION OF MORALITY, SERVICE LEARNING, AND THE PROFESSOR

Common ethical concerns run through any teaching context. Whether one is a preschool or a university teacher, the ethical foundations of charity and fairness, for instance, imbue every teaching–learning relationship. The moral dimensions of teaching have been described in general terms by Goodlad, Soder, and Sirotnik (1990) and Strike and Soltis (1985) who argued that moral actions must be considered first in any teaching context. However, in the existing literature, I could not find any mention of the moral dimensions of requiring students to engage in service learning. Yet, many writers have addressed issues of morality in the professoriate.

Murray, Gillese, Lennon, Mercer, and Robinson (1996) suggested that nine principles should guide the moral decisions of any university or college professor. Of these principles, the three that may impact a service learning requirement are pedagogical competence, dealing with sensitive topics, and student development. Each of these, and its implications for service learning, are now discussed in more detail.

Principle 1: Pedagogical Competence. A pedagogically competent teacher communicates the objectives of the course to students, is aware of alternative instructional methods or strategies, and selects methods of instruction that, according to research evidence (including personal or self-reflective research), are effective in helping students to achieve the course objectives.

Professors who require service learning must clearly justify it as pedagogically sound. Such a justification implies that the professor has an instructional goal in mind when requiring service learning. Of course, some who promote service learning argue that it should be required simply for its own sake (i.e., that its learning goals are quite different than the learning goals of classroom-based instruction). But at the university level, we might imagine that students should somehow connect the knowledge they are acquiring in their courses to service learning. For instance, service learning in an introductory gerontology class holds an obvious connection and application to service. However, what type of service learning would be required of students taking a course in microeconomic theory? If we argue that service learning must relate to a course content, then each and every class may not be a candidate for a service learning component. Naturally, a course in early literacy development for low-income students may have a direct connection to the field, but the professor must balance the service requirement with the pedagogical goals of the class.

We must also be aware that there is only limited research documenting the effects of service learning in the current literature. For instance, Lipka (1997) pointed out that ". . . there is relatively little research available to inform us about whether there is a connection between service learning experiences and adult life, particularly in terms of persistent, long-range effects on behavior attitudes and predispositions" (p. 56). Ward (1997) offered caveats of her own, based on her service learning program at Simmons College in Boston. She observed students who feel frustrated by a service learning experience that fails to connect to their own interests and who find that the service learning was important but did not add to their knowledge of the course content. And if we are to trust Murray et al. (1996), the professor who has not linked service learning to pedagogy may be violating an ethical principle.

Building on this principle, professors should know their subject well. However, nowhere does it suggest professors should be responsible for having knowledge of the same "experiences" as students. Yet, we would be shocked to find physicians employed in a teaching hospital who would ask students to perform tasks that they had not done. Responsible professors would not likely require students to read a book that they had not read, to perform mathematical analyses outside of their own experience, or to read about a theory that was novel even to them. Professors must likewise give each service site or experience great attention before asking students to engage in similar experiences. By extension, professors must consider carefully their role as experts and what this role means to students and their expectations. In other words, should professors be expected to engage in their own service projects similar to those they require of their students? This issue is particularly sensitive to professors in education who are often accused of not having the relevant K–12 classroom experience to guide teacher education students.

I would argue that in any professional school the professor must have the relevant experience in order to maintain moral coherence. Without the experience of service learning, the professor cannot know the context completely and will not be able to build on student experiences fully. Indeed, the professor must organize time to engage in service learning alongside the students, devoting resources and energy in amounts similar to those of the students. Professors cannot require students to serve without asking themselves to commit to helping as well.

Principle 2: Dealing With Sensitive Topics. Topics that students are likely to find sensitive or discomforting are dealt with in an open, honest, and positive way.

Naturally, service learning can raise issues not normally encountered in the college classroom. For instance, a student working in a homeless shelter may encounter a child who reports physical or sexual abuse. Of course, that student should bring this matter to the attention of the university instructor or advisor, who is obligated to help the student with this dilemma. After all, the student would likely not have been in the homeless shelter if not for the university requirement. Clearly, this particular issue is complex and quite indeterminate. Should the student report the abuse directly to the child protective services, or is it sufficient to tell the director of the shelter? As a volunteer, the student would not be required to make a report, but should a report be made nonetheless? The ethical principle suggesting that professors should deal with sensitive issues in a fair and open manner is really of no help in this context. Of course, such an issue should be dealt with in a fair and open manner, but what is the professor's responsibility in this situation? Two conclusions must be drawn from this example: First, the typical ethical guidelines for professors are inadequate for dealing with the kinds of issues raised in service learning. Second, professors are bound to find themselves helping students grapple with the sensitive issues students encounter in service learning.

Principle 3: Student Development. The overriding responsibility of the teacher is to contribute to the intellectual development of the student, at least in the context of the teacher's own area of expertise, and to avoid actions such as exploitation and discrimination that detract from student development.

Murray et al. (1996) suggested that the professor's overriding duty is the intellectual development of the student. If the goal of service learning is to build in students a sense of duty, a new ethical view, and a diffuse belief in helping, as it is in some K–12 service learning programs, then service learning at the university level seems out of the bounds of a professor's normal responsibilities. Such a view is not strictly true, but it is true that most professors do not consider their work to be building morality. Students at the university level are invited to refine their moral claims based on the content of the courses. And it is true that many university students dramatically alter their foundational concept of what is fair, what is truth, or even what "is." But it is rare to hear of university professors who argue that their role is the teaching of morality.

Yet, such an omission does not, of course, mean that the professor is not required to act in morally sound ways, and professors must be considered fair in the strongest interpretation of the term. In the course of understanding the term fair, most university students equate fair with equality in every instance of the course. For example, students are unlikely to consider a professor "fair" who allows some students to omit an assignment while requiring it of others. The professor in such as case may be truly rendering fair (e.g., if a set of students had a prerequisite and did not need to do the assignment), but not equal treatment. Most university students would be troubled by the professor's conception of fair but not equal. Within the dimensions of service learning, fair requirements, I would argue, mean equal assignments. But sometimes fairness in service learning can be difficult to determine and sometimes not equal. An example of this dilemma comes from my own experiences with service learning. Because around 60% of our teacher education students are White and middle class and live in neighborhoods that reflect that cultural view, and because most local schools are not so uniform in culture, we sought for our students to learn something about culturally different children and youth in their service learning. And by different, we meant African-American and Mexican-American culture, particularly those who were poor.

With culture learning in mind, we offered our students, as one of several 20-hour service learning options, a YMCA after-school program in a Mexican-American section of Houston. This location was very effective with our White, middle-class students, who we believe learned much at this site, but some of our Mexican-American students who chose this location had grown up and lived in the neighborhood; one even worked summers at this YMCA. This location turned out to be very convenient for them, but did not really introduce them to another cultural viewpoint. In other words, based on their assignment, we were asking them to act as an outsider in their own community. And, perhaps more serious, the White students saw the ease with which they completed their assignment. Merely the fact that they lived close to the YMCA made the service learning assignment easier. We considered asking them to choose another location, but questioned that move, wondering what message would be sent. Our program has the theme of preparing students for urban, multicultural classrooms, so it would not be coherent if we asked students of color to volunteer in a wealthy, White school just for the sake of experiencing a different culture. Deciding what is fair and what is equal in this kind of situation exemplifies the ways in which teachers must grapple with ongoing moral dilemmas in education.

PROMOTION, TENURE, AND SERVICE LEARNING

The reward structure in universities seems to throw many professors into a moral morass. In research universities, in particular, professors are required to conduct research, but should the research mandate take precedence over student learning? Of course, most beginning professors want to earn tenure, and we should not fault them for working toward this goal. However, does the establishment of service learning present a serious threat to the untenured professor?

Returning to an issue raised earlier, should the professor who requires service learning be knowledgeable of the contexts in which students conduct their service learning? Requiring the professor to engage in service learning alongside students may be more effort than professors can deliver. After all, the reward structure in the university does not reward all types of service.

In perhaps the most influential book on the professorship, Boyer (1990) argued that service by professors must be narrowly defined.

Clearly a sharp distinction must be drawn between citizenship activities and projects that relate to scholarship itself. To be sure, there are meritorious social and civic functions to be performed, and faculty should be appropriately recognized for such work. But all too frequently service means not doing scholarship but doing good. To be considered scholarship, service activities must be tied directly to one's special field of knowledge and relate to, and flow directly out of, this professional activity. (p. 22)

If these are the rules of service, the professor has a moral dilemma if she or he wishes to be a role model for students. I argue that in order to ask students to engage in service learning, the professor must also engage in service learning and at least be knowledgeable of the contexts in which students are asked to serve. Given the visibility of Boyer and his views, professors have little chance of engaging in the kind of service learning often required of students, at least until they reach tenure or some other plateau (full professor status). And even then, with salary decisions tied to the time-honored triumvirate of scholarship, teaching, and service, if the professor can only derive benefits from service relating directly to their research or teaching, participating in service activities may be very difficult to justify within the typical structure.

However, this is not to say that professors are not thinking of creative ways to merge service and scholarship. Kahan (1998), for instance, described a program that joins preservice teachers and schools in a physical education project. Rather than focusing his article on what students did during their service learning, Kahan discussed at length how the service learning project he developed meets Boyer's definition of scholarship.

. . . standards for scholarship assessment were met by the author through the [service learning] project . . . students were taught pedagogical skills and a curricular model and then were given the opportunity to demonstrate their learning in an applied setting. Findings [of the service learning project] were communicated via presentations at the state and national level and in an article appearing in a widely read professional journal for physical educators (p. 53)

Kahan's insistence that his work fits Boyer's definition suggests that professors must make it clear that publications based on service learning projects are indeed scholarship. But Kahan did not argue that it was necessary for him to serve alongside the students in the project. We might imagine why he did not. Service takes time; learning from that service is even more intensive. By its very nature, it is

not efficient: It takes a great investment of time and energy to even begin to derive benefits from the experience. And time is of great concern to the untenured professor. Being out in the community, serving, takes time away from writing. Of course, there are those
professors who can write quickly and efficiently, producing publish-
able papers. But such professors are the exceptions. For most of us,
writing takes deliberation, and long stretches of uninterrupted time
to organize ideas.

Beyond the concerns presented by the university reward structure,
I believe that students will begin to resent service learning if the professor neither knows about it nor participates in it. University students, by virtue of their intellectual and moral development, are always on the lookout for hypocrisy. Professors, by virtue of the reward
structure at universities, often focus their research and specialties on
issues unknown to the common university student. The "ivory tower"
metaphor is often invoked by university students and by the
nonuniversity public in general. Professors who require service learning without actually engaging in it themselves are risking student resentment. Unlike the intellectual skills of many professors, service
learning is not grounded in a purely cognitive realm. Students who
can respect the knowledge professors have obtained will see no hypocrisy when those professors assign intellectual work to be mas-
tered. But service learning is different. Service learning is experiential
at its very core. Students who will not question a professor's academic assignments will call into question a service learning requirement if the professor has not had the same experience. The danger in
service learning is that students may come to resent the assignment
because their professor, the one who is supposed to be an instructional leader, cannot speak from the experiential base. For instance,
a sociology professor can speak with great authority on the theories
of poverty, and students can respect such knowledge. But if that
same professor invites students to engage in service learning in a
low-income community, but cannot speak to students regarding the
lived experiences of the poor, I predict that students will come to resent the professor, and, more dangerous, the service learning experience as well. It is therefore critical that a professor build the cognitive
and experiential base if service learning is to be a required assignment.

In addition to concerns about time for scholarship, what are the effects on student evaluations when professors require service learning? I could find no work addressing this topic, but my own experience suggests that some students see the requirement of service
learning as a failure of the professor to teach. Students who come to

the university for the traditional professor–student relationship (professors lecture, students learn) are unlikely to view service learning as a helpful activity. These same students may use the course evaluation forms to express this concern. How then is the professor to proceed with the service learning component?

Making service learning a morally sound enterprise for professors must include at least a widening of the definition of service for professors. Of course, each academic department and college needs its faculty to work on committees designed to improve curriculum. And serving on editorial boards of journals, for instance, is also important work. But if service learning is to be a widely implemented innovation, I argue that universities must allow service learning to count toward a faculty member's work in the interest of their university and profession. If professors who require service learning and who are morally consistent in their application tend not to earn tenure, the moral dilemmas faced will be vexing indeed.

INTEGRATING SERVICE LEARNING WITH ESTABLISHED CURRICULAR REQUIREMENTS: AN EXAMPLE

I have been confronted with each of the moral dilemmas faced in this chapter, and I have responded by temporarily eliminating service learning in my classes until I can find ways to make it a morally sound endeavor. I have been exploring ways to coalesce the moral obligations of my job with the requirements of service learning. One exploration involves recasting a traditional requirement with a service learning component.

With the growth in service learning activities, teacher educators must begin to explore the varying ways that service learning can be required of preservice teachers while maintaining ethical standards. For example, as I have argued here, it is a moral responsibility of a professor to acquire the same service learning experiences as the students. Similarly, professors must be aware of students' other obligations, especially as they relate to the opportunity costs of service learning. Further, students must see the relevance of service learning in their own development as teachers.

In order for service learning to become a commonplace activity within teacher education, we need to invent ways of integrating service learning with conditions already in place, while maintaining moral obligations to our students and to ourselves. I argue that one strategy is to recast and partially restructure the student teaching experience as an opportunity for service learning. In the typical student teaching arrangement, students are introduced into the tasks of teaching before taking on instructional responsibilities for the entire class. But in the early stages of student teaching, the student teacher is given opportunities for tutoring students (typically those having difficulty) individually or in small groups, an activity resembling service. In nearly every case, student teachers are not paid for their efforts, suggesting that student teaching is indeed service learning.

However, teacher educators have never, to my knowledge, suggested that student teaching was service learning. In an article titled, "Service Learning and Teacher Preparation," Scales and Koppelman (1997) argued that service learning in teacher preparation involves service to community organizations outside the school setting. But are schools not part of the community? Is there any particular reason why student teaching could not be considered service learning, especially if students worked in low-income schools and extended their experience to include additional small group tutoring and providing other help to the school? Such service would not eliminate the possibility of doing service work outside the school. Perhaps student teaching could be extended slightly and defined as moving from a purely service activity to a purely learning activity. Figure 5.1 represents this progression.

In this model, the typical 14-week student teaching experience is extended to 18 weeks to give students extra time to engage in service. Both principals and teachers are asked to consider the early weeks of student teaching as service and should feel free to invite student teachers to engage in activities that may not directly relate to classroom instruction. Student teachers must also understand their role as service agents and not be impatient about taking on classroom activities. For this model to work, however, I argue that student teaching must take place in an underresourced school, where the number of adults who can provide help to school is limited. An upper middle-class school that can rely on parents for extra activities would not serve as an appropriate context.

Reworking student teaching into a combination service and learning activity solves several of the moral dilemmas raised earlier. For instance, every preservice teacher must engage in student teaching; therefore, all teacher education students, including those who may not have time for additional service learning expectations, are prepared for the time and resource demands of student teaching. Second, professors in teacher education must, in general, have at least 3 to 5 years of teaching experience in public school settings, thus eliminating the moral dilemma of the professor's obligation to know the

Service/Professional Development (PD) Ratio

START   FINISH

Service	100%	Service	75%	Service	50%	Service	25%	Service	10%	Service	5%	Service	0%
PD	0%	PD	25%	PD	50%	PD	75%	PD	90%	PD	90%	PD	100%

Sample Activities

Week 1	Week 4	Week 8	Week 12	Week 14	Week 18
• Assisting counselor with home visits • Working in the communities in school's office • Helping with a parent education program	• Working with individual students from different grade levels • Assisting teachers with extracurricular activities (e.g., science fair)	• Taking larger role in community interventions • Choosing a selected area of need in the school and developing a strategy for intervention	• Working with individual students in a selected classroom while watching mentor (cooperating) teacher. • Helping ESL students in small groups • Continuing earlier out-of-school projects	• Traditional transition from teaching smaller to larger portions of the school day • Continuing earlier out-of-school projects	• Full teaching responsibility in a single classroom

FIG. 5.1. Proposed progression from purely service learning to purely learning activities.

service learning context. And because university professors or supervisors must visit the schools during student teaching, this model does not require a large increase in time or resources. Finally, teacher educators can place student teachers on low-income campuses where resources are limited. Such a placement nearly guarantees that teacher education students will be working in the interests of those truly in need, who often represent the urban areas. In other words, place does matter.

This model is only one suggestion. Certainly teacher educators and professors in other disciplines can develop additional strategies to make service learning more effective and more consistent with the needs of students and society. As in all educational development, service learning is an ideal. It will take several years of implementation and honest reflection to develop truly sound programs. At the moment, however, service learning is in need of a provisional definition and the construction of borders that will help to carve its space in higher education. If service learning is to take hold in the life of the university, it cannot be the answer to all the institution's or the country's problems. Furthermore, more evaluative research must be conducted to determine its effectiveness. Professors must clearly understand the nature of service learning if they are to navigate the new moral ground service learning covers. As I have pointed out, the context of service learning cannot be ignored, nor can the students who perform such learning.

REFERENCES

Addams, J. (1972). *The spirit of youth and the city streets.* Urbana, IL: University of Illinois Press. (Original work published 1909)

Astin, A. (1997). Liberal education and democracy: The case for pragmatism. *Liberal Education, 83,* 4–15.

Boyer, E. (1990). *Scholarship reconsidered.* Princeton, NJ: The Carnegie Foundation for the Advancement of Teaching.

Darling-Hammond, L. (1994). Who will speak for the children? How "Teach for America" hurts urban schools and students. *Phi Delta Kappan, 76,* 21–34

Goodlad, J. I., Soder, R., & Sirotnik, K. (1990). *The moral dimensions of teaching.* San Francisco: Jossey-Bass

Herzberg, B. (1994). Community service and critical teaching. *College Composition and Communication, 43*(3), 307–319.

Humphreys, H. C. (1923). *The factors operating in the location of state normal schools.* New York: Teachers College.

Kahan, D. (1998). When everyone gets what they want: A description of a physical education-teacher education service-learning project. *Action in Teacher Education, 29*(4), 43–60

Lipka, R. P. (1997). Research and evaluation in service learning: What do we need to know? In J. Schine (Ed.), *Service learning: Ninety-sixth yearbook of the National Society for the Study of Education* (pp. 56–68). Chicago: National Society for the Study of Education.

Lott, C. E., Michelmore, C. W., Sullivan-Cosetti, M., & Wister, J. A. (1998). Learning through service: A faculty perspective. *Liberal Education, 83*(1), 40–45.

Murray, H., Gillese, E., Lennon, M., Mercer, P., & Robinson, M. (1996). Ethical principles for college and university teaching. In L. Fisch (Ed.), *New Directions for Teaching and Learning,* 66 (pp. 57–63). San Francisco: Jossey-Bass.

Scales, P. C., & Koppelman, D. J. (1997). Service learning and teacher preparation. In J. Schine (Ed.), *Service learning: Ninety-sixth yearbook of the National Society for the Study of Education* (pp. 118–135). Chicago: National Society for the Study of Education.

Schutz, A., & Gere, A. R. (1998). Service learning and English studies: Rethinking "public" service. *College English, 60*(2), 129–149.

Strike, K., & Soltis, J. (1985). *The ethics of teaching.* New York: Teachers College Press.

Téllez, K., & Cohen, M. (1996). Preparing teachers for multicultural innner-city classrooms: Grinding new lenses. In M. W. McLaughlin & I. Oberman (Eds.), *Teacher learning: New policies, new practices* (pp. 133–144). New York: Teachers College Press.

Téllez, K., Hlebowitsh, P., Cohen, M., & Norwood, P. (1995). Social service field experiences and teacher education. In C. Sleeter & J. Larkin (Eds.), *Developing multicultural teacher education curriculum* (pp. 65–78). Albany, NY: State University of New York Press.

Ward, J. V. (1997). Encouraging cultural competence in service learning practice. In J. Schine (Ed.), *Service learning: Ninety-sixth yearbook of the National Society for the Study of Education* (pp. 118–135). Chicago: National Society for the Study of Education.

6

From a Distance: Service-Learning and Social Justice

Rahima C. Wade
University of Iowa

Let us plead with ourselves to live in a way which will not deprive other living beings of air, water, food, shelter, or the chance to live.
—Thich Nhat Hahn (1991, p. 39)

This chapter is the story of my personal journey in attempting to live and work in ways that enhance the quality of others' lives. It is a story of service and social justice, of hope and despair, of success and failing, and, most of all, of questioning and seeking. I write this story now, after 6 years of coordinating service-learning programs at the state and national levels, because I stand at a crossroads in my journey. I am too often disappointed in my own service-learning practice and the projects I see in public school classrooms and I question my own and others' motivations for engaging in service.

It is time in my evolution as a teacher educator and as a person to face these shortcomings in my work and to reexamine my commitment to and efforts toward working for a better world. The focus of this chapter is a personal exploration of my life and struggles as a White teacher educator and thus, should provide opportunities for other academics to reflect on their own work in regard to social justice issues. Teacher educators have written extensively about the importance of reflection and personal narratives. This chapter is my attempt to model these practices; I hope that others reading this will find inspiration here to reflect on their own academic and personal journeys as well.

I have chosen to approach this task in two ways; first, to examine the various aspects of my life past and present that inform my work in the field of service-learning and my commitment to social justice, and second, to intersperse these personal vignettes with the thoughts and inspirations of others who have struggled with similar concerns. Last, I offer concrete plans for the new directions I plan to take in my work and personal life that have emerged from these explorations.

SOCIAL JUSTICE AND SERVICE-LEARNING: EARLY LESSONS

I grew up in a small town on the Eastern seaboard, Scituate, Massachusetts. Scituate is a predominately White, middle- to upper middle-class Boston "bedroom" community on the South Shore. I had little exposure to cultural diversity as a youth and for the most part grew up in a sea of faces that looked just like me. I did have one friend of color, Judy, who was adopted. To this day, I do not know what her cultural background is; we never discussed it.

The earliest community service experience I remember was in high school. In 1971, as a senior at Scituate High, I was a member of Friends of the Earth, an extracurricular environmental service club. One of our projects was to develop plans for a recycling center for the town of Scituate. I clearly remember the May evening we took our proposal before the Scituate Board of Selectmen (no Selectwomen in those days). I'm not sure if our teacher-advisor had spoken with the Board before we delivered our presentations or if the financial climate was positive at the time. Whatever the reason, the selectmen approved our plan on the spot. I will never forget the feeling of elation as I thought to myself, "Wow, I have been a part of something that is really going to make a difference in the world." Although I was an excellent student, involved in many activities, everything I had done up until that point was primarily for me, to develop my skills and knowledge, to prepare myself for college. Never before had I participated in a project that was focused on making a difference for others in my community.

I believe that this early lesson in the power and excitement of community activism contributed to my becoming involved in many other political and civic activities during my college years. I worked on democratic campaigns and participated in antinuclear rallies and I gravitated toward service projects involving senior citizens, from providing chore support for one elderly woman to working at summer camps with elderly blind residents.

Like many college students, I changed my major several times. After just one semester in art, I switched to social work because I wanted to be involved in a helping profession. After taking a year off between my sophomore and junior years in which I worked with special education children at a residential school, I changed my major again, this time to elementary and special education.

The last 2 years of my college education were spent in Buffalo, New York. Having grown up in a small suburban town, this was my first encounter with living in a big city. Although I did not often venture out of the campus environment, I did enjoy a practicum experience at a home for delinquent (and almost all African-American) teenage boys in Tonawanda, an impoverished area of Buffalo. I remember playing ping pong, hanging out, and talking with these youth about their lives, interests, and hopes for the future.

After graduating with an education degree, I spent several years traveling and working part-time as a puppeteer. Although several of my puppet shows had social justice themes and I participated occasionally in community service or political activities, this time in my life was primarily focused on spiritual development. Over a 7-year period, I attended many meditation retreats and worked as little as possible, just to support my basic needs (supplemented by getting some of my clothing from the local "free box"). In retrospect, I see how my growing spirituality contributed to my concern for others and to my commitment to make the world a better place. Through meditation and spiritual practice, I often felt as though I was entering into "the heart of the world." Feeling the pain and suffering at the center of so many other peoples' lives motivated me to enter into my previously chosen profession, teaching elementary school children, and to enter the most intensive period of my life thus far with regard to political and social action.

Working as a kindergarten teacher in Washington state, my husband (then boyfriend) and I engaged in protests at a local nuclear sub base, attended antinuclear rallies in Seattle, and withheld our federal taxes in protest of the percentage of such funds that supported the military in the United States. When we were married, we insisted that friends who wanted to give us gifts donate instead to a social justice organization. We maintained that we had plenty and did not need additional material goods. After a move across the country to rural New Hampshire, I continued to be involved in political and service activities; coordinating a Women's Action for Nuclear Disarmament chapter, campaigning for local candidates for political office, and visiting 2 elderly women at a nursing home with our 2 young toddlers.

All of these experiences undoubtedly contributed to my decision to pursue a doctorate in education with an emphasis in multicultural and global education. Searching for a future professional niche, I enrolled in a variety of courses that could loosely be conceived of as "social studies." For my dissertation, I spent a year in a fourth-grade classroom teaching a human rights curriculum and studying the children's responses to democratic classroom processes, children's rights issues, and social action projects. When it was time to interview for academic positions, I titled my job talk "Social Action in the Social Studies Curriculum." Naively, I did not realize that this title might be somewhat controversial in some academic settings. Despite being vehemently questioned about my stance on educational issues, I was eventually offered two jobs, and chose a position to teach elementary social studies methods at the University of Iowa.

SERVICE-LEARNING OR SOCIAL JUSTICE?: A TURNING POINT

In my first year at Iowa, I remember deliberating over the direction of my "research agenda." Given the Research 1 status of the University, each new professor was strongly encouraged to choose a line of research and scholarly activity through which one could make a name for oneself. Should I stay with "social action" or go with "service-learning"?

I had only recently come across the term service-learning and quickly learned more through readings and attending the National Service-Learning Conference where I met teachers and students whose lives seemed to be ignited by blending community service and academics. I also learned about the Commission on Community Service and federal funds available for service-learning programs in higher education. Might as well go with service-learning then, I reasoned. The two terms seemed similar in nature and I believed that I could make more of a difference using the term *service-learning* by being able to apply for state and federal funds to support program development.

Looking back on this choice made 6 years ago, I have mixed feelings. On the one hand, I have been able to accomplish a lot. With a combined total of close to $1,000,000 in state and federal service-learning grants, I have developed programs involving thousands of preservice teachers, public school teachers, and their students in the state of Iowa. I have also been instrumental in creating a national network for teacher educators involved with service-learning. Much of my writing has been focused on evaluating these efforts and developing practical service-learning resources that are being used in elementary and university classrooms nationwide.

On the other hand, when I look at service-learning practice, in my own teacher education courses as well as in the public schools, the reality too often falls far short of the ideal. I have been frustrated with trying to engender my preservice teachers' interest in getting involved with children through local community agencies and have never felt particularly successful with fostering teacher education students' abilities to question their assumptions and stereotypes and to interrogate societal norms and values. Public school teachers' projects that I have been associated with have been mostly of the "feel good," charitable variety. Typically small-scale environmental or intergenerational activities, few have involved examining the social and political issues that create the need for service in the first place. Whereas several have been substantive and worthwhile, others could hardly even be categorized as service-learning.

For example, a student teacher and her cooperating teacher recently submitted a proposal to me for funding a service-learning project in which their kindergartners would frost graham crackers and deliver them to every student in the school during their birthday month. Where is the problem or need in this project? The school in which these teachers work is in a rural, middle-class community with strong family values. Given that the students in the school did not greatly need their birthdays to be recognized by their peers, I could not consider this project service-learning. Although the activity is a viable means for kindergartners to extend kindness to others, it did not, to my way of thinking, have a central need or problem at its core.

But what is "service" anyway? I often state in class that the best service-learning projects will alleviate suffering, but how many projects actually do that? How many projects make a difference in others' lives or in the societal structures that lead to so much inequity in our country? In my book on service-learning (Wade, 1997), I spent a chapter exploring the meaning of service. One of the central conclusions I drew there was that service should be about working *with* others rather than just *for* them. Service, in the highest sense, goes beyond meeting individual needs to empowering others to work on their own behalf. Kahne and Westheimer (1996) aptly raised the question of "Service to what?," suggesting that perhaps we need to envision service toward an ideal rather than toward an individual.

Yet, service for an ideal (insert social justice or the common good here) is not as easy or simple as service to an individual. Service for an ideal will of necessity take us beyond the "feel good" nature of helping others to wrestling with pervasive, difficult issues at the societal level that cannot be changed quickly or understood easily. Service for an ideal would undoubtedly lead us to squarely facing the enormity of the problems we are addressing. Working toward an ideal may require a long-term commitment and an ability to delay the need to see results from one's efforts. On the other hand, working collectively with others on the root causes of injustice may create greater long-term change. In the process, we will be learning a variety of change strategies; from advocacy to influencing public policy to political action.

In general, service for an ideal is more compelling to me because of its potential power to effect change for more people. However, in practice, service to individuals is more accessible and easier to facilitate with a given group of students over a short time (e.g., a semester). One of the reasons why I chose service-learning over social justice at the beginning of my academic career was because I questioned whether the largely conservative teachers in public schools would even be interested in or able to relate to the notion of social justice. Most teachers are White and middle class and thus do not face the daily inequities that are so much a part of life for many marginalized groups in this country. Indeed, as I encounter teachers who choose to develop projects such as the frosted graham crackers, I speculate about how concerned they are about the social problems and the environmental degradation in our society. Many projects seem to be self-serving. Some teachers seem overly concerned with whether the project will make their students feel socially responsible and empathetic without giving due concern to whether the service aspect of the project is what's needed or will make a significant contribution to others. When I come face to face with the limitations in teachers' commitment to the larger common good, it leads me full circle to thinking that perhaps I should focus more on engendering their commitment to social justice. Rather than help several individuals in the community, I question whether it would be better to facilitate teachers' questioning the status quo, seeking new ideas for creating societal change, and working collectively with others, slowly but surely, to bring about some of those changes.

QUESTIONING MY COMMITMENT
AND PRACTICE

As I consider the shortcomings of service-learning practice among the teachers with whom I work, I must also question the training I have provided to them. Now I wonder if I too, as a White upper middle-class professor who has lived in predominately White suburban towns, have much of a commitment to social justice.

Examining the work I have done in the field of service-learning over the past 6 years reveals both my wavering commitment to social justice and the lack of interest that most teachers have in examining such issues as part of their classroom life. Typically, I have provided workshops of short duration to inservice teachers and several class meetings in my methods courses for preservice teachers on the essential components of service-learning. There are so many logistical issues to be covered; planning, orientation, service activity, curriculum integration, reflection, celebration, and assessment, to name a few, that the focus on social justice can be easily lost, either in my presentation or in the teachers' learning. Also, I am often concerned that teachers simply buy into doing some type of service-learning project (and agree to take university practicum students I am responsible for placing) to help them. For this reason and because I want teachers to be creative in their teaching and design a service-learning project to fit their curriculum, I usually share a variety of ideas and teaching resources without emphasizing any particular type of project as being more valuable than another. I do assert that there must be a need or problem at the center of the project, but without a value base focused on social justice, it is easy for me to see how some teachers choose projects, like the frosted graham crackers, that are very weak service-learning.

I also coordinate a program where student teachers can plan and conduct service-learning projects. As with the public school teachers, student teachers are very busy and so I encourage them to choose simple projects that can be completed during their few weeks of head teaching. I reason that having student teachers start small and feel successful will contribute to their continuing to implement service-learning in their teaching during the early years of their career. In fact, about 20% of the preservice teachers in the University of Iowa's elementary education program who acquire service-learning training and get a full time teaching job go on to implement some kind of project in their first 3 years of teaching (Wade, Anderson, Yarbrough, Pickeral, Erickson, & Kromer, 1999). Their projects are typically small scale with little reflection or formal assessment. The focus of most projects is usually either environmental, intergenerational, or school based; few could be characterized as having a social justice orientation.

Both beginning and experienced teachers struggle with finding sufficient time for service-learning, both for planning quality activities and for integrating service into the school day. I also find myself continually constrained by time in several ways. First, I teach service-learning as part of a two-credit elementary social studies methods class. My obligations to cover other social studies content (e.g., history, geography, multicultural issues, lesson planning, assessment) are considerable. Every semester, I question how much time in the course I should devote to service-learning, given the other aspects of social studies these students will be required to cover as public school teachers. Although I believe that service-learning is a more effective strategy for fostering active citizenship than book learning, I am always mindful that my responsibilities entail giving these soon-to-be teachers the skills and knowledge they need to be competent in the school system, as well as to teach them how to be change agents.

As part of the social studies methods course, my preservice teachers work with children in need through local community agencies such as Big Brothers/Big Sisters, Neighborhood Centers, and Parks and Recreation. I require 10 hours of direct service, which I consider minimal and many of them consider a huge imposition on their busy schedules (even though I explain that this is part of the 4 hours of homework each week they are to spend outside of class). In years past, I have done more in the course with reflection assignments, an advocacy activity (researching a social issue and writing a letter to a congressperson or newspaper), and a portfolio to document their work in the community. Whereas many students have felt these activities to be valuable, others have complained that service-learning takes up too much of the course content and time. In response to their concerns, I have gradually cut back on some of the reflection activities and have included more course content related to other social studies topics.

These changes have solved some problems but created others. I question now whether students are reflecting deeply on their service experience and especially whether they are examining the larger societal contexts regarding the need for service without the advocacy activity. I wonder if students working with low-income and single parent families are reinforcing rather than challenging their stereotypes. At this point in my practice, I conclude that quality service-learning focused on social justice goals takes considerable time and energy at any level, from kindergarten to college.

SERVICE AND SOCIAL JUSTICE
IN MY PRIVATE LIFE

In questioning my commitment to social justice, I cannot separate my work in the field of service-learning from how I live the rest of my life. Although I tithe 10% of my income to social justice organizations, I do little beyond this effort, with the exception of a few community service activities locally such as a Sunday Meals on Wheels route and, once a month, preparing a salad for the Free Lunch program. I still vote and occasionally donate funds to a campaign, but I'm no longer attending evening meetings and going door to door with brochures.

Seldom in my life have I chosen to put myself in situations where I will directly encounter others' sorrows and difficulties. Instead, I tend to choose "safe" activities, those that often keep me at a distance from the difficult circumstances of some people's lives. And I know that the little involvement I do have is motivated, at least in part, by a sense of guilt. I have so much, I owe it to my community to give something back.

As I look at the ways I spend money; buying clothes, eating out, taking vacations, paying for expensive dance, soccer, and music lessons for my own 2 children, I am saddened at how my actions speak to my lack of commitment to work for the common good. I ask myself, how can I pay for my son's competitive soccer club or my daughter's cello lessons, when so many other children do not even have enough food to eat? Marian Wright Edelman eloquently advocated for these forgotten children.

> So much of America's tragic and costly failure to care for all its children stems from our tendency to distinguish between our own children and other people's children—as if justice were divisible. The pervasive breakdown of moral, family, and community values, and the widespread presence of drugs, violence, teen pregnancy, neglect, and abuse in every race and income group should help us realize our common interest in investing in and protecting all children—other people's as well as our own. (Edelman, 1995, p. 110)

I'm not sure where this line of thinking leads me, except to extreme guilt. Like so many other people, I selfishly want to enjoy the "good things" in life and I want the best for my own 2 children as well. I ask myself, if I were willing, what would be the "right" thing to do? Images of Mother Teresa, Martin Luther King, Jr., and Ghandi quickly come to mind. Or should I just buy my clothes at thrift stores like Ralph Nader, grow my own food, and live as simply as possible? My mind vacillates between the notion that I am only one person among billions and therefore that my lifestyle matters little in the scheme of the whole to the thought that individual actions do matter. Ed Ayers, editor of World Watch, expressed the latter point of view.

> The greatest destruction in our world is not being inflicted by psychopathic tyrants or terrorists. It's being done by ordinary people—law-abiding, churchgoing, family-loving "moral" people—who are enjoying their sport utility vehicles, their vacation cruises, their burgers, and are

oblivious to where those pleasures really come from and what they really cost. Oblivious not to what those things cost at the store, but to what they cost when all the uncounted effects of their production and use are added up. (Ayers, as cited in Macy & Brown, 1998, p. 12)

Sometimes I wish that I was ignorant of the impact of my upper middle-class lifestyle on the world, so that I could just live happily and enjoy my wealth and not feel guilty. Yet, in my better moments, I recognize that guilt is not only a burden, it is also a motivator. It is in large part what has led to much of the questioning and self-examination that I write of here. Guilt will prod me to keep inquiring and exploring, to take small steps toward living more consistently with my espoused commitment to social justice. So in some ways, I am thankful for the experience of guilt and its role as a harbinger of potential transformation in my life and in the world.

I look at my life now compared to my years of political and civic involvement in Washington and New Hampshire and I ask myself "When did I make more of a difference?" Although I believe that my lifestyle during the earlier years had more integrity, I also see that my position as a professor and grant program manager has enabled me to have much greater impact in other's lives (even if it is not always to the extent that I would like it to be). The difference between a puppeteer's and professor's salaries has also enabled me to contribute a great deal more money to social justice, political, and environmental causes than in the past. Yet, for the most part, the scholarly life and my own choices have created a lifestyle where my daily actions are at a greater distance than they used to be from the people and causes I try to help. With a full-time job, a husband, and 2 school-aged children, I do not make the time to get personally involved in the community in the ways I used to. I look around me—at my work setting, the neighborhood I live in, the families with whom I come in contact through my children's extracurricular activities—and I do not see the support for living a life committed to social justice. Others have told me that they see me as a positive example of someone making important contributions to the community, but I often feel like I have lost my way and do not contribute nearly what I could. I believe that Peter Marin speaks for me and many others in the following analysis of middle-class life.

Many of us suffer a vague, inchoate sense of betrayal, of having somehow taken the wrong turning, of having somehow said yes or no at the wrong time and to the wrong things, of having somehow taken upon ourselves a general kind of guilt, having two coats while others have none, or just having too much while others have too little—yet proceeding, nonetheless, with our lives as they are. (Marin, as cited in Macy & Brown, 1998, p. 29)

While I sometimes fault our commercial culture as "beating me down," I also take ownership for buying into the seductive life of a university professor. I cannot honestly separate in my mind the power, status, and financial gain that accompany the grants I have received from the good work that the grant activities accomplish. My motivations to engage in such activities are therefore mixed, and the time I spend on these and other scholarly pursuits of necessity limits the amount of time that I can be directly engaged in social action with others.

A couple of years ago, I became very dissatisfied with how I was living my life in this regard, particularly in the way that I chose to keep a distance between myself and others in my service activities. My husband and I decided to put a large amount of our tithing money into a project that we could be personally involved in as well. We spent considerable time exploring several organizations and projects before we chose to contribute to funding a Mayan library in a small Guatemalan town through the Plenty organization. One of my attractions to this particular project was that it seemed to be service with social justice. This project seemed to hold many possibilities for future involvement through my work as well. I envisioned providing the students in our elementary education program with opportunities to gather educational resources, fund raise, and possibly even go to Guatemala to work on building the library or to work with the children there.

As I reflect on our involvement in this project over the past few years, I have mixed feelings. Plenty administrators had told us they would be raising other funds to go along with our initial contribution of $5,000. Although the Guatemalan town had donated the land for the project, building the library building was going to cost close to $70,000. Hiring a librarian and procuring educational resources on the Mayan culture would require additional funds. However, Plenty's fund-raising efforts have fallen far short of these goals; little funds beyond our own contribution have been raised. The project has begun, however, through acquiring a rent-free space provided by the Guatemalan town council. Our contribution has funded a librarian's time and some initial library materials. The situation is somewhat temporary; the long-term future of the project still depends on Plenty's getting other contributions. Whereas some might judge the Mayan library project as a "failure," I see the stumbling blocks along the way as indicative of the difficulties of effecting change in the world and perhaps especially in finding "first world" funders for projects that support indigenous people in "Third World" countries.

At present, I have decided not to give any more funds toward this project until additional funds are raised to actually build the library, as I do not want my tithing funds to go down the drain, but I have not discounted future involvement and I continue to learn from my experience. My original thoughts about getting personally involved in this project are "on hold" as well. I question my motivation with this delay. When I think about going to Guatemala, meeting the people, what would I do? I speak only a few Spanish words and the time it would take me to become conversational in that language feels like hours I do not have time to spare in my busy days. I am fearful about going to a country that has had terrorist acts in the past and where people from the United States have been killed. What about my own children? How could I safely take them to such a place? Would it be right for me to risk my own life? What if I got sick while there? What type of health care is available in the Guatemalan countryside? How will I feel when confronting the poverty in the village? How will the resulting knowledge and feelings make me feel about my own wealth? Will I "have to" change how I live?

My head spins with these and other worries and it becomes much easier to just stay home and to keep my distance from all of these difficulties. Feeling so overwhelmed can make me feel like just giving up on trying to help others. The resultant line of my thinking goes something like this, "What difference does it make? I am only one person and whether I recycle, donate money, or live simply it is just a drop in the bucket compared to the ways humankind is furthering injustice and destroying the earth." Clearly, the stresses and busyness of modern life and the overwhelming nature of the world's problems can lead to giving up. Yet, there is a tremendous price enacted when one denies caring for the earth and its inhabitants.

> Silence concerning our deepest feelings about the world and the future of our species along with the fragmentation, isolation, burnout, and cognitive confusion that result from that silence—all converge to produce a sense of futility. Each act of denial, conscious or unconscious, is an abdication of our power to respond. (Macy & Brown, 1998, p. 37)

So, while I do not want to buy into a "save the earth" syndrome, neither do I want to diminish the individual's role in making a difference. I believe that it is important for everyone to contribute what they can. And, as individuals tutor children, vote, write letters to their congresspeople, and work against injustice, our actions become part of a collective effort that can and often does create change. In their study of over 100 long-term social activists, Daloz, Keen, Keen, and

Parks (1996) noted these individuals' abilities to focus on both the particular and the global at once.

> Because they recognize systems, they are able to link immediate problems to larger, global issues, and to take a broad-based, long-term stance. With a bird's eye view on the partiality of their own work, they can see themselves as "one among many," and carry a sense of both greater humility and enhanced responsibility. (Daloz et al., 1996, p. 123)

Several of the activists have expressed this focus eloquently. Stated one:

> So usually you have to see yourself over a long time span, and your life is just one single flower giving its seeds for the next part, the next stages. But don't necessarily expect to see the next stages bloom. It's for someone else to see that flower. (Daloz et al., 1996, p. 106)

NEW DIRECTIONS

When I began writing this chapter, I had not intended to include concrete ideas for actions in my life. To my surprise, immersing myself in the process of reflecting on my work and personal life, and reading the inspirations of others on some of the issues that trouble me naturally led to new insights and ideas for concrete changes. Daloz and his colleagues noted that "Unless one finds connections between the new insight and lived experience, the new insight will languish. A process of repatterning and reframing connects the 'ah-ha' to our lives in fitting ways" (Daloz et al., 1996, p. 134). Yet, it is not enough to just reflect on these insights and their connections to one's life. It is important to articulate and act on these insights publicly. You, the readers of this chapter, thus serve as my "interested public" and the writing that follows as my articulation of the next steps in my personal and professional life for integrating service and social justice.

To address my concerns about the distance I place between myself and those I serve and my fears about getting involved with culturally diverse individuals in unfamiliar settings, I plan to participate in an intensive cultural "immersion" experience. A recent review of the literature on multicultural field experiences in community settings raised my awareness of the power of such intensive activities for preservice teachers (Wade, 1998). For example, Mahan (1982, 1984) prepared teacher education students for a year on campus before they spent 18 weeks living on a Native American reservation with a family and student teaching in a reservation school. This experience was powerful for many preservice teachers, contributing to their questioning of prevailing stereotypes of Native Americans and their commitment to teaching in diverse communities.

For my first time with this type of experience, I will go on an established trip with experienced coordinators for a short period of time. This might be a spring break week in an inner city or a service-learning project in a diverse community. Through this experience, I will be in direct contact with others and hopefully get beyond my service from a distance position. I also hope to acquire information about what benefits such experiences hold for preservice teachers and how to coordinate such opportunities. My hope is that this learning will lead to involving preservice teachers from my own university in cultural immersion experiences coordinated by myself or others.

Second, I am going to make significant changes in the way I structure the service-learning part of my social studies methods course. After asking myself, "What would service-learning focused on social justice look like?" and reading several works related to educating for social justice, I have developed a plan that includes the following four components; research, direct service, community education, and advocacy.

First, in each class section (I have four sections of about 20 students each), we will brainstorm and identify an issue or population as the focus of our efforts. Several choices suitable for our community would be bilingual education, single parent families, or the homeless. We will research the issue using resources such as the internet, journal articles, and interviews with individuals and social service agency members in the local community. We will divide up these strategies so that every student has a task and is responsible for bringing information on the topic to class.

Next, it will be important to engage in some direct service with the population we are studying. This part of the service-learning component will probably be similar to how it is now. Students typically engage in 10 to 20 hours of service with children in need (e.g., children with disabilities, children living in poverty, children from single parent families) through a local community agency.

The third part of the project will involve some type of community education about the issue. Several possibilities include writing letters to the editor of a local newspaper, creating a display at the public library, speaking at a community meeting, teaching school-age youth, or coordinating a campus forum. Community education will be envisioned as an important aspect of service-learning with a social justice perspective. We cannot create significant, long-term change just through working one-on-one with individuals in the community. It is important that we educate and involve others in learning about the issue and how they can become involved.

Finally, preservice teachers will engage in advocacy activities that address the root causes of the problem and try to affect changes in laws and policies at the local, state, or national level. This step might involve something as simple as writing a letter to a congressperson or a more complex endeavor such as coordinating a small group to lobby a local official.

Throughout these activities, I will emphasize to preservice teachers that service-learning for social justice entails going beyond just direct service to individuals. I will also include assignments in which the teacher education students make connections between their involvement in these activities and how they could effectively incorporate such experiences in their future teaching of school-age youth. We will also discuss the teacher's role in being a change agent in the school and an advocate for both children's rights and the quality of public education. Many of the skills that teacher education students practice in completing this service-learning project (e.g., community research, collaboration, public speaking, writing letters) will be useful in their future efforts to create change in schools.

While I am excited about these changes in the ways I approach service-learning in my methods course, I am also wary of several issues. It will be a challenge to find ways to meaningfully engage all students in these activities and to not spend too much class time on decision making. How will we agree on an issue that all 20 students feel is important? Should all students do all parts of the project or could we divide up the tasks so that several students are doing each part? Will we be able to determine a meaningful short-term direct service activity? Will it take too much of my work time to coordinate this experience? These are just several of the questions that worry me as I embark on planning this project. I am also concerned that I will still encounter student resistance to some of these activities. Despite these concerns, though, I am excited about enacting these changes in my teaching and the promise they hold for having preservice teachers learn about teaching for social justice. Recently, I was able to get my 2-credit social studies methods course changed to a 3-credit course. The extra time will give me a bit more flexibility in enhancing the social justice components of the course.

In regard to public school teachers' practice and inservice training in service-learning, I also have a new plan I am excited about putting into place. The local school district's social studies coordinator and I will convene a small group of elementary school teachers to develop a unit of instruction that meets the following criteria: (a) It is connected to the district's recently revised social studies curriculum; (b) It incorporates service-learning activities, and (c) It has a social justice orientation. The latter aspect of this work will be the most challenging. Undoubtedly we will need to spend some time as a group talking about what social justice is and what it might look like as a meaningful activity in the elementary social studies curriculum.

Through a summer curriculum writing project, several teachers will be paid to work with me on developing this unit of study. The unit will include a number of specific lesson plans as well as details on several options for service-learning activities. We will review available curriculum resources for the unit and put together multiple copies of resource kits for the units that can be checked out by teachers in the district. Public school teachers who would like to use the unit will be paid to attend inservice training in the summer, provided by me and/or some of the teachers who worked on developing the unit and kit. Inservice training will include reviewing the lessons in the unit as well as learning how to use any specialized materials (e.g., computer software). Preservice teachers in our elementary education program will participate in the project as practicum students in the teachers' classrooms.

An example of a possible unit may make this project clearer. The topics for third grade in the district's social studies curriculum include cultures in the local community. A third-grade class could choose a particular culture represented by students in their school (e.g., African-Americans, Latinos, Jews) and then examine the number and quality of the books in the school's library about this culture, using a checklist on stereotypes and discrimination provided in the unit. The class could then examine new books about the culture using the same checklist and recommend to the librarian that certain books either be removed from the existing collection or purchased and added to the library shelves. Additional service activities could include developing a display in the library of the books and what students learned about stereotyping and discrimination, compiling a list of the books about the culture and distributing it to other classrooms in the school, presenting a story hour using some of the new books in a trailer park or Head Start preschool, or asking the town's public library to purchase some of the books. Students could also participate in advocacy activities related to the cultural group such as contacting the local city council about their human rights committee or writing to state or federal legislators about laws promoting equal opportunity for all people, regardless of the color of their skin.

Note that the activities described in the previous example include all of the components of the revised service-learning activities in the social studies methods course. As teacher education students complete both the methods course and the practicum in the same semester, they will be both directly experiencing personal involvement in these aspects of service-learning for social justice and learning how to involve school-age children in such activities.

This program in the public schools will require some additional funding that, fortunately, we have available from several sources. The school district allocates some funds for curriculum writing and purchase of curriculum resources; they also have applied for and received a state-funded service-learning grant for program development and service-learning transportation and supply needs. At the university, we have funds that can also be used for service-learning curriculum development and materials, given that our practicum students will be involved in this program. Thus, funding should not be a problem.

Although I will continue to offer the district's teachers the opportunity to develop their own service-learning projects, I expect that many teachers will welcome the opportunity to use this preassembled curriculum with several service-learning options. Public school teachers are exceedingly busy; although they would like to develop their own curricula, many do not believe they have the time to do so. Other teachers do not possess the confidence, creativity, or knowledge to develop plans such as the sample unit presented here and many feel that the existing social studies materials are lacking. Having district teachers and consultants directly involved in this project will foster the development of practical plans and useable materials. I am hopeful that many teachers in the 16 elementary schools in the district will want to become involved in this project.

The three plans I have previously outlined all relate to my work. I am excited about bringing these ideas to reality; if I am successful, they will transform the way I view my work, the potential of service-learning, and my commitment to social justice. In addition to enacting these projects, I plan to continue to interrogate the choices I make about my scholarly activities and my motivations for engaging in them. I am at an institution that allows professors a great deal of freedom to pursue their scholarship in many ways; having achieved tenure allows me to question which activities are most worthwhile and which may be appealing more for the status and money they provide than for how they can promote the common good.

Finally, I cannot conclude this chapter without returning to the plaguing issues surrounding how I live my life outside of work. Ultimately, there is a balance here between "living simply so that others may simply live" and "enjoying the good life." This is one of the issues

I have struggled with, and will continue to do so. My intention for the present is to remain aware of my conflicting desires and, as many of the activists in Daloz et al.'s study recommended, "acknowledge the contradiction, but do not try to eradicate, hide, or force it into a premature solution." (1996, p. 122).

While I doubt I will ever be completely at peace with my choices, I have come to some helpful conclusions. First, I need to honor and appreciate the contributions that I do currently make to support the common good. I too readily discount the difference that tithing from my income makes, perhaps because I have been donating money for so many years and so seldom see the results. In addition, I ride my bike to work, recycle at home, vote in every election, and always participate in one or two community service activities. Recently, my husband and I decided to cochair the Service and Social Action Committee at our local church. This too is a small but important step that I take toward social justice.

In regard to how I spend my money beyond tithing, I want to look more at where the money goes. For example, if I buy new clothes, is the money going to the CEO of a corporation that involves child labor in foreign countries or am I supporting a small family owned business that makes clothes from materials that do not harm the environment? Along this same line of thinking, I can look at the money I spend on my children's private music lessons as helping to support their teachers' college educations. Vacations, too, can be constructed and viewed in multiple ways; as "indulgences" or opportunities to learn, teach, and make a difference in the world.

The reminiscing and reflection involved in writing this chapter has brought me back in touch with many of the civic activities I used to engage in and no longer do. Although I must recognize that being a wife, mother, and scholar take many hours of the day, I want to make more time to participate more directly in my community working with others. Recently I began taking my junior high daughter and a friend of hers to a local nursing home every Friday after school to paint elderly women's fingernails. Although painting nails is certainly not an earth-shakingly meaningful activity, it is an activity of mutual enjoyment for the 12-year-old girls and the elderly women. It involves caring and human touch, talking and laughing together. Perhaps the best part for me is it brings me into direct contact with individuals who are greatly in need of some warmth and friendship to brighten their days. Thus, I find myself engaging in service a little less from a distance.

Ultimately, I hope that my journey with service-learning and social justice, both personally and professionally, leads me to greater commitment to the common good, to more effective use of my skills and talents, and to richer connections with others. My intention is to stay open to both the pains and joys in the world and to be willing to consider new possibilities and directions as I seek the best path to walk. Ultimately, I am hopeful that my life's journey will reveal the truth of these final words, "to find our calling is to find the intersection between our own deep gladness and the world's deep hunger" (Frederick Buechner, as cited in Macy & Brown, 1998, p. 169).

REFERENCES

Daloz, L. A., Keen, C. H., Keen, J. P., & Parks, S. D. (1996). *Common fire: Leading lives of commitment in a complex world.* Boston, MA: Beacon Press.

Edelman, M. W. (1995). *Guide my feet: Prayers and meditations on loving and working for children.* New York: HarperCollins.

Kahne, J., & Westheimer, J. (1996). In service to what?: The politics of service-learning. *Phi Delta Kappan, 77*(2), 592–599.

Macy, J., & Brown, M. Y. (1998). *Coming back to life: Practices to reconnect our lives, our world.* Gabriola Island BC, Canada: New Society Publishers.

Mahan, J. M. (1982). Native Americans as teacher trainers: Anatomy and outcomes of a cultural immersion project. *Journal of Educational Equity and Leadership, 2,* 100–110.

Mahan, J. M. (1984). Major concerns of Anglo student teachers serving in Native American communities. *Journal of American Indian Education, 23*(3), 19–24.

Thich Nhat Hanh. (1991). *Peace is every step.* New York: Bantam Books.

Wade, R. C. (1997). *Community service-learning: A guide to including service in the public school curriculum.* Albany, NY: State University of New York Press.

Wade, R. C. (1998, November). *Service-learning in multicultural education: A review of the literature.* Paper presented at the National Council for the Social Studies Annual Meeting, Anaheim, CA.

Wade, R. C., Anderson, J. A., Yarbrough, D. B., Pickeral, T., Erickson, J. B., & Kromer, T. (1999). Novice teachers' experiences of community service-learning. *Teaching and Teacher Education, 15,* 667–684.

REPORTS FROM
THE FIELD

7

Developing a Critical Pedagogy of Service Learning: Preparing Self-Reflective, Culturally Aware, and Responsive Community Participants

Kathleen Rice
Seth Pollack
California State University Monterey Bay

California State University Monterey Bay (CSUMB) is one of the few public universities in the country where service learning is a graduation requirement. Since its founding in 1995, service learning has been institutionalized as a core part of the academic program. In each of the university's first 3 years, 50% of the students have taken service learning courses, contributing over 60,000 hours of work to the community and resulting in partnerships with more than 240 community organizations (Service Learning Institute, 1998). Although the extensiveness of these efforts is noteworthy, it is the university's fundamental commitment to issues of multiculturalism and diversity that distinguishes its service learning program. At CSUMB, service learning and multiculturalism are inextricably intertwined.

This chapter describes how multicultural education and service learning have come to be powerfully interrelated at CSUMB, resulting in the creation of a program committed to preparing "self-reflective, culturally aware, and responsive community participants through reciprocal service and learning" (Alexander et al., 1998). At the core of CSUMB's service learning program is the required lower division course, Service Learning 200: Introduction to Service in Multicultural Communities. In this class, students provide service to the community while examining issues related to multiculturalism and diversity, social power, privilege,[1] and oppression.[2] By incorporating this critical examination of issues related to service and society, CSUMB is enabling students not only to participate in community, but to contribute to the creation of more just and equitable communities. Through the development of a critical service learning pedagogy, all students at CSUMB begin to understand how they see themselves, how others see them, and how these identities affect their involvement in the community. In this way, service learners become more aware of the stereotypes that they hold, and develop ways of interacting in the community that are sensitive to the dangers of perpetuating existing systemic injustices. After students become more aware of the existence of oppression and injustice in their everyday lives, they are better able to consciously choose whether and how to work to end racism, classism, sexism, and other forms of oppression that often underlie the service context.

This chapter first describes the unusual context in which CSUMB's service learning program is evolving; namely, a new university "for the 21st Century" that has been created on the site of a decommissioned U.S. Army base. The second section describes CSUMB's service learning program. Being supported by an institution committed to ethical reflection and practice and multiculturalism, CSUMB's Service Learning Institute has begun to build a program that incorporates both service learning as pedagogy (the "how-to's" of active, experiential learning) and service learning as the critical engagement by students, faculty, and community partners with the contested concept of service.[3] The

---

[1]"A resource or state of being that is only readily available to some people because of their social group membership" (Adams, Bell, & Griffin, 1997, p. 118).

[2]Many of the concepts underlying our work with social justice and service learning are well defined in the book by Adams and colleagues, *Teaching for Diversity and Social Justice*. In this book, privilege was defined as: "A systemic social phenomenon based on the perceived and real differences among social groups that involve ideological domination, institutional control, and the promulgation of the oppressor's ideology, logic system and culture to the oppressed group. The result is the exploitation of one social group by another for the benefit of the oppressor group" (p. 118). This same book is cited to clarify the definitions of other concepts as they arise in the text.

[3]The concept of *contested terms* was used by political theorist Connolly (1993) to refer to concepts in society "whose definition is never neutral but always entangled in competing moral and political commitments" (p. 7). As such, their definitions are continually being reinterpreted and renegotiated in response to political, socioeconomic, and cultural forces. Pollack (1997) provides a more thorough treatment of the concept of *service* as a contested term.

third section describes the curriculum and pedagogy of CSUMB's core service learning course, Service Learning 200: Introduction to Service in Multicultural Communities. This foundational course assists students in learning to enter, participate in, and exit communities sensitively, and provides the conceptual framework and language that students need to critically examine their relationship with issues of power, privilege, and oppression in society. Finally, issues that have arisen in teaching this challenging curriculum are discussed, and implications for the wider field are introduced.

CSU MONTEREY BAY'S DISTINCTIVE CONTEXT

There are many factors that have contributed to the centrality of service learning at CSUMB. The local community played an active role during the planning phase of the new campus, insisting that any institution that is built on the decommissioned Army base, Fort Ord, be accessible to and be a part of the local community. This insistence on local involvement and contribution had a significant impact on the character that the new university was to develop.

The U.S. Army decided in 1991 to vacate Fort Ord, a sprawling army base situated outside of Monterey, on California's scenic central coast. Prior to its closing, Fort Ord was the largest U.S. Army base in the world, with an area of 28,000 acres and holding up to 100,000 people at its wartime peaks (Arias, 1998). In late 1994, the governor of California signed the legislation authorizing the creation of the California State University system's 21st campus. As it was designed to be a model for the future, the CSU system came to refer to CSU Monterey Bay as "the 21st campus for the 21st century" (Chance, 1997).

CSUMB is intentionally designed to address the needs of 21st century students (who are increasingly diverse), the 21st century society (which is increasingly global and interdependent), and the 21st century economy (which is increasingly technological). The core values of this very unusual institution are articulated in CSUMB's vision statement, created in 1994 to guide the development of the institution. At the core of CSUMB's vision is the need to prepare students to participate effectively in a diverse, multicultural world. The following excerpt from the vision statement gives a sense of this unique, values-driven university.

> CSUMB . . . will be distinctive in serving the diverse people of California, especially the working class and historically under-educated and low-income populations. The identity of the University will be framed by substantive commitment to a multilingual, multicultural, intellec-

tual community . . . broadly defined scholarly and creative activity, and coordinated community service.

Our vision of the goals of California State University, Monterey Bay includes a model, pluralistic, academic community where all learn and teach one another in an atmosphere of mutual respect and pursuit of excellence. . . . Our graduates will have an understanding of interdependence and global competence . . . the critical thinking abilities to be productive citizens, and the social responsibility and skills to be community builders. CSUMB Vision Statement, 1994

Whereas it is not unusual for a university to lay out such goals in a document and then file it away to gather dust, CSUMB has attempted to make its vision statement a living document, and it has been given a prominent role in the university's formative years of development. The statement has been central to faculty and student orientations, and to the program development, accreditation, and review process. In order to keep the vision statement in sight as the campus grows, CSUMB has distilled from it seven core academic values to guide its program planning. These core values are technology infusion, multiculturalism, globalism, ethical reflection and practice, interdisciplinarity, applied learning, service learning, and collaboration (CSUMB, 1997). Of particular importance to the organization of the service learning program have been the values of multiculturalism and ethical reflection. From the institution's founding, critical multiculturalism has been central to CSUMB's understanding of service learning. Service learning is understood as an active learning pedagogy to help students experience and examine their role in a multicultural society and to further explore the ethical and moral issues related specifically to multicultural community participation.

Centrality of "Critical Multiculturalism" at CSUMB

The university's commitment to multiculturalism has had a significant impact on the formulation of the service learning program. Multiculturalism is a central component of the vision statement, one of the institution's seven core academic values, and is embedded in both the general education curriculum and in the graduation requirements of each of the university's 12 majors. CSUMB's approach to multiculturalism is strongly rooted in social reconstructionist multicultural education (Sleeter & Grant, 1987), and therefore emphasizes teaching about social injustice and the systems of power, privilege, and oppression that maintain social inequity.

One example of CSUMB's approach to "critical multiculturalism" is the way in which multiculturalism has been incorporated into the university learning requirement (ULR) system. One of the 13 ULRs specifically addresses issues of multiculturalism. Rather than being called "multiculturalism," it is called "Culture and Equity," to emphasize the important historical connection between cultural and social inequity. To fulfill the Culture and Equity ULR, students must

> . . . demonstrate a comprehension of one's individual cultural identity in relationship to other cultures and lifestyles within their contexts; and demonstrate critical awareness of relations of power as well as means for creating greater equity and social justice (Culture and Equity University Learning Requirement). (CSUMB, 1998)

This statement is a clear indication of how the study of multiculturalism at CSUMB is inextricably linked with the discussion of power relations and issues of equity and social justice. In addition, other ULRs such as "U.S. Histories," "Ethics," "Community Participation," and "Democratic Participation" have also incorporated a critical multicultural approach to their content area. Critical multiculturalism has also been incorporated into the learning objectives for each major.

CSUMB's multicultural emphasis is not without criticism (Pitnick, 1998; Will, 1998). Nor are the current resources and support structures deemed sufficient to achieve the vision statement's goal of creating a "model, pluralistic, academic community." Yet, the groundwork has been laid to build an academic program that has critical multiculturalism at its core.

SERVICE LEARNING AT CSUMB

From the earliest planning days at CSUMB, service learning has been envisioned as a central element of the educational program of this innovative university for the 21st century. This fundamental commitment to service learning is based on CSUMB's goals of (a) preparing well-educated students for an increasingly multicultural and global society; and (b) building a pedagogy and a curriculum that makes the community and the academy equal partners in teaching and learning (Franklin, 1996).

Growing within a very distinctive context, CSUMB has developed a service learning program that is distinguished by its integration throughout the academic program, by its critical examination of the concept of service, and by the pedagogical focus on issues of compassion, diversity, justice, and social responsibility.

Service Learning Integrated
Into the Academic Program

During the 1994 planning year, a community and national service work group headed by Dr. Timothy Stanton of the Haas Center for Public Service at Stanford University met regularly and recommended that service learning be a graduation requirement for all CSUMB students. The university adopted this recommendation and ultimately developed a two-tiered graduation requirement, embedding service learning in both the lower division ULR system, and in the major learning outcomes developed by each major. Those students who enter CSUMB as lower division students (new freshmen or lower division transfer students) must develop the competencies specified in the Community Participation ULR. Currently, this is accomplished by taking (and demonstrating competence in) the core course, SL 200: Introduction to Service in Multicultural Communities. This course helps students develop skills in entering, participating in, and exiting a community sensitively, and increases students' awareness of dynamics related to power, privilege, and oppression in society. In addition, all students, regardless of when they enter CSUMB, are required to take a service learning course in their major. Thus, students who graduate from CSUMB have at least two opportunities to be involved in community service learning, and those who transfer as juniors are guaranteed of having at least one opportunity. Currently, there are over 40 service learning experiences offered each semester, addressing learning outcomes from each of the university's 12 undergraduate degree programs (see chap. 8 for a description of two courses in the university's Liberal Studies major).

Examining the Concept of Service:
Critical Service Learning Pedagogy

Although the university's service learning requirement ensures that CSUMB students will participate in the service learning process, it is the outcomes-based education format and the values of multiculturalism and ethical reflection that guide their learning experiences. The incorporation of these values related to moral and civic development as an integral part of the course's learning objectives makes service learning distinctive at CSUMB. At many higher education institutions, service learning is regarded as a powerful example of active, experiential pedagogy, designed to provide a real-world context to facilitate the acquisition of what is considered to be "academic" knowledge. Despite the active approach to learning through community involvement, the "content of the course" (i.e., its learning objectives) remains focused on traditional academic learning objectives based in specific disciplines. At CSUMB, the learning objectives themselves have been transformed by incorporating a critical examination of the very concept of service as an integral aspect of the learning experience.

In all service learning courses, students examine issues of compassion, diversity, justice, and social responsibility. By explicitly making the examination of these values part of the curriculum, the concept of service becomes embedded in the learning objectives of the course. Students are able to develop new knowledge and new skills relevant to multicultural community participation. They are also able to deepen and clarify their own understanding of the concept of service, especially as it pertains to their role in a diverse, multicultural society.

CSUMB's academic program is still growing, and the concept of a "critical service learning pedagogy" is not fully developed in all program areas. The critical service learning pedagogy is most fully developed in the required sophomore-level service learning course that enables students to meet the Community Participation ULR. The curriculum and pedagogy of this course is presented in detail in the following section.

INTRODUCTION TO SERVICE IN MULTICULTURAL COMMUNITIES

The curriculum of SL200: Introduction to Service in Multicultural Communities, the core lower division course that fulfills the Community Participation University Learning Requirement, is designed to prepare students to demonstrate competency as self-reflective, culturally aware, and responsive community participants through reciprocal service and learning (see Fig. 7.1). To help students become this type of community participant, the course content exposes them to opportunities to learn about (a) the assumptions they carry with them when interacting in society; (b) larger societal patterns of power, privilege, and oppression, and their impact on groups of people; (c) ways in which their own identities and their views of the world are influenced or shaped by these larger societal patterns; and (d) how systems of oppression impact our communities and in particu-

The purpose of this University Learning Requirement is to foster the development of self-reflective, culturally aware, and responsive community participants through reciprocal service and learning.

Learning Outcomes
1. The student will demonstrate competency as a self-reflective community participant.
2. The student will demonstrate competency as a culturally aware community participant.
3. The student will demonstrate competency as a responsive community participant.
4. The student will demonstrate competency in engaging in reciprocal service and learning.

What does this mean?
1. The student will demonstrate competency as a self-reflective community participant.
The self-reflective community participant will be able to:
- Recognize her/his own beliefs and assumptions and their impact on her/his interactions in community settings;
- Critically and sensitively question, examine, and analyze her/his own experiences and identities in relation to her/his participation within communities and larger systems of inequity.

2. The student will demonstrate competency as a culturally aware community participant.
The culturally aware student will be able to:
- Examine ways in which her/his cultural identities (e.g. abilities, age, class, gender, primary language, race, sexual identity, religion) influence the way s/he perceives and participates in communities.
- Analyze power relations within and between communities and their larger societal contexts and determine how to relate to those structures in ways the community defines as effective.
- Contribute to community in ways that do not replicate/reinforce systemic injustice.

3. The student will demonstrate competency as a responsive community participant.
The responsive community participant will be able to:
- Listen empathically to community identified interests, needs, and strengths.
- Engage in work in the community defined as valuable by the community.
- Hold oneself accountable for one's actions by reflecting upon, learning from and incorporating feedback to respond more effectively in subsequent situations.

4. The student will demonstrate competency in engaging in reciprocal service and learning.
The student engaged in a reciprocal service and learning relationship will be able to:
- Communicate and demonstrate her/his power to contribute to community and the power of the community to contribute to her/his academic, personal, and professional learning and development.

FIG. 7.1. California State University Monterey Bay Community Participation University Learning Requirement.

lar, the service relationship (see Rice & Brown, 1998, for more information on the impact of the course on students).

Course Overview

Each semester, multiple sections of the course are taught by a team of faculty from varied academic disciplines. Instructors use a common core curriculum that prepares students for their service experience and provides them with theoretical and practical constructs to examine the ways in which systems of oppression, privilege, and prejudice are at the roots of many of our communities' concerns. A core reading packet is used in all sections and students are required to participate in at least 30 hours of service with a partnering community organization selected by the faculty. In addition, each instructor incorporates issues from her or his discipline and area of interest to create a thematic focus for the course. The service students provide is related to the theme of the section. For example, students in a section on youth literacy serve as tutors with the America Reads program, those in a section on neighborhood organizations work with parents who patrol their children's school to ensure safe passage to and from school, and students in a section on disease and the environment provide educational outreach on HIV and other sexually transmitted diseases to youth, sex workers, and people who are homeless.

A significant amount of time at the beginning of the semester is spent preparing students to enter a community agency respectfully and sensitively. Students are asked to examine their assumptions and stereotypes about groups of people and neighborhoods. They explore different views on service and self-reflect on their own motivations for being of service. Although many enter the class with the perspective that service is something you do in your spare time, or that service is about "helping those less fortunate," the course gives them opportunities to critically examine the power dynamics of that approach to service and to identify new ways of entering into a reciprocal relationship in the community. As students begin their 30 hours of work in the community, they explore issues of compassion and blame, and learn about the local community. Midsemester, they are introduced to the cycle of socialization model[4] and explore ways in which dominant groups (e.g., people who are male, White, heterosex-

---

[4]The way systemic subordination and domination are perpetuated from generation to generation by passing on misinformation and stereotypes, and behaving in ways that continue to support a system of injustice (Adams et al., 1997).

ual, Christian, wealthy, or able-bodied) in our society receive institutional and individual privilege whereas others are the targets (e.g., people who are poor, female, young or elder, disabled, Jewish, gay, lesbian or bisexual) of prejudice and discrimination. They are then challenged to link this awareness of themselves and others with their work in the community. As the semester closes, students explore ways of respectfully exiting their community site, if they are not going to continue, and consider what role community participation will play in the rest of their education and in their lives.

Facilitating Critical Reflection

Once students are actively involved in their service work in the community, faculty guide them through the process of transforming their service experience into a learning experience through "capital R" Reflection (M. B. Wilmes, personal communication, January 17, 1996). Although people commonly engage in "r"eflection throughout the day, when we look back over an experience to derive meaning from it, "R"eflection is a more intentional, structured, and directed process that facilitates exploration for deeper, contextualized meaning linked to learning outcomes (Eyler, Giles, & Schmiede, 1996). Often in service learning work, reflection encourages students to reflect on others, rather than on their own perspectives that shape how they view their communities and the people in them. This focus on other often leads to a perpetuation of the assumptions and oppression a course such as this one works to help students unlearn. Various readings, discussions, exercises, and creative activities are used to help students develop skills in "R"eflection that are based on awareness of one's own experiences, knowledge, assumptions, biases, and perspectives. These skills include questioning themselves, their assumptions, and their own behavior as well as learning how to observe and describe what they see in their work in the community from a more informed, self-aware, and compassionate perspective.

In this course, "R"eflection activities are designed to provide students with a forum to engage in self-reflection on their experiences, opinions, perspectives, and positionality (i.e., as members of target and/or dominant groups) related to systems of identity and inequality in our society, and to learn about the way their identity impacts others. They are also asked to "R"eflect on their relation to people at their service site, the work of the agency, and its role in the community. The readings and classroom activities are chosen specifically to encourage students to link their experiences with individuals at their sites to a larger context and to explore the root causes of the social issues people they are working with in the community are experiencing (such as homelessness or illiteracy). Students also examine the ways in which oppression is often perpetuated through community service that is insensitive to community-defined assets and needs, or that is performed by people unaware of the impact their privilege and/or internalized oppression[5] may have on their interaction in community. The goal of these strategies is to guide students toward informed, reciprocal, and compassionate ways of being involved in social change in their communities.

Classroom Activities

Experiential activities make complex issues such as oppression easier for students to begin to understand. Star Power (Shirts, 1993) is an effective simulation that demonstrates some of the ways people frequently react to a system where the distribution of power and resources is inequitable. Because this system simulates the power dynamics of life in the United States, students often find themselves placed in groups with whom they have had little experience outside the simulation. Those who have experienced being the target of racism or sexism on a daily basis may find themselves in the position of having the power to make the rules and further benefit themselves or to distribute the resources more equitably. Those who do not understand why people who are poor do not "work harder to change their situation" find themselves in a group denied resources and power. They discover how difficult it is to survive when the system is created to keep some groups from having the power to direct their own lives.

Reflecting on what they observed and experienced in the simulation, students are asked to identify ways in which parts of their identities including race, gender, age, class, physical and mental abilities, sexual orientation, and religious background, bring them advantages, while other parts of their identities systematically put them at a disadvantage. The dynamics of internalized oppression, internalized domination,[6] resistance of oppression,[7] and on rare occasions, ally

---

[5]"The result of people of targeted groups believing, acting on or enforcing the dominant system of beliefs about themselves and members of their own . . . group" (Adams et al., 1997, p. 98).

[6]When members of the dominant group "accept their group's socially superior status as normal and deserved" (Adams et al., 1997, p. 76).

[7]When a member of a target group rejects oppression on an individual, collective or institutional level (Adams et al., 1997, p. 76).

building,[8] are present in this simulation and provide a common experience for all students to draw on when they are trying to come to grips with the real-life applications. Many students comment in journals and in course evaluations that this simulation is "an eye-opener." They say it helps them better understand the systemic nature of oppression, something that had been difficult to see in their day-to-day lives, despite its pervasiveness.

Another exercise asks students to indicate if they are conscious of their gender, age, race, sexual orientation, religious affiliation, or access to financial resources when they are at their service sites. They then discuss what may bring about this consciousness or lack of consciousness. Subsequent questions ask students to indicate if the identities of the staff and people using the services at their sites reflect the demographics of the local community. From these observations, issues of institutional and systematic inequity such as racism, sexism, and classism are explored using the students' own concrete examples. This exercise also helps students question their own preparedness for participation in the community by recognizing how their own identities and experiences, in relation to the identities and experiences of people they are working with, may help and hinder their ability to be culturally aware community participants.

Creating an Inclusive Classroom Environment and Developing Trust

In order to facilitate learning on these challenging topics, faculty work with students to create a classroom environment with a level of trust that enables a diverse group of students to participate respectfully in rich and powerful discussions full of personal and emotional significance. Early in the semester, it is important that the class work collaboratively to define how they want to communicate with one another. The "Poem for the Creative Writing Class, Spring 1982" by Merle Woo (1995) is used to explore what inhibits full participation in class. From this the students generate a list of guidelines they will employ to keep the classroom from becoming an "ugly classroom" (Woo, 1995). When students suggest guidelines like "respect one another," they are asked to define what they mean—what is respect, how might different people need different things to feel respected, and what happens if someone does not feel respected.

---

[8]When a member of the dominant group rejects "the dominant ideology and takes action against oppression out of a belief that eliminating oppression will benefit them and members of the target group" (Adams et al., 1997, p. 76).

Diversity in the classroom provides both pedagogical benefits and challenges. Students bring various experiences to the class, both as members of target groups and as members of dominant groups. However, the presence of this diversity does not necessarily imply that students have reflected on what their membership in a given group has meant to them. Facilitating respectful conversation across differences is particularly challenging. Many White students, for example, are unaware of the hurtful effect their racist comments have on students of color in the class. Similarly, some heterosexual students' derogatory comments about homosexuality exposed their gay, lesbian, and bisexual classmates to pain, often experienced in silence. Diversity in the classroom can also put members of target groups on the spot as when White students expect students of color to "explain racism" to them or to "tell me how I am racist."

Videotapes such as "Skin Deep" (Schmidt & Dunn, 1994) give voice to college students' experiences of racism without expecting students in the class to share their own painful personal experiences unless they choose to do so. Instructors are challenged to assist students in dominant groups to explore their own attitudes and privilege while also being sensitive to the impact their comments have on class members. Caucus and dialogue groups provide structured opportunities for students to learn more about what it means to be a member of a target or dominant group. For example, in gender caucus groups, men and women meet separately. A trained facilitator guides the men through the process of examining gender stereotypes, male dominance, male privilege, the oppression of women, and how these issues relate to their own lives. They also begin to explore how they can work to unlearn their own sexist attitudes, change sexist behavior, and work as allies to educate other men about sexism. The women explore experiences with sexism, ways they have internalized the oppression, and strategies for resisting it. When the two groups reconvene, both engage in dialogue that is better informed, less defensive, and less likely to replicate the dynamics of male dominance or female silencing.

Another challenge encountered in teaching about these issues involves the identities of the instructor(s). For example, as White instructors, it has been crucial that the authors engage in our own work on an ongoing basis to unlearn the racist perspectives and behaviors we have been taught. Self-reflection on our own privilege and on the ways we have perpetuated a racist system is crucial in helping other White students engage in this work. It is also crucial for White faculty to recognize when we do not have the experiences or perspectives of students of color. Creating ways of truly listening to one another in the class, especially when we come from different places of power, is critical. Having classes cotaught by people of differing identities has been an effective strategy. Coteachers can offer students diverse role models, such as the perspective of a target group member working to resist oppression and of a dominant group member working to challenge their own privilege, to educate other dominant group members, and to work in coalition to end injustice.

Journal writing provides an important avenue for students to voice their feelings on these issues without exposing their peers to repeated racist, sexist, classist, or heterosexist comments as frequently. An essential aspect of journal reflection is to create a dialogue between the faculty member and individual students. Responding to journals also provides instructors with the opportunity to challenge in a private forum, the perspectives of students who have difficulty in exploring ways in which they may have benefited from some forms of oppression and may have perpetuated them. By providing feedback that supports deeper, reflective thinking and by posing questions in their journals, faculty encourage students to explore their own assumptions, stereotypes, misinformation, and judgments about others. Equally important, through the journal, instructors are able to support students who describe painful experiences of oppression they or others have experienced in the classroom and outside, or to support students as they begin to take responsibility for their privilege and to challenge their own assumptions.

Pedagogical Support for Instructors

Teaching this curriculum is extremely challenging as faculty are often unfamiliar with either experiential pedagogy or with teaching about issues of power, privilege, and oppression. The Service Learning Institute provides two critical components of pedagogical support. They are (a) the involvement of student leaders as coteachers of the course, and (b) weekly workshops where a learning community of course instructors share teaching strategies and resources and learn from campus and community guest speakers who share their experience and perspectives.

Student coteachers (University Service Advocates, or USAs) are trained in a month-long Summer of Service Leadership Academy where they intensely explore issues of leadership, community, service, and social justice, particularly on the local level. USA coteachers play a variety of roles with this course: They provide peer support for students, facilitate class discussion and activities, develop course curriculum with the faculty member, serve as an additional contact with the community, share their own experiences in the class, and facilitate dialogue groups outside the classroom providing additional support around issues of power, privilege, and oppression. The USAs provide an excellent resource to the faculty as they bring a wealth of experience as previous students in SL200 and in the leadership academy, as well as their own life experience. The involvement of the USAs has lead to important curricular changes that have strengthened the course. In addition, the presence of experienced students in the classroom provides a valuable support for students as they go through this challenging course.

The Service Learning Institute also supports the instructors of SL200 by organizing a learning community made up of current and future SL200 instructors. Learning community members also participate in 1- or 2-day pedagogy workshops at the beginning of each semester. Instructors are provided with a manual of exercises, activities, background readings, and other pedagogical support materials as well. The learning community of current and future SL200 instructors meets weekly to share teaching strategies, to try out experiential activities before using them in class, to gain feedback on challenging classroom situations, and to deepen instructors' knowledge of issues of service, community, and oppression. The weekly meetings provide a time and space for instructors to reflect on their effectiveness as a teacher and partner with the community. The workshops assure the curriculum does not stay static but that it evolves out of our own experiences.

CHALLENGES OF TEACHING
THIS CURRICULUM

The challenges of teaching students to be self-reflective, culturally aware, and responsive community participants are many. Some of the greatest involve faculty development needs, the student development issues encountered in helping students work with this curriculum, and identifying the most appropriate service learning partnerships that provide students with the opportunity to gain awareness of the relationships between systemic injustice and community needs and assets.

Faculty Development

Although many faculty are attracted to CSUMB for its vision statement, in particular its commitment to innovative teaching and learning that goes beyond the classroom, and its commitment to multiculturalism, few have had the opportunity to teach a service learning course that addresses issues of power and privilege in depth and experientially. Faculty have asked for support in gaining skills to facilitate discussion, in designing and implementing experiential activities, in learning how to create true community partnerships, as well as in gaining deeper awareness of their own role in the cycle of oppression. Faculty have also found unique challenges to teaching the course, based on their own identities. For example, faculty of color prepare for accusations of being self-serving and for resistance from White students when White privilege and racism are introduced; White faculty prepare to be attentive to students of color who may question what a White person really knows about racism; and faculty who are biracial prepare to navigate both arenas. The weekly learning community lunches provide very important support for development and reflection on the challenges of teaching this course.

Different Levels of Student Awareness and Development

Some of the developmental challenges students encountered in the class are described earlier. The fact that this course is required, and that many students believe they have already "done" service learning through volunteer work often provides initial frustration for students. In addition, the fact that the course content is so personally challenging, demanding significant introspection and questioning by the students, makes it even more difficult. One of the greatest challenges in teaching the course is in helping students make the connections between new awareness of their own identities in terms of internalized oppression and internalized domination, and the relationship of these identities to their work in the community.

Another important support that instructors can offer to students is to provide them with some frameworks to analyze the role racism, classism, sexism, heterosexism, ableism, and so forth play at their sites. White students working with children frequently say "there is no racism at my site. Everyone is treated the same," or "I don't see their races, I just see children." The work of McIntyre (1997) can help students examine this issue from another perspective. She said:

> Being colorblind allows white people to both ignore the benefits of whiteness and dismiss the experiences of people of color. . . . By minimizing the importance of their students' skin color, the participants accept the fallacy that "kids are just kids." Unfortunately, the partici-

pants' way of thinking negates the essentiality of recognizing and valuing the lived experiences of their students, and understanding the relationship between those experiences and the bifurcation of racial equity in our schools and in our society. (p. 126)

Instructors are able to provide information, such as this quote, from a more macro, societal perspective that can help make these issues clearer to students. For example, instructors can ask students to explore why the majority of people abused by partners, lovers, and spouses are women, or to reflect on the origins of a social service system where a disproportionate majority of agency staff are White women, and a disproportionate number of White men hold the administrative and leadership positions in the field. Providing students with this type of systemic information can also help students see the larger implications of a system of inequity on their particular agency.

Community Partnership Development

Not all community partnerships are appropriate for SL200. Ideally, agency staff who have awareness themselves of the dynamics of oppression and how they play themselves out in the community and in their agencies make some of the best service learning partners. Although the language they use may be different from the academy, those who understand the larger systemic issues at work can ask questions that will help the service learners examine these issues in the context of the agency. Also, organizations that are addressing systemic issues, rather than only addressing short-term solutions, are most conducive to supporting this curriculum. Examples include an organization that provides comprehensive services to people who are homeless including short-term, transitional and long-term housing programs, or an organization that provides safer sex kits, prevention education on AIDS and HIV, and needle exchange programs as well as services for people who are HIV positive or living with AIDS.

The types of activities students engage in is also very important. Rarely does office work provide students with a perspective on how people are dealing with injustice. Partnerships where service learners work with children and do not have the opportunity to understand some of the broad challenges parents of the children face, can also be problematic. This is not to say that students should be investigating particular parent's situations or inappropriately prying for information. Rather, having a broad view of the challenges homeless parents face can help a service learner work more effectively and sensitively with their children in a day-care program, for example. The role of the community partner as coteacher can be powerful in helping draw students' attention to these and other issues.

CONCLUSION

Our work at integrating service learning and critical multiculturalism has evolved in a uniquely supportive context at CSUMB. As a new university, we have not had to battle either tradition-bound approaches to teaching and learning, or rigid discipline-based departmental structures. The faculty who came to teach at CSUMB were attracted by the university's distinctive vision statement and its explicit commitment to multicultural education and community engagement. Although there is still much work to be done in translating the words of the vision statement into policies and high-quality, cost-effective programs and curriculum, there exists a shared commitment to building a university whose graduates are capable of both working to end injustice and creating more caring communities.

Yet, whereas CSUMB provides a particularly conducive climate for critical service learning pedagogy, the core elements of this program are equally as relevant for other higher educational contexts. If community involvement is not to result in the reinforcement of structural injustice and inequity, students must be introduced to these concepts as an essential element of their preparation for service. Furthermore, students must develop heightened capacities for self-reflection to examine their own role in perpetuating or transforming these systems of power and privilege in society. Finally, we have found that community partners are not just valuable supervisors of students' field work, but they are also valuable coteachers, many of whom are also committed to building more just and equitable communities.

After working intensively with this curriculum for 4 years, we have recognized the importance of preparing students for self-reflective, culturally aware, and responsive community participation through reciprocal service and learning. Although references to the importance of preparation are frequent in the service learning literature, they mostly refer to the logistical preparation necessary to connect the learning-centered world of the university with the action-centered world of the community. Preparation takes on another meaning in critical service learning pedagogy as it introduces students to new ways of looking at social issues and of examining the root causes of social problems. In their preparation for community service, students identify and examine their assumptions about people "in-need" and search for the origins of these assumptions in the dominant cultural systems of power and privilege that are at work in society. Preparation therefore includes naming the systemic inequity that underlies a given community service setting, and identifying the interrelated systems of oppression that perpetuate social injustice. In addition to the logistical preparation, students carry these newly acquired conceptual lenses with them as they work in the community, searching consciously for the root causes of the social issues that people they are working with in the community are experiencing.

Our second observation concerns the importance of developing students' capacity for self-reflection. Reflection is also a commonly used term in the service learning literature. It is seen to be the crucial process that transforms experience into learning, a key element of all experiential learning processes (Kolb, 1984). Yet, in critical service learning pedagogy, self-reflection is emphasized. It is not sufficient for students to reflect on "those people," the "others" with whom they might be involved in the community. Students must also reflect on their own identities, actions, feelings, thoughts, and perceptions. As we interact in society, our actions contribute to the existing social structure, and can either reinforce or alleviate the system of oppression that exists. Therefore, to insure that we do not perpetuate the system of oppression, we must develop the capacities to look inward and we must be conscious of the relationship between our identities and our actions in an unjust and inequitable society. Racism, sexism, homophobia, ableism, and so forth is not only about groups who are the targets of these specific oppressions; it is equally about groups that receive privileges based on certain characteristics of identity. In this preparation, all of us are called to examine how we have responded to being both a target at some point in our lives, and to receiving unearned privilege. Self-reflection on the cumulative effect of receiving multiple forms of privilege or being targeted in multiple ways is critical to culturally aware community participation. Developing this capacity for self-reflection—a trait not encouraged in our fast-paced "been there done that" society—is therefore an important aspect of critical service learning pedagogy.

Introducing students to the concepts of power, privilege, and oppression, and stressing the development of their capacities for self-reflection can and should be central elements of all service learning efforts.

REFERENCES

Adams, M., Bell, L. A., & Griffin, P. (Eds.). (1997). *Teaching for diversity and social justice: A sourcebook.* New York: Routledge.

Alexander, Z., Castro, V., Garrison, T. C., Pacheco, S., Pollack, S., Rice, K., Salinas, M. C., Slade, A. M., & Woodridge, B. (1998). *Operationalizing the community participation university learning requirement.* Unpublished manuscript, California State University Monterey Bay.

Arias, A. A. (1998). *On the emergence of a culture of technology at a new university.* Unpublished manuscript.

Chance, W. (1997). *A vision in progress: The decision to establish a public university at Monterey Bay.* San Jose, CA: California Higher Education Policy Center.

Connolly, W. E. (1993). *The terms of political discourse.* Princeton, NJ: Princeton University Press.

CSUMB. (1994). *CSUMB Vision Statement.* Monterey Bay, CA: Author.

CSUMB. (1997). *CSUMB: An overview of the academic program.* Monterey Bay, CA: California State University Monterey Bay.

CSUMB. (1998). Culture and Equity University Learning Requirement, Monterey Bay, CA.

Eyler, J., Giles, D., & Schmiede, A. (1996). *A practitioner's guide to reflection in service learning: Student voices and reflections.* Nashville, TN: Vanderbilt University and the Corporation for National Service.

Franklin, W. (1996). *An overview of service learning at CSUMB.* Monterey Bay, CA: California State University Monterey Bay.

Kolb, D. (1984). *Experiential learning: Experience as the source of learning and development.* Englewood Cliffs, NJ: Prentice-Hall.

McIntyre, A. (1997). *Making meaning of whiteness.* Albany, NY: State University of New York Press.

Pitnick, R. (1998, September 24–30). Making the grade: A critical look at Cal State Monterey Bay. *Coast Weekly,* pp. 14–18, 20–21.

Pollack, S. (1997). *Three decades of service learning in higher education: The contested emergence of an organizational field.* Unpublished doctoral dissertation, Stanford University, Stanford, CA.

Rice, K., & Brown, J. (1998). Transforming educational curriculum and service learning. *Journal of Experiential Education, 21,* 140–146.

Schmidt, S. L., & Dunn, S. J. (1994). *Skin deep* [Videotape]. Berkeley, CA: Iris Films.

Service Learning Institute. (1998). *Service Learning Institute fact sheet.* Monterey Bay, CA: California State University Monterey Bay.

Shirts, R. G. (1993). *Star power: A simulation game.* Del Mar, CA: Simulation Training Systems, Inc.

Sleeter, C., & Grant, C. A. (1987). An analysis of multicultural education in the United States. *Harvard Educational Review, 57,* 421–444.

Will, G. (1998, April 24). Touchie-feelie u. is blooming in Monterey. *San Francisco Chronicle,* p. A25.

Woo, M. (1995). Poem for the Creative Writing Class, 1982. In A. Watters & M. Ford (Eds.), *Writing for change: A community reader* (pp. 142–143). New York: McGraw-Hill.

Social Justice, Service Learning, and Multiculturalism as Inseparable Companions

Herbert L. Martin, Jr.
Terri A. Wheeler
California State University, Monterey Bay

We are poised here on the beginning of the 21st Century with many of the great problems of the 20th Century—war, poverty, hunger, racism, gender inequality, homophobia, and burgeoning environmental disasters—still facing us all around the globe. Having lived through the most exciting and hopeful time in American history, the revolutionary 1960s, both authors have never been able to teach anything but a social justice-oriented curriculum. Service learning, with its philosophical emphasis on multiculturalism and social justice, is the perfect companion to this approach.

This chapter describes two California State University-Monterey Bay classes that feature multiculturalism and pluralism integrated with a social justice approach to service learning in multicultural communities. Terri Wheeler teaches a course in the Liberal Studies major called *Multicultural Children's Literature*. About 85% of those who take this class are headed for the Teacher Credential program. The Service Learning Field component takes place in culturally and linguistically diverse elementary classrooms. Herbert L. Martin, Jr. teaches a Liberal Studies class called *Culture and Cultural Diversity*, which is required of every Liberal Studies major. What these two learning experiences have in common is the powerful emphasis on social justice as the organizing thread that is woven throughout the

135

chosen texts, films, teaching techniques, and service learning partnerships.

Social justice involves teaching in an intentionally pluralistic manner that is aimed at "leveling the playing field" for underrepresented groups (we include not only human cultural groups in this definition, but also all flora and fauna of this planet). Our predominantly Euro-American student population completes service experiences in culturally and linguistically diverse communities. Without the strong social justice/pluralistic focus of both classes, we would have the perfect formula for disaster. Nothing is more insulting in a multicultural community placement than poorly prepared, culturally uninformed service learners, who descend on a community armed only with the types of stereotypes that have been characteristic of the present Eurocentric teaching that still dominates K through 12 American education and far too much university level teaching.

The strong emphasis on a "level playing field" in both our classes is necessary because of the unfailingly Eurocentric curriculum that has been the previous source of our students' knowledge about nonmainstream cultures. To expand students' understanding, *Multicultural Children's Literature* includes texts that offer an "insider's" view of a culture. For instance, Rudolfo Anaya's *Bless Me, Ultima* (1972), gives authentic cultural information about the "curandera," a spiritual healer from Mexican-American tradition who has been erroneously referred to by mainstream anthropologists as a witch. The *Culture and Cultural Diversity* class uses content materials on American History from a diverse range of perspectives.

Both of these courses meet the Culture and Equity University Learning Requirement (ULR) described by Seth Pollack and Kathleen Rice in chapter 7 of this volume. As Service Learning classes, both utilize the resources of the Service Learning Institute and both include reflection components. Both of these classes also align perfectly with the California State University, Monterey Bay Vision Statement, which prominently links Multiculturalism and Service to the community.

MULTICULTURAL CHILDREN'S LITERATURE

The *Multicultural Children's Literature* course at CSUMB examines, in the context of teaching and learning through culturally and linguistically diverse children's books, a number of diversity and social justice issues. Service Learning supports both the students' learning of the course content and the development of the students' commitment to the integration of this literature into the curriculum as a way of contributing to educational and social reform.

The Course

Students read *Teaching Multicultural Literature in Grades K–8* (Harris, 1993) in order to get historical background on the development of children's literature by and about various cultural groups included in this course. The Harris text begins with a look at children's books about Christopher Columbus and shows how each book contains the author's bias. What authors consciously or subconsciously decide is important for children to know about Columbus (in what is usually children's first introduction to history) presents a history that sanitizes, omits, ignores, and justifies genocide and racism.

The great majority of the children's books read in this course are written by "insiders" of the underrepresented groups in the United States, and these previously silenced voices in children's literature provide other perspectives on both history and the present. Students read each chapter of the Harris text to put the children's books about a particular cultural group into socio-political, historical, and cultural context; then, they read children's books from that group. In-class discussions, videotapes, audiotapes, and lectures help students become aware of the literary traditions, cultures, histories, and perspectives of Mexican-Americans and other Latinos, Native Americans, African-Americans, Asian-Americans, and European-Americans (particularly the White ethnic experience). Environmental issues, gender issues, differently-abled people, and gay and lesbian people are also represented in the children's books read as part of this course.

Students are able to gain some understanding, through profound reading experiences, what it was like to grow up African-American in the rural South in the 1930s (Taylor, 1976), to be Jewish in Poland in the 1940s (Yolen, 1988), or to be Ojibway (Broker, 1983). They see the thread of the continuation of tradition in the life of a contemporary Abenaki/European-American girl who is mourning the loss of her great-grandmother (Bruchac, 1993). Other experiences, issues, and perspectives are explored through the 20 or so required readings and in additional in-class readings.

Students read of the difficulty in getting the works of authors of color published, and they see evidence of this in classrooms, libraries, and bookstores. Informal surveys among the students show that most classrooms in which they perform their service learning have no multicultural children's literature available.

The Service

Service learners spend a minimum of 25 hours in area elementary and middle schools. Their purpose is to share literature, to promote literacy, to help children make cross-cultural connections and to help children learn to love literature. In classrooms, after school programs, special reading programs, or through tutoring, service learners read aloud or tell stories to individuals, small groups, or whole classes. They follow the story with book discussions that often include a connection to the students' lives; in addition, service learners involve the children in art activities, dramatization, writing their own books, and other literature response activities.

The Community Partners of the course are elementary and middle schools in the communities surrounding the university. The required book list and learning outcomes for the Service Learners are shared with the Community Partners, and the Service Learning Institute holds training workshops to foster the partnership. In addition, the SLI assigns a University Service Advocate (USA) to assist me in developing the Community Partnerships. The USA works with me in many other areas, including course development, site visitations, and the development and leadership of reflection discussions and activities.

At the end of the second week of the semester, students meet with the course's community partners at the Service Learning Placement Fair, held on campus. Students are able to ask questions of the site representatives and sign up for more information or decide on a placement. They arrange to visit the site and receive an orientation. The usual commitment to the site is for the student to be providing service for 3 hours a week for a 10-week placement.

The Reflection

Because an essential aspect of the service learning experience is reflection, the course includes many opportunities for students to reflect on their service and its connection to children's literature. These opportunities include three papers, ongoing journals, and in-class discussion and activities.

The Reflection Papers. The first of the three papers is written before the students begin their service. In this paper, students describe who they are and what they bring to this experience. Expectations for the course, the site, the children, and the service learning experience are also explored in this preservice paper. For those students who transferred into the CSUMB as juniors, this upper-division course may be their introduction to service learning, and their papers are sometimes full of a missionary-like zeal to enlighten those poor deprived children they are about to encounter. The students who have taken the lower-division service learning course (SL200) usually have the understanding that the children will be teaching them much more than they can ever teach the children. Most students eventually realize that the children bring with them knowledge and ways of knowing that must be valued by the school in order to help all the children reach their potentials.

The second paper is a midservice self-evaluation; it describes what cultural misconceptions the student may have recognized and revisits their original expectations in light of what their experience so far has taught them. This is often a paper filled with new outlooks on their role at their site and recounts their struggle to fit in and be accepted.

The final paper is written after the student has exited the community site (although some students choose to continue to volunteer at their sites after the course has ended) and describes what students found out about themselves and the cultures and lives of the children. For some students who would not previously admit to having any cultural stereotypes, this paper serves as a way to explore their true feelings and explain how these stereotypes were dispelled by the children with whom they worked. One student revealed that she began the semester believing that the children in her bilingual classroom did not want to learn English; she finished the semester filled with respect for the children because they worked both during and after school hours, in their desire to become fluent in English.

The Service Logs. The service logs or journals are used to monitor the student's progress and to choose topics for in-class discussion and activities. The journals allow me to monitor the service learning experience and make comments, suggestions, or to make sure that the experience is going well. I am more informed about the students' perspective on the service learning experience before I check in with the community partner to see how the student is doing at the site. The journals are turned in five or six times during the semester, providing many opportunities for feedback and discussion topics.

Each time students visit their sites, a journal entry is made. The journals list the books used and explore the thoughts and feelings of the service learner in response to their experience that day. One student reported her amazement that her group of 7th- and 8th-grade Mexican-American students did not believe that California had ever been part of Mexico. Others have expressed surprise that 8th-grade students do not believe that the Holocaust actually happened. And, although students of all ages have responded enthusiastically to the award-winning *Family Pictures/Cuadros de familia* (Garza, 1990), service learners have been asked by some teachers to censor parts of the picture book because they want to protect their students from knowing where their food comes from (Garza includes her memories of her grandmother killing a chicken for dinner) or from understanding the tradition of the *curandera*.

At times, students' initial fears are borne out in their first experiences if they walk into their classroom and are asked to read a book in Spanish to the children. Those who do not feel totally proficient in Spanish feel humiliated and inept as they attempt to get through the book. Invariably, the children gently correct their pronunciation and help them complete the book; the students are surprised when the children graciously ask the service learner to come back and read to them again. This experience actually helps the service learner and the children bond more quickly. The service learner is better able to understand the frustrations of the children as they comprehend a book in Spanish and then struggle to express their comprehension in English in timed, written tests.

Topics for in-class discussion and activities often come from issues brought up in the student journals. For example, a recent journal contained statements that almost all of the students (the great majority of whom are Mexican-American) came from broken or unstable homes, and that the parents are very rarely involved in or care about their children's education. In response to these misconceptions (whether they reflect the student's attitudes or those of the school personnel), the instructor and the USA planned a role-playing script to be followed by a free-write prompt and small-group discussions. Readings in the class support the idea that there are cultural differences in what is considered a stable and loving home or in the definition of family; students note that the schools may not be aware of or consider these concepts as valid.

At various times, students are also given specific writing prompts for their journals. For example, students begin by describing their experience at the Placement Fair, where they meet the Community Partners and usually decide on their site. After picking their site, they are asked to brainstorm any words or images that come into their minds when they think of the community that they are about to enter. Seaside, Marina, Monterey, Watsonville, Chualar, and Salinas (the communities in which the school sites are located) have very different reputations, and the various images brought up may be full of negative stereotypes. Some students are fearful about entering a community that they perceive as a low socio-economic area populated by ethnicities different from their own. We discuss these preconceived notions of each community and how these images are conveyed to the children who live and attend school in those communities. It is suggested that the students visit the community, stop at a local café for lunch or coffee, observe the neighborhood in which the school is located, interact with residents and business owners, and compare that experience with the "brainstorming" images they produced. Class discussions and readings in children's literature attempt to help the students dispel mistaken notions about the community and the childrens' cultures and to see how such notions help to keep the status quo in place.

After they have begun their service, students are asked to focus on the school in which they are serving. By this time in the semester, we have discussed different approaches to multicultural education; students are asked to find evidence that the school is committed to multicultural education. How is multicultural education defined and manifested at their school? Students write about their observations and conversations with school personnel. Some note that the school has a vision statement that includes a school-wide commitment to multicultural education; in these schools, the evidence may be apparent in each classroom and with each teacher. Other students find that their schools have isolated classrooms in which the teachers use a multicultural education approach, but there is no support on a school-wide level. Still other students find that the schools are "clueless" about multicultural education and the need to teach about diversity.

Several weeks into the service experience, students are asked to take a close look at the classroom(s) in which they are serving. Does the teacher have any books in the classroom collection that reflect diversity? Do the students have access to a school library with a culturally diverse selection? Is the classroom teacher comfortable with the materials the student is bringing in and the kinds of issues brought up in the books? Is the culture and knowledge brought by each student valued by the school and built on in the curriculum?

By midsemester, at least one student will have written about school personnel attitudes toward parents, which may not take into account cultural differences or parental workload realities. At this point, the students are assigned to find out what efforts are made by the school to provide a welcoming atmosphere for parents. It is usually found that, in those schools with a commitment to diversity, many efforts are made to facilitate parental involvement and community links. In some schools, students have found, bilingual newsletters are sent to the parents, parent–teacher meeting hours are flexible (or the teacher visits the home) and childcare is provided on site while the parents meet with teachers, the teacher is bilingual or has cross-cultural competence, English classes are provided on-site (with child care provided), and parents are consulted about improvements for the school (new playground, after-school programs, etc.). Parents and community members are brought in as classroom resources (for instance, in sharing their oral tradition). School personnel in these schools are often active in community issues; for instance, the administration of the school in Chualar played a crucial role in getting drinking water for the town after the town's water source was declared undrinkable.

In-Class Discussion and Activities. In-class discussions change each semester as different issues are brought up in students' journals. Each semester, however, discussions revolve around power relations and how these are manifested in the schools, social justice, and educational reform, cultural diversity and multicultural education, and the role that multicultural children's literature plays in exploring these issues.

Besides discussions in class, activities include role-playing, free-writing, small-group tasks and discussion, and sharing of experiences as students share our required books in their classrooms.

Other Coursework

The other coursework assigned during the semester both supports and is supported by the service learning experience. The first assignment of the semester is for the student to collect a story, rhyme, poem, or riddle that has been handed down in their family. These "Hand Me Down Tales" are told to the rest of the class. This powerful assignment is often the students' favorite, as well. The "Hand Me Down Tales" establish a personal link to oral tradition as a child's first connection to literature and as a carrier of culture and history. Students become aware of the power of the oral tradition and its importance in keeping culture and history alive. They realize that the children with whom they are in contact also bring their own stories and cultural traditions with them to school.

A semester-long project is the development of an annotated bibliography of literature appropriate for culturally and linguistically diverse learners. By limiting choices to books representing the experiences and perspectives of African Americans, Native Americans, Mexican Americans, and Southeast Asian Americans, this assignment allows students to see for themselves the underrepresentation of these groups in children's literature. Southeast Asian-American books set in the United States are particularly difficult to find, yet the students see the need for the Southeast Asian-American children in California's classrooms to have books that accurately portray their experiences.

An essential aspect of this bibliography is the student's evaluation of whether the book contains cultural bias. The student looks at the qualifications of the author and illustrator, searches for any negative stereotypes or the countering of negative stereotypes, and evaluates the cultural accuracy and authenticity of the work. Although students find this part of the assignment difficult because they are just beginning to learn how to tell the difference between accurate and inaccurate representations of cultural groups, it is important that they develop this awareness. Part of their service learning assignment is to select and evaluate the books they choose to share with the elementary and middle-school students.

Finally, the last two class sessions are devoted to group presentations. The students choose groups of four to six people midway through the semester and plan an interdisciplinary unit featuring multicultural literature. A dramatic, multimedia presentation is made in the class as a highlight of this project. This presentation is a celebration of the growth in knowledge and perspective that each student has gained through the course and the service learning. Each student takes on a character from the course and presents his or her portion of the presentation from that character's perspective. Students often include live musical or dance performances, which add to the emotional impact of the presentation.

Past presentations have included panel discussions on the impact of Columbus on the Western Hemisphere (panelists included Christopher Columbus, Taíno and Apache women, and Laura Ingalls); a video presentation and puppet show featuring the words of Black Elk and Christopher Columbus that explored how each perspective impacted the earth and that connected this impact to the contemporary lives and working conditions of farmworkers; a satirical look at a classroom teacher who tried to cover multiculturalism in one hour by presenting the most superficial and stereotypical portrayals of each group and who shut down any questions or challenges from her puzzled and offended students; and a Civil War drama that showed the impact of slavery on African Americans and Euro-Americans. These presentations can be powerful and moving as they show what students have in their hearts at the end of the semester's experience in the Multicultural Children's Literature course.

Students, by the end of this class, often report a sense of outrage that these perspectives and history, itself, have been omitted, distorted, and hidden from them until now. They see the need for change in how students are taught about history and culture and in the kinds of literature that can be used to let children experience the world. However, they often find in their Service Learning experiences that some schools still feel a need to protect children from the truth and ask the service learners to censor part or all of award-winning multicultural children's books; at the same time, the students hear classmates report the positive responses of children at their sites to those same books. This frustration, ideally, leads to a commitment by the student to become a teacher who will use multicultural children's literature to tell the whole story.

CULTURE AND CULTURAL DIVERSITY

History was once thought of as the story of kings, nobles, presidents, laws, and battles. Contrived and written by the victors, it told of their glories, valor, goodness, and high purpose. It omitted their greed, violence, or bigotry and was more legend than truth.

The original losers lost again when their story was written by their former enemies. Their heroism became savagery, their high purpose treason, and their glories were simply borrowed by the oppressors.

This tradition in writing history has survived long into the current era. Those who have exploited others still justify their greed with cunning words and deprecations. But the oppressed have a proud, interesting, and important history. In this country, their titanic struggle against the forces of nature and man built the nation's railroads, mines, buildings, plantations, and most of its wealth.

Their story deserves a telling, one recounted not from the vantage point of those who profitted from their misery. Without it, the entire tale is incomplete and inaccurate. By including their neglected portion, Americans can gain an understanding of their true national heritage and present problems (Katz, 1974, p. xxx).

The *Culture and Cultural Diversity* Learning Experience described later begins a historical odyssey that often challenges the monocultural historical orientation that the vast majority of our students bring to our classrooms. From the outset, the students are about to boldly go where their previous education has feared to tread. In the area of multiculturalism and pluralism, the idea of a conventional curriculum has long been a Eurocentric one, which limits what is considered important knowledge even within the Western European model. Thus, in addition to the conscious or unconscious assumption that Eurocentric patriarchal ideas are normal, there is also a tacit understanding that ideas from nonmainstream races, cultures, or other microcultural groups are exotic, strange, or possibly immoral or evil. Ethnocentrism is at work, in other words. To challenge this, all course components attempt to help students under-

stand history through the vantage point of those who have been traditionally underrepresented or underserved in education. The vehicles
for making this exploration include powerful classroom activities, an
approach called the *New West* curriculum, an organizing "meta-
question," specially chosen pluralism texts, and service learning partnerships in culturally and linguistically diverse communities.

Exploration of Self as a Cultural Being:
The Long Introduction

The very first class activity that starts students on the path of becoming an interculturally empowered service learner is what is known as
the *Long Introduction*. The purpose of the activity is to have each
class member (including the instructor) acknowledge themselves as
belonging to some ethnocultural group and to have them identify
some cultural heritage. This has not proven difficult for the underrepresented groups (African Americans, Native Americans, Pacific Is-
landers, South East Asians, and Latinos), but it often proves prob-
lematical for those who have grown accustomed to thinking of and
identifying themselves as White or who have never before considered
their racial identity. During this 3-hour-long first-day activity some
really surprising ethno-racial-cultural combinations will self-identify
as White. When the introductions are finished, all have a deeper understanding of the concept of culture and that all peoples everywhere
have some cultural associations. Each student is also asked to identify their earliest racial encounter during this segment. The discussion that ensues simultaneously helps to bond the class as a group
and begins the creation of the safe environment for our future discussions, some of which will be controversial.

Slices of American Life

The next major activity involves a visit to two distinct underrepresented groups through selected film excerpts. The excerpts have all of
the flavor of the contacts the service learner will eventually make with
their own chosen sites, but without the risks. The two movie clips give
a good simulation of what can happen when groups come in contact
who do not really understand each other. In small groups, the class
views the opening 17 minutes of the movies *Grand Canyon* (Kasdan,
Okun, & Grillo, producers; Kasdan, director, 1991) and *Thunderheart* (de Niro, Rosenthal, & Fusco, producers; Apted, director, 1992)
and process the cultural interchange that begins each movie. In each

clip, a potentially violent encounter takes place between members of underrepresented groups and members of the mainstream macro-culture. In *Grand Canyon*, the underrepresented are African American in Los Angeles, whereas in *Thunderheart*, they are Lakota in the Badlands of South Dakota. Both clips contain cultural putdowns and misunderstandings bred from lack of knowledge and insensitivity to another culture and consequently they are great teaching tools. The small groups process the class focus questions on the activity among themselves first, then share with the whole class their impressions. This activity brings out the different cultural lenses we each wear, as the groups come up with various interpretations of the encounter.

The end result of this activity is a dawning of awareness among the students in this class of the great gulf (or "Grand Canyon") that exists between the dominant racial group in the United States and under-represented groups. The concept of ethnocentrism, the human tendency to view your own culture and traditions as right, normal, and moral, whereas those of others are perceived as slightly different, odd, exotic, immoral, or even evil, and dangerous, is introduced here. This helps to explain the many different perspectives they have just experienced while processing the clips. From here, we proceed to one of the most dynamic and unforgettable experiences of the class.

"The Color of Fear"

This 90-minute video was produced by Chinese-American Lee Mun Wah, of Stir Fry Productions, in 1994. It documents a weekend re-treat of men from African American, Latino, Asian, and Euro-American cultures. There were about two men from each tradition. The entire weekend is spent processing "white privilege" (McIntosh, 1988) and racism in America. Interethnic racism is also briefly explored. The exchanges range from mild, gentle, interactions to verbally explosive sections, which leave the audience quivering and taking sides. It is extremely important to process this video immediately after viewing. Under no circumstances should one show it and then send the students home. To go home without discussing the passions that have been stirred by this incredible tape is to lose valuable, intense feelings, which are some of the key components to transformative multicultural teaching and learning. The classroom exchanges from this processing almost always mirror those seen in the videotape. As the class becomes aware of this, we then sit back and discuss why. The earlier lessons on ethnocentrism and cultural lenses come through clearly here. The class is now ready for the next step in their journey to becoming interculturally empowered service learners; the processing of the texts for this class.

The "New West" Curriculum and The Required Texts

The selection of my required texts was based on Patricia Limerick's "New West" curriculum model. This approach, a new multicultural historical model, which is put forth in Patricia Limerick's *The Legacy of Conquest* (1987), calls for a more complete presentation of the many perspectives that exist on the "taming of the West" or the old "frontier" model. She presents a history in which it is possible to see the European settler as an "invader" disturbing the homes and lifestyles of countless diverse peoples and animals, not to mention the environment itself. The truly multiculturally literate person, according to this perspective, is knowledgeable in multiple ways of seeing instead of having to depend only on the Eurocentric model.

The New West curriculum provides gender-balanced curricula and teaching materials by integrating important knowledge about the history, needs, problems, and aspirations of both men and women. It also thoroughly integrates multiculturalism and pluralism to provide a cross-cultural understanding through history, using appropriate curricular materials and techniques. What is particularly unique about this new pluralistic curriculum is the integration of the drama of life of the animals, plants, the environment, and the very earth we live on as important and vital parts of our story of cultural transformation that must be considered in a holistic curriculum.

The first half of the class focuses on ethnoracial cultural groups, while the second half takes every issue from historically feminine perspectives. Within this feminine-centered focus, gay and lesbian issues, shamanic healing, cross-cultural spirituality, and environmental racism are thoroughly explored. Dr. Harry Kitano's *Race Relations* (1997) is used as the first course text because it beautifully lays out underrepresented histories within the context of a neocolonial, dominant-cultural environment. For example, one is allowed to see the current conditions of, say, Native Americans or African Americans painted against the background of dominant culture tactics of prejudice and discrimination. The cultural heritage of each group is explored thoroughly, with emphasis on the Civil Rights period (roughly between the 1950s and the 1970s), but also reaching into the present. Such important historical figures as Booker T. Washington, Martin Luther King, Jr., Stokley Carmichael, W.E.B. Dubois, Crazy Horse, Black Elk, César Chávez, Delores Huerta, John and Robert Kennedy, Mohandes Ghandi, Carol Gilligan, and Betty Friedan are included as important contributors to social justice.

Riane Eisler's *The Chalice and the Blade* (1987), is the second required text. This book chronicles the early history of humankind in a time of gender-equality and reverence of nature, women, and a feminine deity known as The Great Goddess. According to this history (or *herstory*, as some gender historians refer to it), humans lived within these partnership societies for over 90% of our time on the earth. To further explore issues of spirituality and environmental racism, students read *Creation Spirituality* (1991), by Matthew Fox. His concept of the *Cosmic Christ* is posited in this book, which is key to the class concept of social justice. This idea stresses the necessity for all humans to become responsible for the stewardship of the earth— keepers not only of our brothers and sisters, but also of the flora and fauna of the earth. He writes about this all within the context of the Great Goddess tradition.

Course Meta-Question

An important service learning device, which fits into the "New West" model, is the use of the course meta-question. This central question forms the hub of the scholarly wheel of exploration that will characterize the service-learning experience as well as the in-class historical journey. The idea of the importance of both culture and equity echo strongly throughout this question. The following question is used for the *Culture and Cultural Diversity* class: "What is your personal role in contributing to a NEW WORLD where social justice is the NORM rather than the exception?"

This is the central reflection question around which all instruction, pedagogical techniques, service learning, and class content revolves. Rooted in the social reconstructionist philosophies of Paulo Freire (1970) and Sleeter and Grant (1988), this focus question asks the students to engage actively in a class based on pedagogy for liberation. It stresses not only the liberation of oppressed peoples of the earth, but also the animals, plants, and the environment that supports everything. This meta-question is emphasized as we process each lecture or discussion, view each cultural video, share personal cultural family histories, do small-group activities, or when students work in their service placement. This question is the organizer of all class content and service-learning reflection.

The Service and Reflection

Service learners spend a minimum of 30 to 40 hours in area community agencies. The purpose is to help them make cross-cultural connections and to help with matters that are of most concern to their particular agency. The daily struggles and issues of a given community placement become the concern of the student.

Some examples of the kinds of placements and the social justice-oriented work students may do are at homeless shelters to find solutions to the problem of homelessness; are with local Indigenous groups to help clarify and strengthen their ongoing struggles with our government and corporate America over treaty rights; are with farm worker groups to help with achieving safe, affordable housing, pesticide relief, a higher living wage, and health benefits regardless of citizenship; gay rights groups on issues related to gender equity and civil rights; environmental organizations that combat environmental racism and degradation.

In these culturally and linguistically diverse placements, students are exposed to the day-to-day issues that face the particular underrepresented group. To help them process their experiences, there are three required reflection papers. Each paper focuses on the students' developmental progress in dealing with the class "meta-question." This central focus question guides reflection on all class readings, video programs, and lecture/discussion sections. The first of the three papers is written before the students begin their service. The other papers are processed in class at midterm and at the end of the class to chart their growth. Each reflection paper contributes to the growth of the service learners before, during, and after they have been in the community placement.

Other Coursework

Additional video clips support the Native American, the African American, the Latino, the Southeast Asian, and the Pacific Islander sections of the class. Within the gender equity section of the class, there are video segments that augment the teaching of this section, including the incredible *Earth and the American Dream* (Couturié & Mercer, producers; Couturié, director, 1992). This video vividly chronicles through music, art, history, and real newsreel footage the damage that has been done to Mother Earth to support the Capitalist American Dream of wealth and prosperity. The class is often moved to tears (both men and women) many times during the showing of this tape. The processing of this particular video produces some of the most profound moments in this whole class experience. This video finishes the teacher-generated content for the class. The class finishes with student presentations and Service Learning reflection papers.

CONCLUSION

In this chapter, we profiled two very powerful multicultural classes, which are integrated with a service-learning component in meaningful and even life-changing ways. The strong social justice theme runs like a steady stream through each of these learning experiences. Indeed, service learning done with a social justice emphasis is the perfect companion to multicultural classes. The combination of these three potent educational forces has a transformative effect on the learner and the service learning site, as well as the instructor of the class. Combining this inclusive approach to cultural history prepares the student to enter and function in a culturally and linguistically diverse site in a sensitive and resourceful manner. The combined scholarly and interculturally aware skills of the students enhance their chances of being productive and helpful in their placement. Not only is it a good experience for the student, but it also helps create and maintain good relationships with our community partners. Also, the instructor of the class is practically always enriched by integrating a strong community service component in his or her class. Thus, the ideal service-learning experience enriches the student, the community partner, and the university instructor.

We have been engaged in service-learning classes for the last 2½ years at this young institution. It has been our consistent experience that profound changes occur in the learner as a result of the integration of service learning with our academic courses. A comment one of our students recently made exemplifies this for us. At about halfway through our semester in the *Culture and Cultural Diversity* class, a Latino student came up and said: "Dr. Martin, I have finally figured out that all this time I have been waiting for heroes like Martin Luther King, Jr. and César Chávez to arrive to take care of the mess the world is in. What I realize from this class is that that hero can be found in my own heart. It is MY responsibility!"

REFERENCES

Anaya, R. (1972). *Bless me, Ultima*. Berkeley, CA: Tonatiuh-Quinto Sol International.
Broker, I. (1983). *Night-flying woman: An Ojibway narrative*. St. Paul, MN: Minnesota Historical Society Press.
Bruchac, J. (1993). *Fox Song*. New York: Philomel.
Couturié, B., & Mercer, J. (Producer), & Couturié, B. (Director). (1992). *Earth and the American dream* [Film]. (Available from HBO/BBC Productions).
de Niro, R., Rosenthal, J., & Fusco, J. (Producers), & Apted, M. (Director). (1992). *Thunderheart* [Film]. (Available from Columbia TriStar Productions).
Eisler, R. (1987). *The chalice and the blade*. San Francisco, CA: Harper & Row.

Fox, M. (1991). *Creation spirituality: Liberating gifts for the peoples of the earth.* San Francisco, CA: Harper & Row.

Freire, P. (1970). *Pedagogy of the oppressed.* New York: Continuum Press.

Garza, C. L. (1990). *Family pictures/Cuadros de familia.* San Francisco, CA: Children's Book Press.

Harris, V. (Ed.). (1993). *Teaching multicultural literature in grades k–8.* Norwood, MA: Christopher-Gordon Publishers, Inc.

Kasdan, L., Okun, C., & Grillo, M. (Producers), & Kasdan, L. (Director). (1991). *Grand Canyon* [Film]. (Available from 20th Century Fox).

Katz, W. L. (1974). *Early America 1492–1812, Minorities in American History, Vol. 1.* New York: Franklin Watts, Inc.

Kitano, H. (1997). *Race relations.* Upper Saddle River, NJ: Prentice Hall.

Limerick, P. (1987). *A legacy of conquest: The unbroken past of the American West.* New York: Norton.

McIntosh, P. (1988, October). *White privilege and male privilege: A personal account of coming to see correspondences through work in women's studies.* Based on paper presented at the American Educational Research Association conference, Boston.

Mun Wah, L. (Producer/director). (1994). *The color of fear* [Film]. (Available from Stir Fry Productions).

Sleeter, C. E., & Grant, C. A. (1988). *Making choices for multicultural education: Five approaches to race, class, and gender.* Columbus, OH: Merrill.

Taylor, M. (1976). *Roll of thunder, hear my cry.* New York: Harper & Row.

Yolen, J. (1988). *The devil's arithmetic.* New York: Puffin.

9

We Made the Road by Talking: Teaching Education 310, "Service-Learning With Multicultural Elders" at the University of Michigan

Stella Raudenbush
Joe Galura
University of Michigan

As educators, we both are greatly influenced by the "talking books" of Paulo Freire. *We Made the Road by Talking: Conversations on Education and Social Change*, which Freire wrote with Myles Horton (1990), inspired the format of this chapter. What follows is our own "talking book." We have summarized our conversations as we prepared for and actually taught this class, which we see as a dynamic synergism between service-learning and multicultural education.

PERSONAL STATEMENTS: JOE

Since 1988, I have directed programming in Project Community, an innovative partnership between the School of Education, Department of Sociology, and the Division of Student Affairs at the University of Michigan. Project Community is one of the nation's oldest service-learning courses, awarding credit since the early 1970s to students who integrate academic theory with community service.[1]

---

[1] For a thorough description of Project Community from the perspective of the sociology faculty sponsor, see Chesler (1993).

153

My work has been in developing seminars and service projects in the areas of Criminal Justice, Chemical Dependency, and Women's Issues. I founded the OCSL Press, which currently publishes *The Michigan Journal of Community Service Learning*, to provide resources for students and faculty interested in combining service with learning. Much of *The Praxis Series*, which I edited with Jeff Howard was written to support the work of my students in their community placements (Galura, Howard, Waterhouse, & Ross, 1995; Galura, Meiland, Ross, Callan & Smith, 1993; Howard, 1993).

Then my father died.

Perhaps the most profound sense of loss I felt was knowing that my two preschool-aged children, David and Genna, both multiethnic,[2] would never hear him tell his life story. They would never know his firsthand account of how the overlapping oppressions of race, class, and gender shaped our family history.

Their grandfather, Atilano Ocampo Galura, was part of the so-called "Manong generation," Filipinos who emigrated to the United States between the end of the Spanish American War and the middle of the Great Depression. "Manong" is the Filipino word for "uncle." These immigrants were largely young men recruited (and exploited) as cheap labor in Hawaii and on the West Coast.

Dad did not meet my mother, Isabel de la Pena Aguilar, until the mid-1950s. By then the immigration laws had changed. Mom was an international student who had recently graduated from the exclusive Philippine Women's University, an elitist institution where Imelda Marcos matriculated just a few years before.

After they were married, Mom and Dad discovered that there were neighborhoods in the Detroit area that refused to allow them—or any other people of color—to move in. This was despite the fact that they could pay for the full amount of their home in cash. And although my parents told this story often while I was growing up, they rarely mentioned Dad's working-class roots.

The 1930 census stated that 787 Filipinos lived in Michigan. By the time my father died more than 60 years later, there were only three Manongs to attend his funeral. It occurred to me then that I could create a new service-learning course, focusing on Filipino American history.[3] Asian Pacific American Studies is a relatively new field

---

[2]Many Filipino Americans would refer to Joe's children as *mestizo* or *mestiza*. See Root (1997).

[3]In addition to Root, the main sources for this survey of Filipino American history are Takaki, 1989 (a comprehensive overview of the Asian American experience), Cordova, 1983 (landmark work of the founder of the Filipino American National Historical Society), and Bulosan, 1943 (autobiographical, by a Manong who emigrated 2 years after Joe's dad).

and most of the literature is based on research done in Hawaii and on the West Coast. As far as I could tell, no one had studied the experiences of Manongs in Michigan.

This was the starting point for my conversations with Stella.

PERSONAL STATEMENTS: STELLA

I enter this consideration of multicultural education as an African-American woman who came of age in the crucible of the 1960s in the United States. During the 1960s, the political atmosphere provided an arena in which thousands of individuals examined and reexamined value systems, power relationships, and public policy. There was an apparent mandate and freedom to work to rectify social inequalities and injustice. My work began in 1967 when I was hired as a case worker in the Boston Public Welfare Department. The job description required that welfare workers administer social welfare benefits to families of dependent children. There were strict criteria and guidelines to be met by the needy family in order to receive these benefits. When I tried to apply these eligibility requirements to these families, I became acutely aware that the rules were arbitrary and did nothing to ameliorate the ravages of poverty. How could I do my job? Was there no room to manipulate the system? Would I be able to help the poor?

The civil rights movement and the antiwar movements had borne fruit throughout the different strata of U.S. society. Working-class women who were unemployed began to understand that their work of raising children was not adequately remunerated. They themselves were devalued and labeled as parasitic. They began to organize and to demand better pay. Their struggle created the room for case workers to reflect on their own role within the system. The conflict between unfair regulation that they were required to implement and the lives that welfare clients were condemned to lead caused many caseworkers like me to consciously seek alliances with the clients.

Now 30 years later, I continue to grapple with the same issue; the tremendous distance between research and practice, and practice and research. My position as an instructor at a large research university is the context in which I seek to find a language through which I can communicate research to the working-class members of my community and to communicate the rich voice of working-class lives to my university colleagues.

It is within this space that we can explore, understand, and celebrate the culture that people create and live as an affirmation of their intelligence, creativity, resilience, and courage in opposition to a hegemonic system that would strip them of these qualities. A similar space emerges within schools when parents and kids resist beliefs and practices that would deny them access to useful skills and leave them social casualties. Middle-class workers, teachers, and social workers, however, can see this culture of struggle for what it is only when they themselves step outside of the socially prescribed role within the institutions in which they work.

In my view, multicultural education is a system of consciousness and action that promotes the empathetic understanding of the nature of human endeavor in any given human situation. This system has several aspects.

1. It requires the effort to understand from the inside out what makes groups and individuals act in a given situation.
2. It initiates self-exploration that enables individuals to understand their uniqueness and their commonalities with other peoples.
3. It evokes a critical awareness of the material conditions in which people live and of the cause of those conditions.
4. A multicultural education shifts human thought away from the dominant narrative that locates humanity's problems in personal shortcomings toward an alternative view that seeks to unfold the vast potential for positive human accomplishment that results from collective action.

In the United States today, racism, sexism, and antiworking class bias—including both the theories and the practices that appear to prove these theories—are the major hegemonic devices for blaming the victims of oppressive conditions for their own oppression. The content and activities that form a multicultural approach challenge the ideology and practice of racism, sexism, and other biases that exclude children from full participation in school. In the place of stereotypic views imposed from the outside is a picture of how universal human needs and values encourage people to construct diverse pathways in the face of their varied circumstances.

Our conversations about our personal life experiences and philosophies of education led to this course description.

COURSE DESCRIPTION:
EDUCATION 310: SERVICE-LEARNING
WITH MULTICULTURAL ELDERS

This is a service-learning course that integrates traditional academic course work with personal reflection and community involvement. The goal of the course is to explore the dynamics of informal education in a variety of community settings in order to help potential teachers understand the role of social history and culture on the social identity of students and their performance in schools.

Students work closely with members of various cultural and ethnic communities to document cultural beliefs and practices that help to shape social identity of youngsters within the community. Participants then develop ways to share these findings with members of diverse communities.

The semester is divided into two parts. During the first part of the course, students read about service-learning pedagogy and ethnographic research methodology, applying and practicing these principles through in-class activities, such as short interviews, and weekly or biweekly journal assignments. This section of the course concludes with a midterm paper, in which students document the life story of a senior family member.

During the second part of the course, students begin interviewing an elder member of a specific community. (Students are allowed to choose acquaintances but not family members for this assignment: The instructors may also designate an elder for students to interview.) In class, students read and discuss aspects of cultural and local history as they relate to their interviews, particularly Takaki's (1993) *A Different Mirror: A History of Multicultural America.*

Students' final papers are their elders' life stories, which they are expected to present to members of the various elders' communities and to University of Michigan faculty, staff, and students at the end of class.

Six Critical Questions

In our planning for and implementation of this course, six critical questions emerged:

1. Why elders?
2. Community: Does it connote a plurality of meaning?
3. Service: Of what, by whom, and for whom?
4. The democratic classroom: Is it a safe place?
5. Emic versus etic: Whose voice is heard?
6. Family mapping: How can we contextualize social class?

We open each of the next six sections with what our initial responses to each question were—before we actually taught the class. We then attempt to bring our students into the dialogue by restating their experiences with the question. Finally we conclude with some advice we hope our readers find helpful if they are interested in constructing a similar course.

Why Elders?   The death of Joe's father drove home to him the words of one mentor—"every time an elder dies, a book is lost." Most communities or cultures look to their elders to provide continuity, from the past through the present and into the future. Elders offer young people a unique opportunity to connect with the traditional roots of their culture and to gain insights into the way things used to be—and why. Stella convened several gatherings of elders at the National Youth Leadership Council. She is convinced that many successful service-learning projects draw on elders as a rich but often untapped resource. In our class, our students have usually chosen to document the life stories of their grandparents. In our estimation, the understanding our students have reached through seeing family connections from the past through the present and into the future, have been spectacular.

For instance, one student, in concluding his grandmother's life story, took issue with the apparent gender bias of one of the course texts.

> In *Ritual: Power, Healing and Community*, Some (1993) said that grandsons and grandfathers share a special bond because one has just come from the spirit world and one is soon to return. I think that he left something out when he didn't include grandmas. (Student paper)

A second student shared the assigned books with her parents, continuing the classroom discussions on elders and community with them. She told us, "My parents love this class!"

A third student used the midterm assignment as a way to reconnect with his grandfather. While documenting this family elder's life story, he explained that his own reluctance to embrace Judaism was not a personal rejection of his grandfather but rather a reflection of his decision not to choose sides in his parents' divorce. One of the precipitating factors in the divorce was one parent's Jewish ethnic identity versus the other's Christian belief system. With all our students, this understanding, or even reconciliation with their past, seems to energize them for the second part of the term.

Our advice to those attempting to create a similar course is for the instructors to establish their relationships with the members of the community who will be involved in the course at least 3 months prior to their participation. We have attended far too many conferences on "university–community partnerships" where our "community partners" rightly complain that they are not contacted until just before an assignment is due—then suddenly are expected to provide meaningful community experiences for the entire class!

Community: A Plurality of Meaning? Joe's initial concept of the course, qualitative research on Manongs in Michigan, posed dilemmas for both of us. First, neither of us could be considered experts in Filipino American history. Second, neither of us was particularly knowledgeable about qualitative research. These constraints were especially problematic at a research institution like the University of Michigan, where the instructors are expected to act as experts. This is not to say that we saw ourselves as having no expertise. Collectively, we do represent substantial knowledge in the areas of service-learning and multicultural education. We realized we would need to structure the course so that it would revolve around our assets instead of our deficits.

The resolution to these dilemmas appeared during a conversation we had with a colleague in the School of Public Health. She said that if she allowed her students to define "community" among themselves, they would organize themselves into smokers and nonsmokers, and not necessarily along ethnic lines. This organization resulted from the length of her department's graduate-level classes, which necessitated hourly breaks. At those points, one group would leave the building to smoke cigarettes while the other would socialize within the building; additionally, the smokers would on some level grapple with the contradiction of studying public health while simultaneously engaging in carcinogenic behavior.

Why not allow the students in our course to define community for themselves? This pedagogical approach reverses what Freire (1970) denounced as an example of banking education, in which the teacher chooses the program content, and the students (who were not consulted) adapt to it.

For Joe, this resolution was a great relief. This plurality of meaning meant that Joe's personal knowledge of Filipino American history would not be the main focus of the class, any more than Stella's personal knowledge of African-American or Native American history would be. In this conception of the course, the instructors unfold and reveal their connections to elders and the community alongside their students. These experiences, along with those of the students themselves, become oral supplements to the written texts, benchmarks, or guideposts as students learn to define community for themselves.

Many levels of guideposts or benchmarks were built into the course. On a more theoretical level, students read Some's (1993) *Ritual:*

Power, Healing and Community and Peck's *The Different Drum: Community Making and Peace* (1987) to begin to identify the essential elements of community. Students also read Takaki (1993) and Zinn[4] (1995) to orient them to the experiences of different ethnic groups in the United States. Students were also given written life histories of African-American, Native American, Filipino American, Japanese American, Vietnamese American, and Finnish American elders.

Interestingly, the reading that students liked the most was *Tuesdays with Morrie: An Old Man, a Young Man and Life's Greatest Lesson* (Albom, 1997). The book chronicled the weekly visits of sportswriter Mitch Albom to his former college professor, who was now dying of Lou Gehrig's disease. To the students, Morrie appeared to be the kind of elder they wanted to learn from, both in the classroom and in the community. The class also noted that Mitch seemed changed by the experience. One student concluded, "How could he not?"

Our advice to instructors on this point is to be inclusive in generating your reading list. By this, we mean both a diversity in the communities represented by the elders and a diversity within the actual chroniclers of those life stories. In our class, for example, students read works by faculty and high school students, scholars and popular writers, undergraduate and graduate students, as well as the "works in progress" generated by their classmates and their instructors.

Service: Of What, by Whom, and for Whom?   We are embarrassed to say that despite our professional standings as service-learning educators, service was the aspect of the course given last consideration.

It was clear to us that students needed to be taught specific skills in doing ethnographic research. It also made sense for them to understand the pedagogy of service-learning and to engage in experiential exercises during class. It was less clear how students should be meaningfully involved in the community, other than through interviewing their elders.

Stella began by suggesting that key questions in the interviews of elders be specifically about service, that is, service of what, by whom, and for whom? Students would be asked to present in class during their midterm and final projects on their understanding of what the terms service, elders, and community meant. It made sense for them to begin defining these terms for themselves during the very first class.

Since the first time we taught the class, we developed additional ways of understanding what we mean by service. One way was to

---

[4]We devoted most of one class session to posters summarizing Zinn's (1995) *A People's History of the United States 1492–Present.*

dramatize the central importance of service—and reflection on that action—to the class by not formally meeting for two sessions so that we could work in the community together during those times. Another way was to assign student participation in one of the Martin Luther King, Jr. Day symposium-related service events, then have them reflect on how they might use that experience to organize our in-class service project. This proved to be a useful assignment. The students wrote a letter to the student newspaper about how diverse groups acting through community service begin to realize King's dream.

Eventually we decided to participate in the ongoing creative writing group at University of Michigan's Turner Senior Clinic. This is an established group of community elders that had been meeting for years and welcomed our participation. As a class, we were invited to listen to and comment on the poetry and prose the seniors had been writing, and also to bring in our own works. As a final service project, the class decided to collect favorite recipes from the combined elder and student group, along with a story about the memories the recipe evoked. At the last meeting, students presented the recipe books, along with our approximations of selected dishes.

In addition to what we as instructors did, we also brought in a number of facilitators to the class to help us think through the implications of our service. One facilitator was Deling Weller, a faculty member in the University of Michigan's Department of Asian Languages and Cultures who described community-based research methods for "The Healthy Asian American Woman," a study of health behaviors. She made the point that ultimately, her work is political because the data generated would eventually be used to advocate for a reallocation of health care resources that would address the needs of the Asian American community.

A second facilitator was Ann Pham, a graduate student in education who documented the oral histories of Vietnamese who emigrated to this area between 1975 and 1980. She too emphasized the political nature of our work, pointing out that for people of color in general, and immigrants in particular, there is often very little information available to lawmakers who may be making far-reaching policy decisions.

A third set of facilitators was the service-learning class from Brethren High School in Kaleva, Michigan, a small town founded by Finnish immigrants at the turn of the century. This class has the goal of community economic development: The high school students have researched the town's history and are using their service hours to transform the town into an historic and cultural center. In the future, we will also work closely with a local clinic in a service project documenting the life stories of their patients with Alzheimer's.

Our advice to instructors is to specify, as much as possible, the weekly hours students are expected to serve in the community, and to make this information available to students before they enroll. Simply hoping that there will be a match between the enrolled student's availability and the community need places all the parties involved in a compromising position.

The Democratic Classroom: Is It a Safe Place? We made an intentional instructional choice to assign bell hooks' (1994) *Teaching to Transgress: Education as the Practice of Freedom* the first week, followed up by an in-class free write during the second class based on chapter 3. hooks argued that instead of focusing on safety, the democratic classroom should instead strive to articulate some "shared commitment and common good that binds us" (p. 40). One former student, an Asian Indian American woman, put hooks' argument into perspective for us.

> I HATE those stupid ice breakers that you do at the beginning of every "alternative" class! Get a group of students together and give me an issue to work on and I'll show you how to build community! (Student paper)

Additionally, another dilemma arose for us. We are both social workers by profession and often highlighted this in our introductions. Because we emphasized the socioemotional aspects of the class, some students mistook the supportive environment for therapy, and even resisted suggestions from loved ones that they seek professional help. These students argued that they were already a part of an ongoing support group and could fortify their positions through a therapeutic-sounding use of course-related jargon.

To counter this, we emphasized academic rigor at the beginning of the class, then framed subsequent discussions of teacher and student roles in light of the literature (instead of our past experiences as social workers). In this way, students did not connect the feelings associated with building classroom community with being in therapy. When we did talk in class about our personal and professional experiences, we did so only to supplement the texts.

We stress this last point because we believe that a democratic classroom is not a therapy group, and even as our students explored deeply personal topics in their family of origin, this exploration was a class assignment with clear educational objectives in mind. We further believe that it is unethical for educators to challenge their students to examine the "blind spots" in their lives without providing adequate support throughout the process.

Our commitment as instructors to support and challenge our students through written and verbal dialogue on a class-by-class, assignment-to-assignment basis wherein the agendas for our meetings are driven by the outcomes of these dialogues, is very labor-intensive (Sanford, 1966). We imagine that our instructional method consumes more time and energy than if we constructed a class where we deposited information through lectures and checked for understanding through multiple choice tests. However, we have noted a deeper engagement between students and the course content, as well as a willingness to apply the material to real-life situations that we simply could not envision happening in any other way.

It was exhilarating to read one student's paper. An established poet, she formatted her assignment in two columns. On the right, she retold her elder's life story. On the left, in response to particular themes or events, she broke into stream-of-consciousness prose poetry. The effect was breathtaking.

A second student used what he learned through the class to develop a proposal for his former high school. He would help them establish a service-learning course where high school students would be elders-in-training for underresourced children in the Chicagoland area.

A third student wrote a letter to her unborn daughter. She explained that the class not only gave her the opportunity to document her family history, which she was passing along to her daughter, but also crystallized her decision to become a science teacher.

Our advice to instructors here is to know your personal and professional limits. Although it is true that in teaching there is always more you can do, the opportunities to do more grow exponentially when students are making the intellectual, personal, and professional connections that they did in this class.

Emic Versus Etic: Whose Voice?   We started this class discussion with two simple drawings of stick figures. Under each was a critical question. Under the etic worldview was the question "What do I (the usually White, usually male, usually privileged anthropologist) see" when observing "the other" (often a non-White resident of the Third World). We noted how this worldview is rooted in a "scientific" paradigm, how reality is what the dominant culture says it is, how "the other" is treated like an object for manipulation, study, and, quite possibly, exploitation. We also noted that the "banking" model of education is also rooted in this paradigm.

Under the emic worldview was the question "How does the native view the world?" Implicit in this view is the transformation of the other from object to subject—she or he is fully human and therefore can be related to on that level.[5] Moreover, within that relationship, knowledge is created as the two parties hold conversations—dialogic encounters—about how they see the world. This view also holds out the promise that all sides may be deeply and personally changed as a result of this relationship.

During our second class, each student described one classmate's clothing, first by observation only, then through a dialogic encounter. To respond to our former student, this was not a pointless ice-breaker. Although students could, for example, correctly identify which brand of jeans their peers were wearing, the resulting conversations—about which store to shop at, when, how much to pay—helped students develop technical competence within this theoretical framework.

Our students built on this idea of emic voice throughout the term. As instructors, we felt privileged to have our students share their elders' life stories with us through the elders' own words. Because of our students' work, we heard the voices of Jewish elders describe World War II. One was a young man in Europe fleeing the Holocaust; the other was a medical officer in the Pacific Theater. We also got a glimpse of life in the Deep South during the Great Depression. One elder was a polite White woman who was fired from her job because she served African Americans, against her boss' directives. Another saw two members of her family lynched by the Ku Klux Klan.

We were all blessed to learn these life stories, told in the elders' own voice and with their own words. Our summary only begins to convey the transforming power of these multicultural, intergenerational connections created through service-learning.

Our advice to instructors is to know your own voice. By this we mean having some awareness of how our multiple social identities, such as race, class, and gender, have influenced how we see ourselves and how we interact with others. Moreover, we advocate for instructors to build this awareness into how they teach. Our belief is that good teaching emerged from who we are, as well as what we know.

Family Mapping: Contextualizing Social Class. We discovered how to use family mapping as a tool for students to contextualize class issues quite by accident.

A few years ago, a number of Joe's students were placed in chemical dependency treatment facilities, often observing and assisting with family therapy. Joe had these students read about family sys-

---

[5]For a further discussion of ethnographic techniques, see chapter 2 in Kottack (1994), a widely used introductory text.

tems theory and then diagram their own families to supplement their fieldwork.[6] He was quite surprised by some of the questions that these students posed regarding the assignment. For instance, they asked:

- Where on this chart would I put my au pair?
- What should I say about the careers of my mom and her aunts? I call them "professional volunteers" because they're active on the boards of all the big community agencies back home who only want them because of the family's "name" recognition.
- Why can't I drive my BMW when I volunteer at the shelter?

Moreover, these questions tended to silence working-class students during discussions, even when more than a few were present.

In subsequent terms, we have shifted the focus. Instead of concentrating on the family system, students read about social class issues before we meet.[7] Drawing a family tree becomes an in-class assignment. Students are given directions in three phases. First, they simply name their relatives and attempt to map the last three generations. Second, they write a brief description of each relative and what they did for a living. Third, we encourage students to connect the exercise with the readings. Do the descriptions seem to reflect a person's ability to choose professions, or the necessity of having to work for a living? Do the family members seem to explore career options, or need to take jobs to make ends meet?

Connecting this assignment with readings on social class seemed to embolden working-class students to identify themselves as such. Additionally, they would describe how they felt excluded throughout their university experience. For example, they would walk to class from the dorm, even in bad weather when others would call a cab. They would have to deflect questions about vacation plans and attending social events because they did not feel understood when they told peers "I have to work—there's no choice involved—if I want to go to school here, I have to work." Even academic counselors seemed unsympathetic when they explained "I just couldn't afford to study abroad."

We have learned that the timing of this activity is crucial. In a recent class, this exercise did not ignite much discussion. We think this was due to where the topic was actually scheduled on our syllabus.

---

[6]Usually we assign Satir (1995) to help students with the "how to's" of family mapping and Napier and Whitaker (1978) for the underlying theory.

[7]We select these readings from Part II of Andersen and Collins (1998).

We held this discussion during the week before the midterm paper was due. Thus, instead of initiating a conversation on social class, in this case the family mapping raised new questions for them to pose to their elders at an already busy point in the semester.

It is still our belief that this is a useful exercise that helps students explode the myth of the United States as a "classless society." However, in addition to scheduling it earlier in the term, we would also advise potential instructors to complete the exercise for themselves at least one week earlier. Our hope here is that if there are any skeletons in the closets of potential instructors, they will not conflate these with attempts to facilitate this activity with students.

CONCLUSION

Parker Palmer (1990) described the epistemology of higher education in this country in general, and of research universities in particular, as "objectivism." This is the belief that knowledge, in order to be valid, must be objective, analytical, and experimental; that there must be a distance between the investigator, or subject of knowledge, and the topic or object studied. Palmer (1998) concluded:

> That kind of teaching creates the most dangerous creatures on earth: people who know much about the outer world but who know little about their inner selves, who have technical competence but no understanding of their own drives and desires . . . people who want to transform the world but who refuse to be transformed. (p. xxx)

We believe that the counter to objectivism may be found in what Freire (1970) called "historicity," the notion that we are all historical beings in the process of becoming. Through service-learning with multicultural elders, we hope that as progressive teachers in solidarity with our students, we become aware of and celebrate our historicity, and make it the turning point for our burgeoning critical consciousness.

REFERENCES

Albom, M. (1997). *Tuesdays with Morrie: An old man, a young man and life's greatest lesson.* New York, NY: Doubleday.

Andersen, M., & Collins, P. (1998). *Race, class and gender: An anthology.* Belmont, CA: Wadsworth.

Bulosan, C. (1943). *America is in the heart.* Seattle, WA: University of Washington Press.

Chesler, M. (1993). Community service learning as innovation in the university. In J. Howard (Ed.), *Praxis I: A faculty casebook on community service learning* (pp. 27–40). Ann Arbor, MI: University of Michigan Office of Community Service Learning Press.

Cordova, F. (1983). *Filipinos: Forgotten Asian Americans*. Dubuque, IA: Kendall/ Hunt.

Freire, P. (1970). *Pedagogy of the oppressed*. New York: Continuum.

Galura, J., Howard, J., Waterhouse, D., & Ross, R. (Eds.). (1995). *Praxis III: Voices in dialogue*. Ann Arbor, MI: University of Michigan Office of Community Service Learning Press.

Galura, J., Meiland, R., Ross, R., Callan M. J., & Smith, R. (Eds.). (1993). *Praxis II: Service-learning resources for university students, staff and faculty*. Ann Arbor, MI: University of Michigan Office of Community Service Learning Press.

hooks, b. (1994). *Teaching to transgress: Education as the practice of freedom*. New York: Routledge.

Horton, M., & Freire, P. (1990). *We made the road by talking: Conversations on education and social change*. Philadelphia, PA: Temple University Press.

Howard, J. (Ed.). (1993). *Praxis I: A faculty casebook on community service learning*. Ann Arbor, MI: University of Michigan Office of Community Service Learning Press.

Kottack, C. (1994). *Anthropology: The exploration of human diversity* (6th ed.). New York: McGraw-Hill.

Napier, A., & Whitaker, C. (1978). *The family crucible: The intense experience of family therapy*. New York: Harper & Row.

Palmer, P. (1990). Community, conflict and ways of knowing: Ways to deepen our educational agenda. In J. Kendall & Associates (Eds.), *Combining service and learning: A resource book for community and public service* (Vol. 1, pp. 105–113). Raleigh, NC: National Society for Internships and Experiential Education.

Palmer, P. (1998). *The courage to teach: Exploring the inner landscape of a teacher's life*. San Francisco, CA: Jossey-Bass.

Peck, M. (1987). *The different drum: Community making and peace*. New York: Simon & Schuster.

Root, M. (Ed.). (1997). *Filipino Americans: Transformation and identity*. Thousand Oaks, CA: Sage.

Sanford, N. (1966). *Self and society*. New York: Atherton.

Satir, V. (1995). Your family map. In J. Stewart (Ed.), *Bridges not walls: A book about interpersonal communication* (pp. 335–345). New York: McGraw-Hill.

Some, M. (1993). *Ritual: Power, healing and community*. Portland, OR: Swan/Raven & Company.

Takaki, R. (1989). *Strangers from a different shore: A history of Asian Americans*. Boston, MA: Little, Brown.

Takaki, R. (1993). *A different mirror: A history of multicultural America*. Boston, MA: Back Bay Books.

Zinn, H. (1995). *A people's history of the United States 1492–present*. New York: HarperCollins.

10

Teaching Diversity Through Service-Learning Immigrant Assistance[1]

Robert E. Koulish*
Bentley College

On October 3, 1998, five members of the Bentley Immigrant Assistance Program (BIAP) shared the stage at Boston's Faneuil Hall with representatives of Boston-based immigrant rights organizations, state politicians, and 1996 Nobel Laureate Jose Ramos Horta, who delivered the keynote address. All were assembled to commemorate the 50th anniversary of the United Nations Declaration on Human Rights. Once on the stage, the moderator introduced the BIAP with the following statement:

> The Bentley College Immigrant Assistance Program (BIAP) is the most recent addition to the highly successful Bentley Service Learning Center (BSLC), which was established in 1990. BIAP endeavors to engage college students in community service activities that address human rights issues together with structured opportunities for integrating this experience with Academic curriculum. It engages students in civic engagement chiefly by partnering them with community based organizations. BIAP focuses attention on the Greater Boston's immigrant community. In conjunction with community partners, BIAP endeavors to

---

*I would like to acknowledge the Bentley Service-Learning Center, the Bentley Immigrant Assistance Program, and all the student participants since 1997. In addition, special thanks to Mauricio Poodts, Marion Bishop, Lucille Ponte for their editorial assistance, to Jim Ostrow, and the Campus Compact National Center for Community Colleges 2+4= Service on Common Ground.

[1]Information and sections of this chapter build upon Koulish (1998a, 1998b).

dissolve the separation between "We and Them," as students experience the fundamental principles celebrated in the Universal Declaration by forging partnerships with community organizations based upon principles of social justice, responsibility and peace.

The BSLC develops and coordinates innovative service-learning projects such as BIAP, which provides a common programmatic theme (human rights and immigration) for cross-disciplinary service-learning. The image of Bentley College students on stage with Jose Ramos Horta—an activist whose ceaseless struggle on behalf of the East Timorese for independence from Indonesian oppression earned him the 1998 Nobel Peace Prize—challenges popular perceptions of students at a business college. In the self-centered and civically disengaged late 1990s, it seems incongruous for business students to spend a Saturday morning at a grass-roots event called, "The Many Voices of Human Rights: A Testimonial for the Universal Declaration of Human Rights," an event that celebrates what has been called the single most important statement of human moral solidarity.

And yet, whether one is speaking of students from a liberal arts college or from a business college such as Bentley, this image does make sense. It provides an example of a fairly recent curricular-based response to the American public's increasing disillusionment with higher education. Such projects have been termed "service-learning," and the learning that occurs through these projects is two-pronged. First, students learn about others. Their experiences with international human rights issues exposes them to what Salmon Rushdie termed "a migrants-eye view of the world." Rushdie believed that, from the "uprooting disjuncture and metamorphosis" of this perspective, "can be derived a metaphor for all humanity" (Rushdie, 1991, p. 394). Second, their involvement challenges students to achieve a new level of awareness about the relevance and meaning of human rights and to foster citizen action to guarantee those rights. In the process, students learn about themselves. Their involvement enables them to examine the social and personal significance of their activities and to acquire the skills needed to effectively participate. And somewhere in the process, they learn about the world and its diversity.

College offers many undergraduates their first experience with diversity. This is particularly the case for Bentley students because about 60% of them went to high schools in somewhat homogenous communities in Massachusetts. Because Bentley is a business college, the challenges of diversity are even more immediate because graduates are expected to assume positions of authority within sectors of multicultural global markets. Such BSLC programs as BIAP endeavor to meet the needs of its students by offering hands-on experiences in diversity of thought, culture, and approach, something not traditionally done in a university that relies on conveying specialized knowledge within strictly defined departments and disciplines.

PHILOSOPHICAL AND PEDAGOGICAL REASONS FOR SERVICE-LEARNING

Service-learning programs like BIAP are on the rise in higher education because they provide a response to increasing criticism of higher education's failure to prepare its students for life beyond graduation (Lucas, 1996). More precisely, service-learning is well suited to meet the challenges of the "information age," an age of an expanding plethora of media for interacting with one another and with the physical world. The information age presents new priorities in the contemporary world with respect to the nature of "knowledge" and its development through education. These priorities require new and complex perspectives—imaginative persons who can acquire, sort through, and interconnect information, and extend beyond *kinds* of information to understanding the sources and uses of information across fields, across sites, and across different media (see Koulish, 1998b).

The information age demands more of higher education than isolated and discipline-specific learning. It remains commonplace for colleges to produce students who neither see the connections between the different disciplines, nor synthesize data into a more holistic way of thinking critically about the information offered by such discrete learning experiences. Wherever the specialized character of learning translates into separation and isolation, the contents and methods of collaborative learning are rendered irrelevant for employers, the ordinary citizen, or anyone beyond the enclosed circle of the traditional, discipline-specific classroom. The consequence is that modern forms of learning are disconnected and have no clear purpose or meaning within the social world, leaving students with neither the tools nor the incentive they need to function effectively in the marketplace (Thurow, 1998).

If education is to serve us well personally and professionally, then we must move beyond the inherent limitations of traditional pedagogy to highlight the more dynamic, less predictable meanings created when we engage communities over time and experience and make sense of the world. Service-learning follows John Dewey's proposition that education is fundamentally about finding "the ends for the sake of which man acts," and those ends consist of a diverse and open-ended program of experiential inquiry and constant revision of beliefs, based on collective interaction, or team building (Dewey, 1916, p. xxx). It considers knowledge as dynamic and socially constructed, not something that exists, in Paulo Freire's words, "out there, somewhere as static entities; it is something that is occurring" (1970, p. 83).

Diversity in understanding, culture, and approach becomes the thread weaving service-learning objectives into particular courses. BSLC students learn how to work well and live with a massive variety of experience, and they gain the ingenuity and sensitivity to be creative and caring of one another in the midst of this variety. In BIAP projects, students and community partners from diverse backgrounds collaborate to initiate and develop new projects, perspectives, and approaches as well as to manage existing projects, thus creating a community of shared meanings from diversity. Immigrant groups bring to a project knowledge and skills about how and what work needs to get done in their community, and show more than one right way to get positive results. All the while, by grappling with a diverse field of study as applied to problem solving, Bentley students come to experience the relevance and value of the very different kinds—sources and uses—of information that are out there, and to choose among them.

SERVICE-LEARNING AT BENTLEY COLLEGE

The BSLC was established in fall 1990 to integrate classroom learning with hands-on, course-related work in the Waltham and Greater Boston communities. Bentley is the only business school in the United States with a comprehensive, cross-disciplinary service-learning program with an extensive scholarship and work program at the undergraduate level; the college also supports service-learning projects in various graduate courses.

As a result, Bentley is unique in its understanding of the benefits of a strong service-learning program to business education and, by extension, to the career aspirations of business school graduates in the country. The BSLC's programming is unique in its focus on inculcating values of social justice in service learning options for business courses, and on building experiences that will enhance the career development for its business students. The program is key to learning valuable skills through projects tied directly to business disciplines, thus raising the prospect of students advancing to upper levels of management.

Service-learning also advances students' abilities to become leaders in the business world. The job market demands that professionals cross the specific boundaries of discipline-specific learning. BSLC wants its students to be able to have the opportunity to be involved in collaborative and community projects that help them to implement what they are learning in their courses and that engage them in community life. Such learning gives them practical knowledge and makes them sensitive to and competent in dealing with people with different approaches to problem solving and from different backgrounds. Never has it been more important that business employees, executives, and leaders have the ability to design, implement, manage, and work with others on projects.

It is through service-learning that students learn to display initiative, follow through, and the capacity to deal effectively and sensitively with diverse populations. They learn firsthand about social issues that have major significance in contemporary life and in the workplace. Students engage in activities through which they acquire a disposition toward the welfare of others that is present in all their ways of thinking and acting.

BSLC's academic programs consist of field-based project assignments within three credit courses, one credit service-learning options (e.g., fourth credit option presented in regular courses) and internships. In projects within three credit courses, students work one-on-one with people of different ages, races, and cultural backgrounds throughout the Greater Waltham and Boston communities. Faculty members may offer fourth credit options early in the semester. In order to complete a fourth credit, students conduct a community service project and also produce either written or oral reports as agreed on with a professor. Once a student has accumulated three fourth credits, they have fulfilled a three-credit Arts and Sciences or Unrestricted elective.

Student programs consist of the Community Scholars Program and Community Work Program. Both programs (about 70 students) concentrate on expanding students' understanding of local community and societal issues as they develop leadership roles in service-learning project design and management. For example, 7 student leaders from these programs comprise the BSLC student steering committee that serves as an oversight and strategic planning component for student programs.

SERVICE-LEARNING IMMIGRANT ASSISTANCE

I came up with the idea for service-learning immigrant assistance (BIAP) in fall 1997, and introduced the project as a service-learning requirement in my three credit Politics of Immigration course, which also offers a fourth credit service-learning option. Some students selected the fourth credit, thus assuming additional project responsibilities and writing an additional paper integrating their service-learning experience with the concepts and theories presented in class lectures. The service-learning project for students taking the course for three credits included about 6 hours of training and 6 hours of working as a naturalization advocate for Citizenship Day (C-Day), assisting immigrants to complete their naturalization packets. Students taking the fourth credit also served on one of three co-committees preparing for C-Day. The fourth credit option allowed for a more extensive experience. All service learning activities required journal entries that directed students to describe their service experience, their personal reactions to the events, and to connect the service with course readings and class discussions.

The C-Day project is a collaborative endeavor with multiple immigrant-based nongovernmental organizations (NGOs). At each C-Day session, students assist immigrants in completing their packets for naturalization including N-400 application forms and passport-style photos. Students with previous C-Day experience and community practitioners teach students new to the program what the legal requirements for naturalization are, how to assist immigrants in completing applications through role-playing Immigration and Naturalization Service (INS) interviews, and how to provide students with a real sense of what lies ahead in C-Day events.

On the day itself, about five supervising immigration lawyers respond to problems and questions that arise and also "eye-ball" each completed application. As immigrants arrive, they sign in, receive numbers, and take their seats to await their turn at the prescreening table and then the application tables, where they meet one of the naturalization advocates. After the immigrants complete their applications, BIAP students take passport-type photos of the immigrants. Lunch and such featured speakers as students, immigrants, faculty, community representatives, and state and local politicians make for a festive celebration of citizenship in all its forms. To allow the process to continue and to reinforce Bentley's vision of service-learning as collaborative, applicants are invited to participate in such future activities as helping with C-Day training, and serving as tutors in our English as a Second Language (ESL) and citizenship training classes.

During that first semester, a handful of students assumed the added responsibilities of the fourth credit (about 5 from a class of 19), and, together as an informal team, we commenced planning, organization, and implementation of activities. Because these individuals were highly motivated, committed, and in constant communication with each other, the classroom and ad-hoc discussion structure served the project well. In April 1997, about 100 immigrants came to Bentley to inaugurate the event. The project has certainly grown since its origins. The number of attending immigrants leaped to 140 and 190 in November 1997 and April 1998 respectively. Despite some logistical obstacles, in fall 1998, 120 additional eligible immigrants came to Bentley to apply for citizenship. As of November 1998, almost 600 immigrants have applied for citizenship as a result of the Bentley activity. In addition to C-Day, students work with community partners on naturalization drives throughout the area.

The ad-hoc discussion structure has evolved into a more formal, albeit horizontal, team-based learning structure to accommodate about 100 students a semester from several different academic units now participating in a multiproject immigrant assistance program. This learning organization succeeds in integrating community service into the course objectives of several different academic units. In 1998, BIAP formed a student steering committee. The steering committee consists of seven student project coordinators in charge of managing events and leading specific projects. They coordinate students from several different classes around Citizenship Day, ESL for immigrant projects, citizenship classes, and more. The main purpose of the steering committee is to provide coordination and direction as well as to demonstrate leadership to the students, ostensibly by example, and to strengthen camaraderie among participants.

In addition to C-Day, BIAP students may select among several other projects sharing the specific goal of assisting immigrants to become full-fledged contributing members of their community and society by teaching them a variety of skills necessary for this end. The projects take place on campus and at community sites. Since its inception, BIAP has created partnerships with about 12 immigrant-based community organizations, one of which is Centro Presente, a direct social service and education provider for immigrants from Central America. Bentley students have assisted Centro clients in obtaining work permits, relief from deportation, and in teaching Centro's ESL and citizenship classes. Students have also helped design a Centro logo and have worked with this organization to design a newsletter and marketing campaign.

Besides having direct contact with immigrants, Bentley students serve as designers and managers of large-scale communitywide projects. For three semesters, BSLC students have collaborated with the Waltham Alliance to Create Housing (WATCH CDC), a local community development corporation, and have managed and facilitated an ESL discussion group for local immigrants who also have housing needs. The ESL project has been one of the BSLC's most rewarding. As one student described the discussion group process:

> I can see the connection between the Bentley students and immigrants; the immigrant appreciates what the teacher is doing, and at the same time, the teacher feels great about helping them. It's the most rewarding feeling when I see my own students learn a new thing. (Student reflection paper, 1998)

One evening a week, students drive the BSLC van to WATCH to pick up about 20 immigrants, most of whom are Guatemalan and Haitian. They then return to campus for a 2½-hour session in ESL that includes reading, writing, and conversation. A similar session, which a certified ESL instructor oversees, is held at WATCH on a second evening. Much of the real-world learning for Bentley ESL participants occurs outside the ESL classroom. This includes van drivers as well as ESL instructors. Early on in one semester, a student driver compared the immigrants' demeanor to those of his own and his Bentley colleagues on certain days. He remarked that the van is "usually quiet on the ride to Bentley—quite as it is for us before we are being tested—," but that on the return trip "as we all walked out to the van, they were practicing the phrases they had just learned. This time, instead of being quiet, all were talking their heads off, myself included."

One Bentley ESL tutor was invited to a couple's house to tutor them in English and join them for a meal. That evening he interacted with immigrants on an equal footing, perhaps for the first time, and found common ground with his hosts by observing striking similarities and differences between the United States and their homeland of Turkey.

> Tonight I had a most gratifying experience. I went to Nubar and Manu's house, working with Nubar on grammar. I used the same lesson plan that we used in class on Monday. Except for a few words that bugged him, Nubar understood much of what I said and got 100% on the vocabulary quiz I gave him. But the best part of the night came later. Manu made teas and some Turkish food. It was excellent!! I sat with both of them and talked politics, Turkish and family life for almost an hour. I learned that Manu came to the U.S. because her father was sick, and that Nubar had to stay behind and could not see his family for 5½ years because he could not get a visa. . . . They said that people in Turkey took an interest in government whereas in this country, we are apathetic as a people. . . . Just being able to experience a different culture for a short time was amazing. (Student reflection paper, 1998)

It is not often that a Bentley student recounts enjoying a discussion about Turkish politics. Such interactions go a long way toward developing critical thinking skills. In this instance, the student referred to his real-world interaction during a class-time discussion about "demystifying the American Dream." The student synthesized the knowledge he gained around the table with class readings to contend that decisions to immigrate are difficult for immigrants to make and often quite personal. He invoked the image of "roads in America paved in gold" as entertainment rather than as accurately representing underlying realities. Such comments provide evidence that BIAP may enrich students' ability to think critically about U.S. culture and society.

The citizenship classes held on campus and at community sites also provide students an opportunity to learn from the immigrants who are enrolled in the class. The standard course curriculum for citizenship classes teaches a rather ethnocentric view of U.S. history and civics to prepare them to answer the questions on the INS citizenship exam. The classes often turn into informal discussions about the topics specified to be covered in the session. As the students engage immigrants in dialogue, it is the Bentley students who often begin questioning events they teach as "facts" in the class. One student questioned whether Columbus really discovered America, and another student wondered whether South Texas-born Chicanos or Boston-born Protestants have a stronger claim on being considered of immigrant stock. As one Mexican-American student reflected after returning from facilitating a citizenship class:

> I think I learned more than my students did today. I think people have preconceived ideas about who is and is not an immigrant. One of the immigrants asked if I was an immigrant. . . . My father's family along the border held a land grant from Spain. . . . We are more American than folks who came over on the Mayflower. I hate to be judgmental, but as I continue getting more involved, I'm finding that my own ideas or judgments have been changing. I never saw myself as an immigrant before. (Student reflection paper, 1998)

In addition to the citizenship and ESL classes, other service-learning projects include computer classes; presentations to Latino youth on HIV, sexually transmitted diseases, and other health concerns of young people; job counseling; youth tutoring; and ESL discussion groups.

The collaborative nature of service-learning is an important component of the Bentley vision. It encourages students to see community members as actual partners rather than as individuals in need of assistance. It encourages students to examine the differences in charity and community in service-learning. The skills the immigrants gain prepare them for an active role in the job market and community.

Once completing these projects, immigrants are invited to share their experiences with students and to collaborate with BIAP in providing assistance to other new arrivals to the community.

COURSE CONTEXTS

One of BIAP's strengths lies in its ability to attract faculty from across disciplines to collaborate in common projects. Indeed, faculty members in courses from five to seven departments participate in BIAP projects each semester. In fall, 1998, BIAP participants came from the following departments; Government, English, International Culture and Economy (ICE), Operations Management, Marketing and Computer Information Systems (CIS). Faculty from the liberal arts, particularly those teaching courses on diversity, immigration, or cross-cultural communication are attracted to the topic of immigrant assistance for obvious reasons. Although the match between BIAP and business disciplines is less obvious, the lessons learned by students and immigrants alike are just as rewarding. Marketing classes have worked with BIAP to create advertising campaigns for the program itself and for particular community partners endeavoring to spread the word of the services they provide to community members and funding foundations alike. Operations management classes have partnered with community organizations to enhance the quality of their service delivery systems; tax classes have assisted immigrants in preparing tax returns; and accounting classes have established accounting systems for immigrant organizations. Two examples of course contexts are described in more detail later.

Civic Education and Introduction
to American Politics

One of service-learning's biggest challenges is to maintain the connection between service and learning, and reintegrate immigrant assistance back into specific course syllabi. One Introduction to American Government class that I taught explained the course content this way:

> In this course we will investigate the theoretical basis for political process in the United States and how it operates in practice. The following question will serve to guide us as we proceed: Does our system of government still serve the country well as we bid adieu to the 20th century?

This is a foundations course in government, and thus our objective is to examine concepts essential to the understanding of politics as well as their application to actual institutional processes. We will try to understand the way our democracy works or fails to work by focusing on civic participation and voter involvement, as well as learn how fundamental institutions of government operate. The Course includes a fourth credit option which allows you to engage in course related service-learning activities and earn an additional 1 credit which is attached to this class. The topic is: Voter registration and education. The fourth credit includes 15–18 hours of service—with one immigrant organization in Cambridge—a journal with descriptive and reflective components that integrate classroom learning with service experience as well as one 8–10 page paper. (From course syllabus)

Students taking the fourth credit option were instructed to interview immigrants during C-Day about the immigrants' views on U.S. politics and civic engagement. This activity was intended to supplement the class readings and discussion about civic disengagement especially among college students. In my class lectures I emphasized that voter turnout in elections is commonly alluded to as the fundamental indicator of civic disengagement (Rimmerman, 1997), directed students to relevant data about presidential and off-year voting patterns, and emphasized that young people are even less inclined to vote and participate in civic activities than are their elders. I noted Jean Bethke Elstain's (1997) comment that citizens are experiencing "a spiral of delegitimization that has its origins in widespread cynicism about government and politics, the disintegration of civil society, a pervasive sense of powerlessness, and other cultural phenomena" (p. 11). However, students' service-learning experiences jettisoned the limiting character of the class discussions. One student on a fourth-credit option worked on a voter registration drive in Cambridge's Portuguese speaking community as well as with the Red Cross to package and send hurricane relief materials to Honduras after Hurricane Mitch. He reported that the service-learning option allowed him to

> get out into a community that is not familiar to me. . . . It may be easy for us to get stuck in our own little routines and forget about all that is going on around, but I was able to actually help out in situations I otherwise pass by in the street or ignore on the news.

His reflection on his experience offers a challenge to Elstain's observation of a spiraling sense of powerlessness. (Student reflection paper, 1998)

A second fourth credit student led a focus group at the fall 1998 C-Day. She reported that although she expected the experience "to be a flop," she was surprised by how rewarding it was to get involved. Her report contributed her observation that immigrants seemed more attuned to the nuances of American politics than were her classmates. According to her report to the class, one immigrant, who was born in Cambodia and moved to the United States in 1982, "already felt like a citizen. She was politically aligned with the reform party and wanted legal citizenship so she could vote. She even scolded me when I said I never voted." According to a second group of students, one immigrant, Carlos, born in Chile,

> told us that he would vote for or against a candidate depending on how that person felt on abortion and other social issues. He told us voting is important because it gives people an individual right to make a differ- ence. . . . Carlos went on to tell us he considers himself an independent politically. . . . He said that he never participated in government in Chile but that now (as a citizen) he had an opportunity to earn a living and have equal rights, he would want to be involved in government and play a role in his community.

This exercise gave students "a different mirror" with which to experi- ence and reflect upon civic engagement. (Student reflection paper, 1997)

English Department and Minor Literature

The English Department offers a rich field for diversity service-learn- ing collaborations. Recent debates on multiculturalism and the canon of Western literature opens this field to a plethora of innovative teach- ing methods. In one English Department class, Women and Literature, the professor introduced her class to how the canon serves to marginalize and even silence minority voices in society, and how lis- tening to the voices of groups thought to be "voiceless" may actually en- rich the canon and expand the learning experience.

This class provided a laudable example of integrating personal re- flections with specific course objectives. Professor Marion Bishop in- tegrated service-learning with specific texts to forge the course objec- tives that, as described in the syllabus, were "to learn about dominant and muted discourse, and to apply theory by helping immi- grants gain citizenship and come to voice in the Bentley Immigrant Assistance Program." Service-learning—including completion of a journal—counted for 20% of the students' grade. The professor de- voted 10 minutes at the end of each class for student reports on service-learning experiences. Students took turns reflecting on their activities and drawing connections between their work with immigrants and their class readings. One student noted:

> In the stories of the *Red Convertible* by Louise Erdrich, *The Rich Brother*, by Tobias Wolff, and *Sonny's Blue* by James Baldwin, the protagonists all have the same answer to the question, "Am I my brother's keeper." Although they experience different situations, the protagonists all feel responsible for the well-being of their siblings. Upon reading these stories and reflecting on my learning experience with the Bentley Immigrant Assistance Program, I have come to understand and appreciate more the answer to this same question. By giving help, the helper completes the cycle of humanity where the receiver and the giver both benefit the same. By taking responsibility for others, one is taking responsibility for himself. (Student reflection paper, 1998)

According to a second student:

> I found a passage in the book, *Joy Luck Club*, that relates directly to my involvement in BIAP. It tells of a woman who travels to America with a swan, in the hope of giving it to her daughter one day. "But when she arrived in the new country the immigration officials pulled her swan away from her, leaving the woman fluttering her arms and with only one swan feather for a memory. And then she had to fill out so many forms she forgot why she had come and what she had left behind. I hope we have made this process a little easier for the immigrants that showed up at Bentley. I hope they felt comfortable with us helping them . . . (Student reflection paper, 1998)

A third student returned the discussion back to the idea that diversity indeed is the thread that binds service and learning together.

> In class, Professor Bishop asked if we should all strive to be part of the dominant circle. I think that is not the goal. It is important to preserve your heritage and culture, which makes us unique and sets us apart from everyone else. It is even more important not to be ethnocentric and respect those who are not exactly like us. It is OK to be different. (Student reflection paper, 1998)

Professor Bishop observed that although many of her students started the semester with rather simplistic and ethnocentric perceptions of immigrants and of people they considered "not like themselves," service-learning encouraged the students to develop a more critical appreciation of diversity and how their own culture is both similar and different from (but not better than) the backgrounds of others.

STUDENT OUTCOMES IN SERVICE-LEARNING[2]

One of the problems inherent in service-learning is assessing its out-comes. Although quantitative assessment tools provide information on trends and patterns of the effectiveness of service-learning, they are less effective in measuring such intangibles as "synergetic collaborations," or "community building" (see Koulish, 1998b). The large number of community partners and classes involved in any given academic year further complicates any effort to use a quantitative assessment tool. Further, such quantitative tools as a Likert scale, for example, formulate attitudinal categories in advance, thus stipulating in advance what the community members' attitudes can be and thus imposing limitations on their experiences (see Ostrow as cited in Koulish, 1998b). The immigrant assistance is offered precisely to empower students in transcending such "narrowly constricted, stylized representation(s) of community" (Koulish, 1998b, p. 34).

Anecdotal hints about service-learning's effectiveness can be derived from comments faculty make about the scores of their service-learning students on in-class exams, or the rich and more complicated questions service-learning students may ask in class. However, reflection journals provide the most consistent evidence of BIAP's and the students' own strengths and weaknesses. The journals provide data about (a) the lived-through character of learning as students anticipate, engage in, and reflect on site visits; (b) the sense and value of community involvement for students engaged in the project throughout their college careers; and (c) the extent to which service-learning prepares students for lives outside of Bentley. In particular, student journals include detailed accounts of any activities, thoughts, anxieties, hopes, fears, concerns, ambitions, surprises, disappointments, or discoveries that are either formally or informally related to the student's service-learning role. Students should be encouraged to write on whatever matters, without faculty placing constricting limits.

Reflection journals of C-Day reveal growth in students' civic commitment and personal comfort with multicultural realities. The months of preparation for Citizenship Day provide important lessons. Certain patterns emerge as students develop from self-absorbed and hesitant students to public-spirited and emboldened citizens. During the first several weeks of the semester, after being introduced to the project, students are likely to voice their fears and perceptions of incompetence. A particularly revealing statement focuses attention on a student's feelings of powerlessness.

---

[2]An earlier rendition of this section appears in Koulish, 1998(a).

I am quite uncertain about myself. I do not know if I am up to the challenge. I do not know what to expect. In class we discussed the different aspects as to what was going to go on, but I do not have any hands-on experience. Our only knowledge is what we read, word of mouth and the diagrams we keep drawing on the board. . . . I just keep thinking what a big deal this is, I mean, important government papers where the future of somebody's life depends on making sure I do my job precisely. That's a lot of pressure. (Student reflection paper, 1997)

Indeed, students find the project involves lots of pressure. There is nothing wrong with such feelings. The key factor in terms of the project is facing fears and struggling to overcome barriers. The first step for students is to deal with their fears by giving voice to them. One student said:

On a personal note, my main fear is the one that I always have when facing something new . . . failure. I have always gone into new things thinking to myself that I am going to do something wrong or something involving me will go wrong or screw up. (Student reflection paper, 1997)

A second student voiced a similar refrain: "I feel nervous and scared that I wasn't doing enough. . . . It's as if I cannot do enough no matter how much I try." During the several weeks that follow, however, the students undergo a journey from awkward victim to a more self-confident and proactive citizen. The students' journals also make clear that the process itself becomes a tool to enhance the students' education in team building. As the second student reflected:

I feel that as time moves on, the others feel nervous just like me and we were all there to help one another. The close interaction of everybody working together for a common goal made me feel so good inside, it is unbelievable to see this event really begin to take shape . . . we are all becoming friends . . . we all care about what is going to happen. (Student reflection paper, 1997)

Student observations acknowledge interactions with others, a sign of students stretching beyond their own biography. By C-Day, they expand further to connect the student to the larger multicultural community, thus also acknowledging the lure of community service learning (CSL):

He [an immigrant] talked about his life when he came over here and how he worked in a candy factory in Cambridge. He gave us the advice of working as hard as we could so we can relax and have fun later on, and that learning different languages couldn't hurt. So many different cultures, there was no avoiding learning and inquiring from others about their own culture. (Student reflection paper, 1997)

Indeed, the path to making students into more effective citizens also provides the opportunity for students to transcend the barriers of their own biography to work collaboratively and begin to see the world as others experience it. By the latter stages of the process, the social distance diminishes between the students and "strangers" in the community. As one student claimed of C-Day:

> It wasn't anything like what many in the training sessions had us envision. I worked with one entire Armenian family and found myself in a regular conversation with them. As the day continued, I felt good that I was opening myself up to other cultures. I guess this was one of the goals of the whole project. (Student reflection paper, 1997)

This particular student who had previously participated in some community service was not aware he could have regular conversations with foreign-born residents until this event. For this student and others similarly situated, C-Day provides an introduction to a great mosaic of ethnic, racial, and religious difference. Another student remarked about the common bonds she shared with one of her applicants:

> He was a bubbly man from Puebla, Mexico. . . . I happened to have studied abroad in Puebla at the same University his daughter almost attended. As we chatted about the city and the people from Puebla, I realized this was the first time I shared my story with somebody who knew what I was talking about. (Student reflection paper, 1998)

The distance between service and learning also diminishes for some as students begin making connections between C-Day and topics the Politics of Immigration class had covered: "I know how disruptive deportation can be on immigrant families. I just kept telling myself, you have to fill (the application) out completely and correctly because you could get them deported."

SERVICE-LEARNING OBSTACLES

Although not all students achieve this level of project expectations, their struggle in the early stages is to move beyond their own biographies and overcome feelings of inadequacy and disinterest. Most students engage their work along these lines; some of them of course do not. It is not uncommon, for example, for students failing to incorpo-rate the overall BIAP vision into their service-learning to "free-ride" on the back of others. These students fail to show up for required meetings and often blame others for shortcomings they perceive in the project. Other students undermine the significance of their activi-ties by focusing solely on completing specific tasks rather than on stretching beyond narrow assignments. Two weeks before a recent C-Day, for example, one student involved in outreach for C-Day told me, "Forget about service-learning . . . it's all about the numbers, get-ting people to the event, we're behind where we were last semester." At about the same time, a community partner voiced a similar con-cern, complaining that students pushed and cajoled them to deliver clients to Bentley rather than spending additional time educating cli-ents on the benefits of citizenship.

Most students forge ahead and take responsibility for completing tasks, maintaining hands-on contact with immigrants, and building their capacity to design, implement, and make sense of the "big-picture." As many students find they are up to the challenge, they begin working in a collaborative spirit. They find the time to meet and begin to create a social product. One student claimed:

> This [project] is all about a group working together towards making a difference in the community, and creating a new program at the college. What makes it more gratifying is that without the other—students and immigrants—our goals would not have been achieved. (Student reflec-tion paper, 1997)

By the project's end, the first student's fears had been replaced by a sense of wonder that the project really did make a difference in the lives of community residents.

> I never saw so many smiles on people's faces. I didn't feel uncomfort-able or timid at all at that point to answer any questions they had. . . . I even got a chance to speak a little Portuguese with somebody in their 50s who was there with his sister to bring their 82-year-old mother to fill out her application. He must have shaken my hand and said thank you about 50 times. (Student reflection paper, 1997)

Similarly, the second student's initial fear by now had turned to "an adrenaline rush" as all the plans became real.

> . . . I was not expecting to see what I saw when I opened those doors. The room looked fantastic. It was exactly as envisioned on the class-room board. The tables were set up just as imagined, there were post-

ers, signs, and flags. I was in a state of disbelief . . . unaware of our potential. I just did not give us enough credit. . . . By 9:30, people were
arriving, adrenaline was rushing, excitement was building. All our
months of hard work and commitment finally realized. Let the games
begin. (Student reflection paper, 1997)

CONCLUSION

Perhaps the most valuable lesson for students is the melting away of
ethnic and racial stereotypes and the recognition that diversity matters. Service-learning students come to recognize that sources and
uses of knowledge expand beyond the classroom and mere transmis-
sion of information. As they compare classroom readings with community service, students become adept at critically deciphering the
accuracy and usefulness of assigned texts and classroom recitations.
As undergraduates experience the diversity of approaches to reaching
a common project-related ends, they learn to think "outside the box,"
as well as the value of teamwork. All the while, the tools students use
prepare them for effective lives in the mind, civic square, and marketplace.

Service-learning immigrant assistance provides a vehicle for students to experience the multitude of ways of seeing the importance of
civic involvement. Immigrant assistance embraces the revered vision
that teachers should educate for the purpose of constituting productive members of civil society. As Benjamin Barber warned, "in disen-
gaging the classroom from real-world settings, schools . . . fail to do
their job and democracy . . . fail[s] to secure the responsible citizens
it needs to flourish" (p. 229). Barber's perspective is especially salient
as we enter the new millennium. As Robert Putnam (1995) pondered
the "strange disappearance of civic engagement in America" (p. 664),
Juan Gonzales from Centro Presente provided, as Rushdie would
view it, a "migrants-eye" view of citizenship:

> In Guatemala, the people are prepared for civic action through educa-
> tion and external political and social circumstances, but for genera-
> tions they have been denied the freedoms needed for getting involved.
> In the United States, citizens have all the liberty they need, but lack the
> preparedness and incentive for involvement. (interviewed by author,
> July 1998)

Gonzales' eye-view of citizenship provides "a different mirror" for students to reflect on their own role in the community and classroom. In
the same way, BIAP projects represent a challenge for students

through exposure to a diversity of cultures, and encouragement to transcend the limitations of their own discrete biographies. As undergraduates participate in field projects relating ideas to real life, they increase their comfort with "the other, while they begin to see their connection to it, as well as its presence within themselves" (Guarasci, 1997, p. 132).

REFERENCES

Barber, B. (1997). "Afterword." In R. Buttistoni, & W. Hudson (Eds.), *Experiencing citizenship: Concepts and models for service-learning in Political Science*. Washington, DC: AM. Association for Higher Education.

Dewey, J. (1916). *Democracy and education*. New York: Macmillan.

Elstain, Jean Bethke. (1997). The decline of democratic faith. In R. Battistoni & W. Hudson (Eds.), *Experiencing citizenship: Concepts and models for service-learning in political science* (pp. 91–94). Washington, DC: American Association for Higher Education.

Freire, P. (1970). *Pedagogy of the oppressed*. New York: Continuum.

Guarasci, R. (1997). Politics, community and service. In R. Battistoni & W. Hudson (Eds.), *Experiencing citizenship: Concepts and models for service-learning in political science* (pp. 127–140). Washington, DC: American Association for Higher Education

Koulish, R. (1998a). Citizenship service-learning: Becoming citizens by assisting immigrants, PS: Political science and politics. 31(3), 562–567.

Koulish, R. (1998b). Community impact: Defining and assessing the intentional community. In T. Pickeral & K. Peters (Eds.), *Assessing internal and external outcomes of service-learning collaborations* (pp. 29–44). Mesa, AZ: Campus Compact National Center for Community Colleges.

Lucas, C. J. (1996). *Crisis in the academy: Rethinking higher education in America*. New York: St. Martin's Press.

Putnam, R. D. (1995). Tuning in, tuning out: The strange disappearance of social capital in America. The 1995 Ithiel de Sola pool lecture. *Political Science and Politics* 29(1), 664–683.

Rimmerman, C. (1997). *The new citizenship: Unconventional politics, activism, and service*. Boulder: Westview Press.

Rushdie, S. (1991). *Imaginary homelands: Essays and criticism 1981–1991*. London: Granta Books.

Thurow, L. (1998). *Economic community and social investment in the community of the future*. New York: Jossey-Bass.

Tocqueville, A. de. (1945). *Democracy in America*. New York: Knopf.

11

Service-Learning and Social Reconstructionism: A Critical Opportunity for Leadership

Verna Cornelia Simmons
University of Minnesota

Wokie Roberts-Weah
National Youth Leadership Council

The expectations for higher education to graduate students who are knowledgeable, skilled, and critical thinkers and who can also effectively live and work in a growing ethnic and culturally diverse society is higher than ever before. Specifically, industry expects higher education to produce workers and leaders who can provide vision, insight, and creative management solutions in an increasingly complex and complicated business environment and world. These expectations require that higher education integrate diversified approaches to teaching, research, and learning where students can simultaneously learn about theory and apply it to "real work" situations. However, the academy often fails to educate students with an understanding of social problems, awareness of democratic citizenship, or the skills to participate effectively (Gardner, 1990). In the *Carnegie Report on Higher Education and The American Resurgence*, Newman (1985) contended that higher education has not only failed to provide a structural means for linking classroom study with students' direct experience of social problems and issues, it has also failed to educate students with an understanding of these social problems, and with an awareness of the traditional responsibilities of democratic citizenship. In short, we teach our students about what others think, say, and do, but rarely do we challenge them to think a new thought, identify an authentic societal need, and work to solve that need. Leadership in the 21st century

189

will demand new dimensions of learning and application that extends beyond top-down decision making to shared-decision making models that seek to address and solve societal issues that can bring about social change. Social change, however, is most likely to occur when a leader works within a group that comes together around a common concern and for a common purpose (Astin, 1996, p. 37). In higher education, we must create intellectual spaces and structures that inspire and teach students to apply their academic work to helping solve authentic societal problems.

This chapter explores the connection between service-learning and multicultural social reconstructionist teaching strategies and experiences as a vehicle that provides critical opportunities for higher education to facilitate leadership capacities and to teach leadership skills to undergraduate students. Since the 1980s, both service-learning and the social reconstructionist approach to multicultural education have gained momentum as effective pedagogies for teaching students about social action, citizenship, and social responsibility. Social reconstructionism focuses on challenging social stratification, as well as on celebrating human diversity and equal opportunity (Sleeter & Grant, 1999). The societal goal of "reconstructionist" is to promote social structural equality and cultural pluralism, whereas school goals are to prepare citizens to work actively toward social structural equality while promoting cultural pluralism and equal opportunity in the school (Sleeter & Grant, 1999).

One of the warnings that Sleeter and Grant (1999) highlighted is that advocates of multicultural and social reconstructionist education do not expect students to reconstruct the world. Rather, these advocates view school as connected with other institutions in society to either reinforce that inequality exists or to work with opposition movements to institute change. Advocates of this approach also view the educational system as a laboratory or training ground for preparing a socially active citizenry. Within this framework, Bennett (1986) noted that students begin to see themselves as powerful agents of change within social institutions where they can begin to examine issues and consider courses of action to take. We believe that service-learning provides an authentic and effective context for students to pursue a course of action around issues of social inequalities. The opportunity to act in this democratic and civilly responsible manner motivates students to develop leadership skills and capacities that may not result in "positional" leadership but will definitely enhance "personal" leadership. The underlying principle of this framework is that when a student develops personal leadership capacities, they are more likely to address critical multicultural issues that could lead to social change.

To think of leadership development as both individual and personal development neatly fits with the value of individualism. The notion that leadership capacity can be developed by almost everyone clearly reflects the value of equality, and the idea that skills are acquired by doing reflects the orientation of action (Hoppe, 1998). In higher education, the connection between the goals of social reconstructionism and service-learning provides opportunities for students to learn and exhibit leadership capacities.

This chapter is organized into three sections. The first examines the definition of leadership from a multicultural perspective. The definitions are based on the results of a survey of individuals from across the country who are involved in leadership and who utilize service-learning strategies in their lives and work. The second section explores programs where social reconstructionist strategies are linked with service-learning to motivate and inspire students to become social change agents who, in the process of working to address the issues, develop specific leadership capacities. In the third section, we wrestle with the question of "leadership for what"? Does our society embrace individual leadership development? Will the students continue their efforts to help solve social inequalities without the structure of service-learning in higher education? Is service-learning a help or a hindrance to disadvantaged communities and people? Can a strategy of connecting service-learning, social reconstructionism, and leadership also positively impact academics? The chapter concludes with a vision for higher education to create comprehensive disciplines that promote academics, service-learning, social reconstructionist ideals, and leadership in undergraduate students.

LEADERSHIP FROM A MULTICULTURAL PERSPECTIVE

As the 21st century approaches, we see a resurgence of new initiatives, theories, and programs relating to leadership. Colleges and universities are beginning to revisit the importance of leadership as a discipline and the corporate sector has increased its attention to what makes for an effective leader. However, the word and concept of "leadership" is commonly used, has multiple definitions, and represents multiple perspectives, ideals, and theoretical frameworks. Our intention was not to explore the vast definitions of leadership, but to focus specifically on leadership from a multicultural perspective. This exploration was accomplished through guided interviews with a select group of service-learning and multicultural education practitioners and scholars from across the United States. The purpose of the interviews was to explore cultural interpretations of leadership, to define leadership in a multicultural context, and to probe for perceptions of whether service-learning in a multicultural and social reconstructionist educational perspective enhances a student's personal capacities for leadership and social change. The interviews, although limited in sample, are important to exploring this topic because those represented are actively working to create critical connections between service-learning, multiculturalism, and leadership in their organizations and higher education institutions. As a result, these perspectives contribute an authentic and realistic context to the framework of this chapter.

The interview consisted of six questions:

1. With what cultural or ethnic background do you most closely identify?
2. In your culture, what are the characteristics of an effective leader?
3. Is this definition different from the mainstream White American definition of leadership? If so, how?
4. In your view, how would you define leadership from a multicultural or multiethnic perspective?
5. How is service-learning connected to the development of personal leadership skills in students?
6. What is the goal of society in developing personal leadership skills in students?

Of the 10 respondents, 6 were female and 4 were male. Four identified as European/White American, 2 as African American, 1 as Asian American, 1 as Native American, and 2 as African. One respondent resisted providing an ethnic or cultural identity because she identified herself as "spiritual," which she believes transcends culture. Occupations included high school principals, a director of professional development, a youth worker, college professors, executive directors, and graduate students.

Cultural Characteristics of Effective Leaders

The interview responses provided provocative and affirming perspectives about leadership. When describing cultural characteristics of an effective leader, the Asian American respondent noted that the most important characteristic of a leader was one who seeks harmony in a nonconfrontational way and has a relational, group mentality. The Native American respondent described leadership as the embodiment of the spirit of a servant leader, one who is humble, empowers others, does not look for recognition, and values the group. One European/White American noted that leadership was traditionally dominant, a hierarchy in which persons in the highest positions make decisions, a chain of command, and is only for a few people with privilege. This contrasted with one of the African-American respondents who described a leader in terms of skills versus position. She noted that an effective leader is fair, firm, consistent, respected, knowledgeable, and one who leads by example and is a calculated risk taker with good common sense. She also noted that in her culture, it helps if one is also charismatic and a good communicator. One of the African respondents from South Africa explained that cultural leadership is earned from a spirit of "Ubuntu," which means caring for the common good of those being served. He further explained that Ubuntu was also core to Nobel Peace Prize winner, Archbishop Desmond TuTu's leadership to help eliminate apartheid. The principle of Ubuntu leadership is that the essence of living is the gift of yourself that you are willing to give to the world. As this respondent described it, a person is a person through another person. Our humanity is bound up in us and when we dehumanize another person, we dehumanize ourself. A leader seeks the common good and leadership is not hierarchical for monetary gain or enrichment.

An implicit but powerful implication generated with this particular question was that cultural values are intrinsically linked to effective leadership. Even though the cultural characteristics of leaders differed greatly, one common theme was that effective leadership is transformational and that, as a White male respondent noted, leaders have the ability to "create conditions that enable everyone in the setting to manifest their highest and finest thoughts and behaviors."

Cultural Characteristics Versus Mainstream Definitions

Although there were some commonalties across cultural lines about skills and characteristics critical to effective leadership such as visionary, service, integrity, fairness, and consistency, there was also definite divergence in opinion about how cultural-specific definitions differ from mainstream European/White American definitions of leadership. At least 8 of the respondents agreed with Hoppe's (1998) assertion that mainstream leadership practices tend to focus on the individual as leader rather than conceptualizing leadership as a function of the group. The Native American respondent noted that in the mainstream society, "drawing attention to oneself is the norm. People are more individualistic in the mainstream. Humility is not as common." This sentiment was also shared by the South African respondent who described leadership in the mainstream as hierarchical, positions of power, and controlling people and things. The African-American professor, however, emphasized that the perception of leadership as a solitary activity was more indicative of corporate culture than of mainstream Whites. She described corporate culture as emphasizing individual accomplishments and competition. Working-class Whites, she said, have less competitive ways of relating to the world. Another White female respondent noted that

> while a mainstream Caucasian definition of leadership is pervasive, it is changing in many sectors. The old perceptions of leadership are hierarchical where the person with the greatest power is in charge. The new model of leadership is based on internal power and modeling. The new leader knows how to bring out the gifts of others and to be inclusive, rather than exclusive.

Leadership From a Multicultural Perspective

The ability to be inclusive in an intentional way was viewed as the most important characteristic of a leader with a multicultural perspective. Leaders who operate from this perspective, said the Native American respondent, "work on consensus building, think about the benefits of the group and are patient and tolerant of differing point of views." An African-American respondent expressed that this type of leader works toward operating an environment that promotes respect for everyone, promotes understanding and a shared sense of common ground. One of the White respondents noted that, "Good leadership should create learning situations that allow individuals to develop their values." Overall, the respondents characterized this leadership as reflective and empathetic where there is much dialogue and a great deal of give and take.

While all of the respondents discussed the value of inclusiveness as a core trait of multicultural leadership, most readily agreed that we, whether as a country or an educational movement, have not quite arrived in this area. One White female respondent explained this in terms of the power and privilege held by Whites, particularly White males in leadership roles. "I had to be aware of how the Whites' dominant perspectives have shaped my leadership, for example the ways in which White men talk more and take up more space in conversations versus listening to the perspective of others. As Whites, we have to learn to deal with silence." Similarly, another White female respondent noted

> I feel that there is a corrupted sense of leadership, particularly in government. . . . Justice is readily compromised, verbiage is stronger and more distinct from delivered actions, integrity is the exception rather than the rule. Many leaders proclaim inclusivity, but continue token gestures and exclusivity.

In summary, the question of "what is leadership" from a multicultural perspective still remains a debate and certainly a nonreality in most of our society. We have learned that leadership is interpreted differently across cultural backgrounds, but some common elements such as integrity and service do seem to transcend culture. We have also learned that multicultural leadership is definitely perceived as being different from mainstream forms of leadership especially as it relates to transformational leadership practices, and valuing the group and the unique contributions of individuals.

Connecting Service-Learning, Social Reconstructionism, and Leadership

One profound reality about trying to connect service-learning, social reconstructionism, and leadership is that each concept represents a unique set of ideals, theories, and assumptions that could easily overshadow and/or compete with the others. However, an effective connection of the three can provide higher education with powerful insights for teaching, learning, and research. In this section, we examine four examples in higher education where this strategic connection has occurred with some success.

One of the most notable connections is represented by a model developed by a team of researchers lead by Helen and Alexander Astin (1996) from the Higher Education Research Institute at the University of California, Los Angeles called, a social change model of leadership development. The basic premises underlying the model are that values demand a conscious focus, that leadership ought to bring about desirable social change, that leadership is a process and not a position, that all students are potential leaders, and that service is a powerful vehicle for developing leaders. This model calls for a group of students to undertake a service project where they learn about and practice seven core values that fall into three groupings; personal or individual values (consciousness of self, congruence, commitment), group values (collaboration, common purpose, controversy with civility), and a societal community value of citizenship (Astin & Astin, 1996). When referring to citizenship, this model takes the position that societal and community value of citizenship clarifies the purpose of the leadership. In other words, citizenship means more than membership, but rather it implies social and civic responsibility and active engagement of the individual and leadership group in an effort to serve the community (Astin & Astin, 1996).

At Miami University in Ohio, the social change model of leadership development was used as the conceptual framework for a new initiative aimed at ensuring that all students have access to opportunities to develop their leadership potential. A collaborative leadership program task force involving faculty, staff, and students worked to create a comprehensive leadership development strategy for the campus using this framework. In addition, the task force created a set of leadership values that they believed would help to guide leadership at their campus in the 21st century. These values include concepts such as awareness and development of potential (personal values, strengths, and abilities), critical thinking and reflection, appreciation and respect for human dignity and diversity, and responsibility and accountability for one's actions (Astin, 1996). The vision of the task was that throughout the university, numerous exemplary organizations would begin modeling the values and framework in their daily affairs. For Miami University, learning to walk the talk of the leadership values could be a powerful source of learning for students, faculty, staff, and the administration. One of the core principles of the Wingspread Declaration (Porter Honnet, & Poulsen, 1989) for service-learning and civic engagement in higher education is that universities prepare students for engaged citizenship through multiple opportunities to do the work of citizenship today. Such work involves real projects of impact and relevance through which students learn the skills, develop the habits and identities, and acquire the knowledge to contribute to the general welfare. The social change leadership model provides an authentic context for the Miami University students to take leadership for transforming their campus culture and environment.

Another example of this critical connection occurred at the University of New Jersey, on the Rutger-Camden campus in southern New Jersey where students from the Latina College took on a service-learning project to facilitate the upward mobility and economic development of Latina women in Camden City. In particular, they organized other young Latina college students to advocate for legislation that would address the needs of poor Latina female single heads of households. Eventually, they drafted a bill called the Hispanic

Women's Demonstration Resource Center Act. The success of their efforts to publicize the plight of Latina women was evident when major newspapers began to cover the issue in detail. The group met weekly to monitor the progress of lobbying efforts and to address other current issues relating to the work. In addition, the group wrote to the governor and kept him informed of the development and progress of the bill, its success, and support for it. The group also organized women support groups all over the state that were prepared to visit the governor and speak on behalf of the bill. The governor, with each of the three centers receiving $150,000, signed the bill into law (Astin & Astin, 1996).

At Cornell University, making the connection between social change, service-learning, and leadership focused on placing minority students in a situation where they had to work together, serve together, and lead together to create Cornell's first Minority Leadership Conference and Town Hall meeting on race. According to Nasha London-Vargas (1998), Associate Director for Counseling and Advising in the Office of Minority Educational Affairs, "This was the first time minority students from different backgrounds had to work on a problem of mutual benefit and concern—to bridge the gap among them" (p. 4). During the conference, students presented a variety of issues to faculty, administrators, staff, and peers around Cornell's racial legacies, contemporary race relations, the need for stronger student leadership and activism, and offered nine steps toward racial harmony both at Cornell and in the society as a whole. London-Vargas noted that campuses often have programs designed to foster minority leadership or community service, but we must be more intentional about using these programs as contexts for community building and leadership development. By working together on a daily basis, said London-Vargas, our students have acquired skills and knowledge about leadership, conflict resolution, and working together across social and cultural differences.

The final program example is a course offered to preservice teachers at Michigan State University entitled Human Diversity, Power and Opportunity in Social Institutions where efforts are focused on engaging middle-class White students in the application of leadership skills through placements in urban service-learning sites. The course involved a social analysis of education, especially in examining ways in which schools continually reproduce and challenge social hierarchies. The service-learning sites, which included elementary and middle schools, community service agencies, and the homes of newly arrived refugees, brought students into direct contact with members from diverse ethnic, socioeconomic, and linguistic communities. The service-learning projects were balanced with heavy doses of critical reflection around issues of diversity, student empowerment, and reciprocal learning through a process where the students were required to write a narrative case study on a child or adult whose background differed substantially from their own. The instructor required students to critically reflect on their experiences through journal writing and reflective class dialogue sessions. For example, one student wrote of her first encounter with her school setting:

> As we entered the school for the first time, the people immediately noticed our presence. The long stares, the sharp glances, and the loud whispering were increasing. For the first time in my life, I was a minority. Never before have I felt so out of place. It felt as if they had something against me. Then I saw a smile. Another smile crept across a custodian's tired face. A friendly hello, a shy wave, and a firm handshake from a student helped to revive my positive expectations about the school. (Hones, 1997, pp. 7–8)

This level of reflection challenged the students to face their own perceptions, biases, stereotypes, and fears about issues of diversity and social inequalities. Furthermore, the students were also building a cadre of leadership competencies approved by the Council for the Advancement of Standards in Higher Education for Student Leadership Programs (1996), such as personal development, group dynamics, problem solving, conflict management, ethics, community building, human relations, and social change.

The course instructor found that as students became immersed in serving others, they were compelled to raise critical questions about social inequalities in schools and society, such as: Why does the drug trade appear to be one of the few economic alternatives in many poor urban neighborhoods? Is there a lack of educational opportunity in public school for some children? By connecting service-learning to preparing teachers to teach in diverse educational settings where social inequalities were present, the students were challenged to reflect on their own roles as change agents in the classroom, in the community, and in the society.

These four examples used very different approaches to connect service-learning, social change, and leadership but they all had the same goals. First, all of the models created intellectual spaces and experiential learning structures as a way to effectively integrate the academic and "real" work of the student. For example, the students at the Rutgers-Camden University essentially learned to be policymakers, whereas at Michigan State University, the students learned how to critically examine one's place in society relative to others without judgment or assumptions. Second, all of the examples provided structures whereby the students would demonstrate social action through applied citizenship. Third, all of the programs have elements of transformational leadership. In other words, the students were provided opportunities to seek ways to test their abilities and look for innovative ways to make social change, were able to inspire others to act on behalf of social inequalities, and were able to take action to solve the problem (Kouzes & Posner, 1998). Finally, these programs and the service-learning paradigm in general suggest that a key characteristic of an effective leader is one who serves others.

Most importantly, all of the programs challenge students to look into themselves and then beyond themselves to examine the perspective of "others." Service-learning only results in transformational change if the program is designed to be reflective and relevant to social change. Service-learning too often falls short of the transformational ideal and instead stagnates on the board of "doing nice things" to help "those people" on "those issues." Providing the critical connection between service-learning, social change, and leadership challenges students to go beyond just appreciating differences and doing nice things so you can feel like a "good" person. Instead, it affords them the opportunity to gain an authentic understanding of multiculturalism and to begin to take action to address social inequities in a meaningful, knowledgeable, and reflective way. As noted by one the respondents, "Who I am as a leader is based on who I am. I have to understand all aspects of my identity to understand how to share leadership." Service-learning helps us discover who we are in terms of privilege and in relationship to others.

LEADERSHIP FOR WHAT?

The question of "leadership for what" provides us with a unique pause to consider the implications of our theory of action and how it encompasses the critical connection between service-learning, social reconstructionism, and leadership. The reality is that we must wrestle with how our society views leadership, particularly personal leadership in students. Are we developing leadership capacities in students that will inspire them to be responsible and knowledgeable social change agents who are helping to solve problems or leaders who work to protect the traditional systems that perpetuate the problems? By promoting this theory of action, are we placing our students in a predicament of having the capacities but being prohibited from taking leadership?

When asked about the goal of our society in developing leadership skills in students, the respondents tended to concentrate on two divergent perspectives. As illustrated in the following quotes from the respondents, the first perspective is idealistic and visionary:

> The goal is to assure continuing vision and hope in sustaining and building a civil society. To work to develop these skills passes the mantle of leadership from one generation to the next and has greater value to the society than just passing on material wealth. (White male)

> Service-learning encourages social responsibility while unleashing and promoting good character. Students become connected to their communities and in many cases become social advocates for the important causes in their local communities and in the broader world. We are becoming a more multicultural society. Service-learning has the potential to bring people of many different backgrounds to do needed work in a context that is team oriented and respectful of culture, assets, and shared voice. (White female)

> Service-learning moves problem solving and decision making into the community. It creates laboratories for change and development. It makes clear that responsibility for the larger society in not only in paid officials but also in the hands of people. It moves people from thinking and theory to action. It provides realities for creating leadership. If that's not good for society then I quit!! (White male)

> Service-Learning is an absolutely beneficial, positive, and fertile ground for leadership because it teachers you to serve. Service-learning could include a philosophy of "my well-being is your well-being and it should not come at the cost of someone else." (African male)

However, the second perspective articulated by the respondents cautions us about what we can realistically expect from society:

> I don't see leadership development as a goal of society. As a society, we only want to develop leadership to the extent to which you stay in your own box. Corporate programs are much more concerned about getting things done versus learning to be a leader. (African-American female)

> In service-learning we often perpetuate the perception that everyone has a culture except White people. We seem to be replicating the oppression and racism that exists in our society. I don't see service-learning practitioners willing to look at issues of race and diversity. (White female)

> I think that society's goal for developing leadership in students is focused more on conforming to society's laws and, in general, being a good citizen. Society's focus is more on personal achievement and lead-

ing by good example, with less emphasis on serving others as an integral part of a lifestyle. (African-American female)

While there may be elements of service, most often students have attitudes of supremacy, which says "If I did something for someone else then it promotes me." I have found that students want a position of power when they are finished with their education that will enable them to practice their skills from a more powerful position. (African male)

Most American schools are designed to feed children into some slot within the corporate economy based on race, gender, and social class. Service-learning only hints at challenging these elements in public schooling. The movement is gutless about dealing with race, gender, and social oppression. (African-American female)

These two streams of thought differ dramatically in that they compel us to further explore the realities of what our society truly values and beckons us to question whether service-learning is a help or hindrance to social change and leadership development in students. In essence, many of the respondents felt that service-learning could actually hinder the development of leadership capacities if students are not properly prepared, lack understanding about the context of their service, or fail to understand their own position of privilege or lack thereof. In an effort to help, service-learning connected to social reconstructionist ideals could further perpetuate biases, oppression, and stereotypes. Furthermore, many academic programs utilize service-learning as a vehicle for engaging students in learning and increasing academic performance but fall short of asking the question, "For what reason do we want students to excel academically?" In addition, we must also seriously consider who the key players are in service-learning at many levels including the organizational leaders, policymakers, teachers, and professors in higher education. Presently, most of the players are European/White Americans who, although well intentioned, represent the privileged and politically powerful segments of our society. As noted by Chesler (1995), we who maintain a comfortable lifestyle while providing service generally are not engaged in making the sacrifices that would be required for dramatic reallocation of privilege and opportunity in our communities. Chesler (1995) concluded with a very serious conjecture that "by and large, then, there is no congruence between service-learning, community service, and social change" (p. 139).

Balancing the two extreme perspectives will be challenging to any higher education institution. However, as Miami University has worked to demonstrate, we must realistically address and confront these perspectives with our faculty, students, and staff. Any higher education service-learning program, course, or practice must provide students with authentic opportunities to address social inequities in which they can acquire leadership skills and capacities.

VISION FOR HIGHER EDUCATION

In this chapter, a number of provocative perspectives and theories of action that strategically address the critical connection between service-learning, a multicultural social reconstructionist ideal, and leadership have been presented. Having looked at leadership from a multicultural framework, program models, and having examined the question of "leadership for what," it is clear that this theory of action is complex and potentially challenging to higher education institutions. Nevertheless, we are convinced that higher education can implement such a theory and we recommend the following visionary strategies and processes for this implementation.

- **Working to make an explicit connection between service-learning and multicultural education can prove to be a promising strategy for higher education in teaching social responsibility, democratic citizenship, and developing multicultural leadership capacities in students.**

As one of our African-American female respondents noted, multicultural education has the potential for creating an environment that promotes respect and understanding for everyone through a shared sense of the common good. Dewey (1938) noted that when the school introduces and trains each child into membership within the community, saturating the child with the spirit of service and providing the instruments of effective self-direction, we have the best guarantee of a larger society that is worthy, lovely, and harmonious. As higher education institutions, our greatest service is providing educated men and women who understand the cultural dynamics of our society and who are willing to authentically lead and serve. This will require that we change how and what we teach. Therefore, we must creatively build bridges internally for linking social responsibility, democratic citizenship, and leadership into the undergraduate experience in increasingly effective ways.

What are some examples? First, this connection requires the integration of multicultural education, social change, service-learning, and leadership into curriculum development, course syllabi, teaching strategies, and research efforts. Second, interinstitutional grant opportunities must be provided for faculty who seek to design research teams that include undergraduate students to pursue problems specific to service-learning, multicultural education, leadership, or social change. This would provide students with both the opportunity to conduct research and a context for critically analyzing how these factors impact communities, schools, and society. Third, we must incorporate and infuse the undergraduate research experience into actual course work. For example, the University of Minnesota is working to make this happen in a number of ways: (a) A critical component of the undergraduate experience initiative is to offer a freshman seminar consisting of small class sizes, interactive instructional strategies, and a guided study of a specific topic. Faculty who choose to teach are provided with resources and time to create seminars specific to their research agenda; (b) An interdisciplinary undergraduate leadership minor is being developed for undergraduates to integrate both service-learning, multicultural education, experiential learning, social change, and research into the required courses. The minor would be taught by faculty and staff from the College of Education and Human Development, College of Public Affairs and the Office for Student Development and Athletics.

These changes in how and what we teach could change the student's perceptions about the higher education experience as expressed by the following student who participated in service-learning at the University of Colorado in 1996:

> I didn't know why I was here at this university until I joined this program. I felt like I was lost and I was just a number and I didn't really want this to be my life and I had never really heard of service-learning. Then education really started to make sense for me. It enhanced what I learned in books, not just memorizing before a test, but it made it stick and click for me. (Eyler, Giles, & Schmiede, 1996, p. 30)

- **Explore program models and profiles where this theory of action has been successfully implemented. However, one should resist hastily replicating existing program models but rather seek out unique interventions and strategies.**

Utilizing and maintaining authenticity in how we implement this theory of action is critical. Why? Because every higher education institution has a distinct culture, vision, and set of values that affect student learning and institutional outcome. Schorr (1997) in her latest book, *Common Purpose: Strengthening Families and Neighborhoods to Rebuild America*, found that effective programs had specific attributes and that there is no simple model that can be "parachuted" in. On the contrary, "successful programs are shaped to respond to the needs of local populations and to assure that local communities have a genuine sense of ownership" (p. 7). For instance, programs such as the Latina College at Rutger-Camden University worked to address an authentic need in the community and demonstrated that it is possible for communities of color to overcome a sense of political apathy and strategically confront social inequalities. The students' efforts made the social inequities faced by poor Latino women a vivid reality that needed political and monetary attention.

As noted by Stanton (1990), linking responsible participation in an "untidy world" with a complete cycle of self-reflective learning, provides an essential bridge for linking personal empowerment and community empowerment with cognitive growth. As such, service-learning has to play a key role in leadership development. As illustrated in this quote from a University of Washington student (1996), these experiences provide new perspectives on social issues:

> I kept hearing things like—people are poor because they don't try or people are on welfare because they don't want to work. I hear things like that and it's definitely made me aware of how complex people's problems really are. That you can't answer it by saying—here's the answer and if you would just do what I say you should do, then your life would be better. It's just not like that. (Eyler, Giles, & Schmiede, 1996, p. 34)

An important strategy for higher education will require exploration of other program models that utilize "new knowledge" to create an authentic integration that has community ownership from students, staff, faculty, and administrators.

- **Allow students to participate actively in decisions that affect their lives and sense of global interdependence.**

According to Greenleaf (1977), students should learn accountability, responsibility, teamwork, problems, and the principles and ethics of citizenship. Then as servant-leaders, they can demonstrate that individual effort, inspired by vision and a servant ethic, can make a substantial difference in the quality of society. These capacities, said Greenleaf, should be modeled and taught by the faculty linked with the authentic service experiences.

For instance, at Cornell University, the students were asked to decide and plan town meetings on race, which could potentially change how issues of race, culture, and ethnicity were handled both on the campus and in their community. Furthermore, these students were challenged to create a community where all students, regardless of color, could effectively work together to solve a problem. The National Youth Leadership Council's (NYLC) Youth Fellows (Fulfilling Engagement in Lifelong Opportunities with Service) Project mobilizes students as experts on service-learning and civic leadership by combining the strengths of a national nonprofit with resources available through Hamline University's Active Citizen Initiative and Center for Global Environmental Education. College students from the Twin Cities complete an internship at NYLC where they serve as Fellows Coordinators—program officers (disbursing $500,000 over a 3-year period), trainers, and consultants to seven middle and high schools around the country. Hamline University provides specialized training in civic education and technology to Fellows who in turn teach middle and high school students how to merge experiential education, service-learning, and social reconstructivist thinking to bring about lasting change within their own communities. The Project offers fiscal and positional responsibility, links to civic organizations, multiple resources, and mentoring to college students who are genuinely interested in service, social change, and leadership. More importantly, it embraces the abilities of young people of all ages to drive social change, address authentic social problems, while simultaneously building the leadership skills.

We must rethink the role of student action organizations in higher education. Many student organizations are actively working to address social change and multicultural issues in the broader society but rarely are these experiences integrated into existing course work, curriculum development, or research projects. This aspect of the vision provides higher education with a unique opportunity to teach the "whole" student by strategically connecting the curricular and cocurricular aspects of student life in higher education through teaching, research, and citizenship.

CONCLUSION

Our research, findings, realizations, and reflections have lead us to new questions and emerging insights about the complexities of leading in an increasingly interdependent world. We are convinced that leadership is a relationship of influence, shaped by culture and informed by the perceptions and perspectives of diverse others. Leadership, we learned, is not a thing to be merely acquired, but something to be shared. Becoming a leader is a process that is often accelerated by the intersection of the two paradigms of service-learning and multicultural education. Both fields unite key leadership concepts and place particular emphasis on social reconstructivist leadership. Both fields focus on the practical and the philosophical, and both are aimed at helping undergraduate students locate their sense of citizenship and responsibility.

But even as we advance a new vision of leadership that forges a stronger, more prominent integration between service-learning and multicultural education, we caution against programs that lack quality and depth and stagnate on the border of doing nice things to help those people around those issues. Our task is to challenge our colleagues in higher education, service-learning, and multicultural education to think about how the integration of service-learning and multicultural education can be used to build the personal leadership capacities of all students and facilitate quality learning experiences. As we ask you to consider the realities of this integration, we leave you with a reflection offered by one of the White female respondents:

> We need leaders in every field of work who have the skills, traits, and attitudes of transformational leadership. This will only occur if they have opportunities or experience a sense of voice and servant leadership when they are young. The more they feel a positive connection to their communities and a sense of themselves as contributors, the more apt they are to continue contributing. The more they see the assets of their communities and the worth of all people, the more likely they will honor the dignity of all that they meet. As we grow technologically, it is critical that we balance this with an expansion of the heart and the wisdom needed for leadership in the 21st century.

REFERENCES

Astin, H. S. (1996, July–August). Leadership for social change. *About Campus* pp. 4–10.

Astin, H., & Astin, A. (1996). *A social change model of leadership development: Version III: Guidebook*. Los Angeles, CA: Higher Education Research Institute, University of California.

Bennett, C. I. (1986). *Comprehensive Multicultural Education*. Boston: Allyn & Bacon.

Chesler, M. (1995). Service, service-learning, and change-making. In J. Galura, J. Howard, R. Ross, & D. Waterhouse (Eds.), *Praxis III: Voices in dialogue* (pp. 137–141). Ann Arbor, MI: OCSL Press.

Council for the Advancement of Standards in Higher Education. (1996). *Student leadership programs guidelines*.

Dewey, J. (1938). *Experience and education*. Collier Books.

Gardner J. W. (1990). On leadership: Experiences for an untidy world. In J. Kendall & Associates (Eds.), *Combining service and learning: A resource book for commu-*

nity and public service (pp. 335). Raleigh, NC: National Society for Internships and Experiential Education.

Greenleaf, R. (1977). *Servant leadership: A journey into the nature of legitimate power and greatness.* New York: Paulist Press.

Hones, D. (1997). *Preparing teachers for diversity: A service-learning approach.* East Lansing: Michigan State University College of Education: Outreach programs.

Hoppe, M. H. (1998). Cross-cultural issues in leadership development. In C. D. McCauley, R. S. Moxley, & E. Van Velsor (Eds.), *The center for creative leadership handbook of leadership development* (pp. 336–378).

Kouzes, J. M., & Posner, B. Z. (1998). *Student leadership practice inventory.* San Francisco: Jossey-Bass.

London-Vargas, N. (1998). *Minority student leadership: Taking the initiative and learning across differences.* Ithaca, NY: Cornell University.

Newman, F. (1985). *Higher education and the American resurgence, A Carnegie Foundation Special Report.* Pittsburgh, PA: Carnegie Foundation for the Advancement of Teaching.

Porter Honnet, E., & Poulsen, S. J. (1989). *Principles of good practice for combining service and learning.* Racine, WI: Johnson Foundation.

Schorr, L. B. (1997). *Common purpose: Strengthening families and neighborhoods to rebuild America.* New York: Doubleday.

Sleeter, C. E., & Grant, C. A. (1999). *Making choices for multicultural education: Five approaches to race, class, gender.* Englewood Cliffs, NJ: Prentice-Hall.

Stanton T. K. (1990). Service-learning and leadership development: Learning to be effective while learning what to be effective about. In J. Kendall & Associates (Eds.), *Combining service and learning: A resource book for community and public service* (pp. 336–351). Raleigh, NC: National Society for Internships and Experiential Education.

12

The Construction of Meaning: Learning From Service Learning

Marilynne Boyle-Baise with Patricia Efiom
Indiana University

Constructions of meaning: what do preservice teachers learn from community-based service learning? Does it "make a difference" in their perceptions of diversity, equality, and equity? Or, does it reinforce stereotypes and attitudes of supremacy? Presently, research that explores the effects of service learning as part of multicultural education is limited. However, research suggests that service learning can assist the aims of multicultural education. Particularly, service learning can foster increased awareness and acceptance of cultural diversity (e.g., Boyle-Baise, 1998; DeJong & Groomes, 1996; Dunlap, 1998; Hones, 1997; Sleeter, 1995; Tellez, Hlebowitsh, Cohen, & Norwood, 1995), heighten commitment to teach diverse youth (e.g., Fuller, 1998), and motivate prospective teachers to examine their prejudicial, stereotypical beliefs (e.g., Fuller, 1998; O'Grady, 1997; Seigel as cited in Wade, 1998). Alternatively, it can be difficult to spur social critique and activism through service learning experiences (e.g., Boyle-Baise, 1998; Vadenboncoeur, Rahm, Aguilera, & LeCompte, 1996). Regardless of this latter challenge, research suggests promise for the linkage of service learning and multicultural education.

Yet, theoretical views of this connection are cautious, even pessimistic. Potentially, service learning may do more harm than good. It may suffer from benefaction: People with more give to people with less, service starts in privilege and ends in patronage (Radest, 1993; Rhoads, 1997; Varlotta, 1997). Consequently, service learning might reinforce, rather than confute, deficit orientations to culturally or socially different "others" (e.g., Cruz, 1990; O'Grady & Chappell, 2000). Service learning might represent, as O'Grady and Chappell argue, a new form of "noblese oblige." These concerns are weighty for multicultural education; service learning could mitigate the intentions of the field.

Caution is warranted, yet skepticism seems premature. Rather, exploratory studies are very much in process and the verdict is far from in. Judgments should depend on evaluation of ample descriptive data. This study bolsters the database about service learning for multicultural education. Specifically, the study explores preservice teacher's constructions of meaning within a multicultural education course. The study considers the following questions: (a) What impact do prior expectations have on service learning, (b) What meanings do preservice teachers make from service learning, and (c) What influence does reflection have on meaning making? Additionally, implications for teacher education are suggested.

THE INQUIRY

This is an interpretive case study. Twenty-four preservice teachers in my multicultural education course represented the case studied. Of 24 class members, 7 were females of color, 6 were African American, and 1 was Filipino American (this student did not complete the course). The other 17 class members were Euro-American; 13 were females and 4 were males. One prospective teacher was bilingual, most were Christian, middle-class, college age, and from within the state.

Community-based service learning was a credited, 20-hour course component. Prospective teachers were placed in community organizations that served culturally diverse and low-income youth, and they selected their own placements. Cultural border crossing was a goal of placement, but was mitigated somewhat by self-selection. Service sites included Bethel African Methodist Episcopal Church, Boys and Girls Club, Banneker Westside Community Center, Diversity Theater (a troupe focused on plays about disability), Girls Inc., and Headstart.

Inquiry teams of three to six preservice teachers worked together at each community organization. Services responded to site-based needs and included tutoring, teaching small groups, and assisting recreational programs. A field-based project, developed in concert with site directors, went beyond usual volunteer activities. Three inquiry teams taught a series of lessons to small groups; one team organized a minisports camp, another developed a safe alternative to Halloween, and another lead an audience discussion about issues raised in a play about disabling conditions.

In-class reflection occurred biweekly. An African-American family, familiar with the neighborhood served, acted as mentors. The family participated in two reflective sessions and answered questions that arose from service learning.

Data were generated from the following sources. Preservice teachers wrote introductory letters and a series of reflective essays. Three reflective sessions were videotaped, and the tapes were transcribed. Additionally, class assignments and field-based projects were collected. This database was limited to the extent that it was based on self-reports, which commonly tilt toward positive self-perceptions and satisfied evaluations of service learning.

These data were read and reread to ascertain points made by each preservice teacher and, then, to determine themes and trends. Constant comparison analysis (Glaser & Strauss, 1967) was used to search for diversity within responses. Special attention was paid to influences of race, social class, gender, and geographic background on responses. Several preservice teachers, who differed in background and in perceptions of service, were selected for in-depth profiles.

Three voices are presented in this narrative; mine, preservice teachers, and a parent mentor. As author, my voice is ubiquitous, yet in the final section, I distance myself from the data and offer my own perceptions of the project. Parent mentors are community people, knowledgeable about local affairs and members of minority or low-income groups, invited to assist in class reflections. In this case, the Efiom family had a 3-year history with the course. The family's involvement stemmed from Patricia's participation in a planning group that considered ways to engage the community in multicultural teacher education (Boyle-Baise, 1997). Patricia writes about her experience as mentor. To indicate voice, our names are noted, prior to our comments. Preservice teacher's voices are depicted traditionally as quoted material.

CONSTRUCTIONS OF MEANING

What might preservice teachers learn from service learning? As this study evolved from my own multicultural education course, my views of this question are significant. To me, service learning is a perspective and a process. It is a form of community-based learning in which students volunteer in local organizations and respond to site-based needs. It is an opportunity to work with community brokers, knowledgeable about local affairs. As part of multicultural education, service learning should be attentive to and supportive of cultural diversity, cultural pluralism, and social justice. This means that relationships of reciprocity and mutuality should characterize service learning: Local leaders should participate in planning projects, and students should learn from and give to community ventures (Rhoads, 1997). Additionally, service learning is a process of experiential, relational learning: Students learn from the community, from personal experience, and from classmates (Palmer, 1990). The aims of this approach are greater understanding of and respect for culturally and socially diverse groups and a heightened awareness of social conditions that impact communities.

How might preservice teachers learn from service learning? Scheckley and Keeton (1997) proposed that individuals construct meaning through the confirmation or disconfirmation of prior understandings. Confirmation is a comfortable learning preference whereas disconfirmation is an unsettling event. Further, individuals filter their experiences through a "perceptual screen composed of cultural norms, individual values, and personal experiences" (Scheckley & Keeton, 1997, p. 36). Radest (1993) referred to cultural screening as a confrontation with familiarity and strangeness. For Radest, "the community service project always involves crossing some cultural line and entails a meeting with strangers . . . in the meeting of strangers, I also meet myself as a stranger" (p. 120).

For many of the preservice teachers with whom I work, service learning is a "first" direct exposure to cultural diversity and poverty. For others, preservice teachers who identify with racial or ethnic minority groups or who come from low-income backgrounds, deprivation or discrimination is "nothing new." Given this diversity, the construction of meaning in a multicultural education course likely is a complex, varied, and somewhat idiosyncratic process.

PROFILES

These profiles sketch individuals who represented varied interpretive stances. The profiles relate to a conceptual framework that Christine Sleeter and I developed (Boyle-Baise & Sleeter, 2000). For that project, we compiled data from 117 preservice teachers who completed service learning within our multicultural education courses over a 4-year period. Data from this case were part of that project, however, the aggregation of information glossed over categories and points emphasized here. These profiles amplify that conceptual framework.

Prior Expectations

In introductory letters, about half of the White prospective teachers, male and female, shared their interests, described brothers and sisters, and noted things important to them. They related special talents, such as playing the piano, and sketched their campus lives. Many disclosed their reasons for selecting teaching as a career: They liked children, they thought teaching would be rewarding, they intended to coach, or they had family who were teachers. The lack of cultural or racial markers in these self-descriptions was striking.

The other half of this group, all female, were a little nervous about pending community service, but thought it a beneficial opportunity to interact with populations previously distant to them. For example, one European American preservice teacher wrote that "in [name] county all the students I have come in contact with have been from my same ethnic and economic background. I think the experiences in this class will be to my advantage" (L.C.P., September 2, 1997).[1] Similarly, another European American preservice teacher wrote: "Coming from a small town, I was not exposed to a lot of diversity. We had approximately five African American students throughout our entire school. I think this course will be a great help to me, as I have not been exposed to a diverse setting" (K.S., September 1, 1997). As noted in a previous study (Boyle-Baise, 1998), expectations for cross-cultural "exposure" through service were pronounced, at least among those who stepped outside their comfort zone to consider it.

Alternatively, all of the preservice teachers of color referenced their ethnic backgrounds in some way in introductory letters. For example, "I'm from [name of city], the urban population is not that large there. It is mostly White, as were the teachers. Still, I had a good experience in high school. I enjoyed singing and traveled with the choir to sing at Carnegie Hall " (E.P., September 2, 1997). Four of the six African Americans wanted to teach in order to give something back to home communities. For example, "I plan to open a daycare center when I graduate. . . . In my area, teens drop out of school because of lack of daycare that is affordable to all. I really want to do something with my life" (J.P., September 1, 1997). As another example, "I had good, strong, supportive teachers in my past and I would like to repay them by becoming the same for some of today's troubled youth" (K.J., September 3, 1997). All of these preservice teachers were from

---

[1]Student quotations included in this text were taken from letters, essays, videotaped reflective sessions, and field notes.

cities of some size and diversity, several came from large families. To the extent discernable from brief letters, this group perceived the service experience through different cultural lenses than did their European American counterparts.

A Deficit View

Leslie was a European American preservice teacher who eagerly anticipated interactions with people culturally and economically different from herself. She lived in a rural area, was married and a recent parent, and commuted to campus daily. She was openly religious, and embraced all children as part of God's human family. In her first reflective essay, she described the children at her community center placement as "underprivileged." She considered the children "wonderful," but "rowdy," and she was concerned with behavior management. "With these kids you cannot say behave or you get a time out. It simply does not work. I think we are learning some tricks. We gave kids attention if they were being good" (L.C.P., October 6, 1997). In an early reflective session, Leslie wondered how to respond to an active African-American boy at the center: "We have a boy . . . who is anxious, well he's mean. [Maybe] he feels out of place. He is the only black boy. Yesterday, another black boy came and he was better. I never dealt with anything like that before" (L.C.P., October 8, 1997).

The theme of behavior management recurred in Leslie's second essay, "My experience at [community center] is going better than I expected. I had some trouble getting the children to behave. They got upset over little things. They craved attention" (L.C.P., October 22, 1997). She felt her inquiry team handled things well; they ignored rambunctious behavior and rewarded considerate actions. Yet, behavioral issues were paramount, and she questioned parent mentors about them during a subsequent reflective session. In regard to the African-American child, she queried: "what can we do to make him feel more comfortable and not threatened?" (L.C.P., October 22, 1997).

In her final essay, Leslie returned to management concerns, still uncertain about "dealing with" the African-American youth. Also, she discussed her team's field project, a series of story readings, again, in terms of conduct. "After we finished the story, we asked the children questions. They knew the correct answers. That really surprised me. They talked all through the reading" (L.C.P. October 17, 1997).

This preservice teacher expressed deficit views in behavioral terms. She did not realize that her interpretations were grounded in her middle class, White cultural frame of reference, and that she possibly misread children's actions. This perception is difficult to disrupt, as it is couched in seemingly normative behavioral expectations. The need to control active children was mentioned by 7 of 13 European American women. Related to this management orientation was the perception of oneself as a role model, particularly someone to provide "stability," offer "attention," and "be there for them." Six European American women perceived themselves in this role. This interpretation assumed that the children lacked permanency, and needed to be "saved" through the provision of constancy and control (Boyle-Baise & Sleeter, 2000).

A Pragmatic View

Learning to deal with or handle children also characterized the statements of the four White males in the class. However, the meaning of these terms differed for males and females. For the men, service learning seemed to be a first opportunity to interact with children. For the women, it was a first effort to manage youth of color or from low-income situations.

One of the men found the experience "eye-opening." In fact, he utilized this descriptor in each of three reflective essays. For Will, "this opportunity really opened my eyes to the great aspects of teaching elementary kids." For him, the most "outstanding part of the project is that you have the opportunity to build relationships with younger people, who worship you." The children's welcoming smiles helped Will "feel really appreciated." The experience "enhanced my ability to communicate with kids" (W.H., October 6, 1997).

Themes of "first contact," "learning to work with kids," and "making a difference" reverberated through Wills's writing. In his second reflective essay, he wrote, "It is my first real experience to interact with the same kids on a regular basis, and really get to know them." Will was satisfied to find "different ways to work with different kinds of kids," and to "make a difference" (W.H., October 22, 1997). Like many classmates, Will defined "making a difference" as offsetting assumed deficiencies in children's lives. Will wrote the following question for a reflective session, "Sometimes I feel I am the only male figure kids have to look up to. Is this true? What does it mean for me as a future teacher?" (W.H., October 22, 1997).

In his final essay, Will evaluated his experience at the community center in the following way, "I learned a lot of things I will carry with me throughout my future educational experiences." He learned the "importance of caring for children and how easy it is to work with a different bunch of kids." Most problems were "behavioral and easy to correct." In general, the experience was an "eye-opener. I saw first-hand some of the problems children have and the way in which an individual can make a change in that child's attitude" (W.H., November 17, 1997).

Will and his male classmates tended to express confidence about their engagement with children. They searched for practical ways to guide diverse youth. One of the men described service learning as "very helpful training for teaching" (B.A., October 22, 1997). Yet, their pragmatism was tinged with compensatory views. Will's descriptions of what was "eye-opening" included increased awareness of children's "problems." Additionally, three of four men considered themselves role models, perhaps children's only positive male role model. This perception exemplified further the savior stance taken by many White women.

A Self-Exploratory View

Wanda, a European American preservice teacher, took steps to educate herself about cultural diversity prior to the course. She volunteered to be a CommUNITY Educator (CUE) in the residence halls, leading discussions among fellow students about issues related to cultural diversity. In her introductory letter, she hoped that service as a CUE, in conjunction with community-based service learning, would assist her in "learning more about myself and others around me" (W.B., September 1, 1997). Wanda chose to do her community service in a local African-American church, along with two African American preservice teachers. In her first reflective essay, Wanda described her initial perceptions of the church in this way:

> My first visit was quite awkward for me. I was really nervous going there, thinking that I would be the only White person. This was the first time that I had ever been truly aware of the color of my skin. Every time I shook someone's hand, I wondered what he or she was thinking of me. (W.B., October 8, 1997)

She realized that in Sunday school, when teacher and students discussed slavery as something "we" experienced, the "we" did not include her. "I knew I could not be included in how they felt because neither I nor people like me had been through the experiences their people endured" (W.B., October 8, 1997). She described her experiences as "uncomfortable" and "insightful" (W.B., October 8, 1997). This experience emotionally jolted her to realizations about the realities of Whiteness.

In her second essay, Wanda wrote that she "continued to learn more about young people and myself" (W.B., October 22, 1997). She felt more comfortable, and she was able to concentrate on the children in her charge. She noticed that young children wandered the aisles and talked freely during church services, in contrast to her own childhood. She wondered how this freedom might translate to the school setting. During a subsequent reflective session, Wanda puzzled this through with parent mentors. She queried, "At [name of church] children move around freely, like walking up and down the aisles during services. Will this influence how these children interact at school? Should I expect them to sit quietly during class?" The mentors, also members of this church, explained that there was little for children to do during long services, and that movement was necessary. They taught their own children to abide by the rules of the situation. Thus, from their view, sitting quietly at school was appropriate.

Overall, Wanda thought her experience was a "great opportunity to be in a place not natural for me. I was often the only White person in the room, which rarely happens to me" (W.B., November 17, 1997). Additionally, she "learned to appreciate the perspectives of others on a deeper level" (W.B., November 17, 1997). This orientation toward self-exploration was mentioned by five White women in reflective essays. However, only Wanda and one other classmate probed their middle-class, White status. The realizations of the other three preservice teachers tilted toward the pragmatic; they pondered their views of "at-risk" or "disadvantaged" children and were "surprised" to find it "fun" to work with these children.

An Activist View

Kayla was one of the African-American female preservice teachers who wanted to "give something back to her community." In her introductory letter, Kayla wrote that, as a teacher, she hoped to return support given to her as a youth:

> Most people do not have as supportive a mom as mine. She managed to work and raise us on her own and still attended all my games. I also have some of my teachers to thank for my motivation. This is another reason why I wanted to become a teacher. I want to show kids there is a future waiting for them if they want it. (K.J., September 3, 1997)

Kayla completed her community service at a local African-American church where she found herself learning "what I feel a good teacher should be able to do . . . relate the subject being taught to everyday life" (K.J., October 7, 1997). Like some of her classmates, Kayla viewed service learning pragmatically, but unlike them, her thoughts were oriented toward the discovery of student's cultural backgrounds. "I feel this will help me to understand more of where students . . . are coming from" (K.J., October 7, 1997). She hoped her future students might feel as "at home" in her classroom as they did in the church.

Kayla realized that life was tough for some of the children, yet she saw them as resourceful. "These kids are not from Beverly Hills 90210. They live real lives with real problems, and have more insight on the world than teachers give them credit for" (K.J., October 22, 1997). As an African-American woman, she felt attuned to these children. "These families welcome you versus the high class moms at the 'Y' (YMCA, where she volunteered previously) who are leery of what a young black woman can impress upon their children" (K.J., October 22, 1997).

Kayla wanted to make a difference in her student's lives. She started a breakfast program at the church, beyond course requirements, to help increase Sunday School attendance. After the first breakfast, she wrote: "It made me feel that, one step at a time, I can really make a difference in the lives of my students" (K.J., October 2, 1997).

In her final essay, Kayla noted that education went beyond teaching subject matter, "it is about providing guidance for the students as well." From her community service, Kayla learned that religious conviction helped some children survive and "should be taken into account when trying to teach the student" (K.J., November 17, 1997). Additionally, Kayla observed great diversity among the African-American children in church. She concluded that it was false to think multicultural education was not needed in a classroom of African-American children.

Four of six African-American preservice teachers wanted to "give something back to their communities." This translated into community improvement, spiritual and moral guidance, and culturally responsive teaching. Most of these preservice teachers were on their way to becoming activists for children, both inside and outside the school setting (Boyle-Baise & Sleeter, 2000).

REFLECTIONS

In order to prompt reflective discussion, preservice teachers were encouraged to express questions anonymously, via a question box, or to raise questions within reflective essays. Thus, our sessions began with a series of class-generated questions. Partially for this reason, reflection scratched the surface of diversity concerns. As suggested by the profiles, preservice teachers focused on disciplinary queries, cultural concerns, or moral issues. In order to illustrate the nature of reflection, two reflective exchanges, captured via videotape, are described.

Reflective Exchange I

Wanda, the student profiled earlier, shared her insights from the African-American church with the class. She recalled:

> In Sunday school the teacher was talking about slavery. She said "our" people and "we" did. For the first time I felt like an outsider. In our classes, teachers say "we" and they are referring to White people. In my teaching when I say "we," I will have to be careful of who I mean. (W.B., October 8, 1997)

I responded, "lots of times we don't specify what we mean when we say 'our' history or 'our' story. Can anyone add to this?"

Rather than pursue the point about racial discrimination, several class members picked up on Wanda's discomfort with her service situation. They turned the conversation to their own uncertainties about interactions with youth different from themselves. As they expressed initial fears and first impressions, perceptions of family life as fragmented and sensational emerged. For example, a European American female confided that, at the outset of her service, she feared the girls at Girls Inc. would not "like or talk to her." Instead, they openly discussed their lives. Yet, their lives were troubled and differed from her own. "A lot of the girls are from single parent homes. One girl told me her mom had a fight with her boyfriend and the police came. She asked me if I had a mom and dad and I was embarrassed to say yes" (J.J., October 8, 1997). Another European American female responded that "you just assume that everyone has a mom and dad. It is something to think about when we teach" (R.C., October 8, 1997).

I asked the group what these realizations meant for them as teachers. They discussed alternatives to "dear mom and dad" salutations on school notes. I pushed consideration of family norms by asking if they knew of any strong single-parent homes. Two women, one European American, one African American, described the strengths of their own mother-headed households. A short discussion followed in which I encouraged the class to imagine their lives at this moment—with the responsibilities of children, home, and job—without parental support for college. What would their homes, families, and job opportunities be like? A European American female responded: "I think this is a reality check for all of us" (K.S., October 8, 1997).

Then (and now), I recognized that these exchanges only pricked the consciousness of many preservice teachers. The "why" papers described by Sleeter (1995), for which prospective teachers research a field-generated question and examine it according to in-group and out-group perspectives, might prod further exploration of these topics. Unfortunately, I did not assign "why" papers for this class, and the field projects resulted in fairly uncritical activities.

Reflective Exchange, II

Both parent mentors, along with their daughter, led this reflective session. To initiate discussion, inquiry teams were asked to develop a question pertinent to their sites. A European American male in service at a Boys and Girls Club asked, "after you spend a couple of hours with kids, they start telling you personal stuff about their families. I don't think I should hear it. I'm not sure how to react" (D.S., October 22, 1997). One parent mentor replied:

> I disagree. I think you should listen to kids. The kids participating in programs sometimes need someone. Sometimes you can't talk to your parents. . . . Or, some kids are more needy. My 6-year-old needs a lot of attention. . . . The best thing you can do is be a friend, that is what you are there for. (P.E., October 22, 1997)

Following this exchange, another question was raised, this one by an African-American preservice teacher in service at Girls Inc. "I haven't done anything to leave an impression on the girls. I just help them with homework. Do you have any suggestions" (P.S., October 22, 1997). The same parent mentor replied, "We all have the responsibility to be role models. You are out there shining. . . . You will leave an impression just by being there. Make sure you don't make assumptions about why the girls need attention" (P.E., October 22, 1997).

At this juncture, I interjected, "you make an important point. We are starting to make judgments, yet we want to be positive. What kinds of things should we try to learn about the children?" This remark was followed by a question from Leslie, the preservice teacher profiled earlier. "We need to know how to deal with [the African-American boy] at the center. We try to reward him for being good. He seems to enjoy going there now. Did it have anything to do with what we did?" (L.C.P., October 22, 1997). The parent mentor answered, "It did, absolutely. He saw how he needed to work with you. . . . I work with my own kids to let them know what is acceptable behavior" (P.E., October 22, 1997). I probed this response, "Many of us are White and interacting with children of color. Are there differences in the ways different groups approach discipline?" The parent mentor responded, "I'm making a generalization, but typically black parents are stricter, more no nonsense than White parents." She gave several examples, then concluded: "it doesn't mean kids are less loved, there are just two different styles [of discipline]" (P.E., October 22, 1997).

Subsequently, a question was raised by an African-American preservice teacher, "In class we were talking about teaching morals. Some people thought morals should be taught at home. I think I will teach morals because I feel the school is your second home. What do you think?" (R.M., October 22, 1997). Both parent mentors responded to this question. One explained that she taught her children to follow the teacher's rules, yet expected the teacher's rules to be fair. The other was saddened that his children still heard derogatory terms like "nigger" and "redneck." He hoped preservice teachers would not disregard insensitive remarks in their classrooms. As the session came to a close, both mentors encouraged the class to avoid judgments of children based on preconceived notions.

This exchange illustrates some contrast between queries by preservice teachers of color and White preservice teachers. The former raised questions of ethics: How can I be of service to this community, how can I teach morally? The latter raised questions of conduct: How should I respond to stories about family life, how should I handle a situation that has racial overtones? Additionally, the exchange indicates the impact of minority group parents as cultural teachers.

Perceptions of a Parent Mentor

(Patricia's voice) *Teaching in a formal setting was something I never aspired to. However, I have always felt an obligation to use my experiences to educate those around me. As an African-American woman, I learned early in life that I had experiences I could share with non-African Americans, experiences that when shared in a nonthreatening environment could prove to be one of the most useful teaching tools I have ever seen. If I were willing to take the risk, and with all of the emotion attached to the experience, tell my story, people were moved in a pretty powerful way.*

Once I understood this, I realized that getting angry was a waste of valuable time and energy and that the only way to fight ignorance was through education. So when I was asked to be a parent mentor for preservice teachers as part of their multicultural educa-tion, I knew that another opportunity to make a difference was be-ing presented to me. Of course, as I approached the classroom on that first day, I could not help but wonder how the class would re-ceive me. I knew that I had to speak from my heart and share expe-riences about my own children—experiences that were not always positive. I had to be clear and give solid examples. I had to fight my own prejudices and not give in to the anger that I knew would well up inside of me from time to time. I had to be able to share emo-tional experiences, but keep my emotions in control. I had to teach these students, but not alienate them. I knew they were coming with a lot of stereotypes, and I had been called in to help dissemi-nate some of those stereotypes. I needed to let these students know that I could not speak for all parents. They needed to be comfort-able enough in my presence to ask the questions that were really disturbing them, questions we all knew could be perceived as prej-udiced. How could I do all of this in a question and answer session that would last one hour?

In introducing myself, I tried to be as warm and welcoming as I could. I let the students know that I would answer any question that was presented to me. As expected, questions at the first ses-sion were tentative. We were getting to know each other, could they really trust me?

By far the most meaningful session for me was when I went back the second time. I passed the test the first time, I did not get angry or defensive, and I answered all the questions. This time I returned with my husband and 10-year-old daughter. The instructor and I agreed to offer students the opportunity to write out their questions, which would be given to me at the beginning of the session. It seemed to me that the questions were more well thought out, that students were less inhibited, and that once we answered a particu-lar question, students seemed to want open discussion. The bolder the questions, the more comfortable we became with each other. By the end of the session, we were going strong and none of us wanted to end. Following the session, students took the time to approach each of us and continue the discussion. It was clear that this session had been very beneficial. I attribute this to the fact that it was our second session together, and the written questions were definitely a success.

The parent mentor program was a vital part of the learning expe-rience for these preservice teachers as they explored unfamiliar cul-tures and dealt with their own prejudices and stereotypes. It was clear from the sessions that they needed the opportunity to discuss their new experiences and understand what was happening to them. They needed to hear that a lot of what they experienced had nothing to do with race or ethnicity, but with children in general. For example, they needed to understand that most children come home from school "starving," not just underprivileged or minority children.

I got a great deal of satisfaction from watching these students develop new perceptions. It was refreshing for me to see what our future educators will look like.

LEARNING FROM SERVICE LEARNING

What did preservice teachers learn from community-based service learning? This case indicates that the process of confirmation or disconfirmation is not simple. Fears of children of color, from poverty, or with disabilities tended to decrease. Often, they were replaced by hunger to know more about diverse youth. Unfortunately, the desire to know often was couched in behavioral rather than in cultural terms. The most intensive disconfirmation generated new understandings of Whiteness among a few European American preservice teachers. There was some confirmation of stereotypes, particularly in regard to problematic family lives. Certainly, this was an area of presumption; family conditions were dealt with minimally as part of this experience. Simultaneously, confirmation was an affirmative experience. Across the board, preservice teachers hoped to "make a difference," and service learning validated these hopes. Some assertions smacked of patronage, especially perceptions of self as a stable, positive role model for youth from low-income families. However, to a small degree, role models also were considered "shining stars," lights needed by all children. For the most part, service learning was considered "very helpful training for teaching." It confirmed the possibility of teaching in culturally diverse or low-income situations for all preservice teachers. Also, it yielded some strategies for culturally responsive teaching. Although a pragmatic effect may be less than ideal, in the long run, students will gain from culturally informed instructors.

Preservice teachers encountered strangeness and seemed to grow more comfortable with it over time. Even teachers with deficit notions conquered initial fears and enjoyed service with children and adults different from themselves. To some extent, preservice teachers examined themselves and questioned their perceptions of the familiar. However, it appeared that in-depth analysis of the impact of race or social class on one's life choices was limited. Even given this caveat, service learning provides a venue to explore notions of similarity and diversity, closeness and distance.

IMPLICATIONS FOR TEACHER EDUCATION

(Lynne's voice) *It is difficult to take something apart, then put it back together again. Should these interpretations be considered separately or cumulatively? Separately, some prospective teachers held deficit views, feared unruliness, and sought techniques to control children of color or in poverty. Cumulatively, preservice teachers utilized the experience to gain teaching expertise, prompt self-assessment, or initiate activism. Rather than denigrate or celebrate service learning, what can be learned from these perceptions?*

What preservice teachers learned seemed dependent on their readiness to learn. Most European American prospective teachers were at a "first exposure" level, a place where they had "never dealt with this before." They struggled to overcome deficit views and to gain comfort in pluralistic situations. Many confronted strangeness, but needed to control it. However, two White preservice teachers, one involved in campuswide diversity activities, the other in tune with self-esteem problems, seemed more developmentally able to wrestle with issues of equality than their counterparts. In comparison, preservice teachers of color seemed ready and eager to tackle culturally responsive teaching and to assist diverse youth beyond school settings.

The perception of service-learning as part of a developmental process of engagement with difference is supported in the literature. Particularly, Dunlap (1998) compares her student's reflections about racial issues in service settings to theories of racial identity development (Helms, 1990). I, too, have noted the emergence, over time, of awareness and appreciation of cultural diversity among preservice teachers (Boyle-Baise, 1998).

Our teaching can be informed by "first exposures" to pluralism. For example, I now realize that deficit (and pragmatic) views might be linked to issues of control. This knowledge enables me to confront and question connections between poverty, ethnic minority identity, and chaos. I can ask, what is there to control? Further, I can improve reflective sessions and activities to grapple with assumptions and presumptions more robustly. As instructor, I, too, learn from service learning, especially from in-depth analysis of my work.

Yet, perhaps it makes sense to ask ourselves: What is enough to expect from service learning? Certainly, expectations should stretch to include preservice teachers for whom this is a first encounter and those for whom this is an additional experience with diversity. For many preservice teachers, it might be enough to jolt awareness

*and to challenge stereotypes. For many, it might be enough to real-
ize children learn differently and to gain techniques to reach them.
For some, service learning might serve as a springboard for further
community involvement. For all, service learning engagements often are too short to motivate major conceptual shifts or to spur activism.*

*Finally, learning from service learning extends to community re-
lations. For example, relationships with my community partners
tend to strengthen and deepen over time. Trust develops. Care
ensues. Over time, I express my intentions and intervene more
strongly. I learn which placements assist affirmative perceptions or
assert compensatory views and change future placements accordingly. The development of community relationships takes time, but
no more than that necessary to interact with teachers and schools.
It is a matter of focus and priority.*

The verdict is still "out." Constructions of meaning do evidence
some thoughts of noblese oblige. There is a savior mentality that un-
dermines equality. However, it does not follow that there are inherent
problems with service learning. In this case, preservice teachers re-
mained open to reconsideration of deficit or supremacy views. Potentially, an instructor can strongly support rethinking through reflective
exchanges and class activities. Perhaps we, multicultural educators,
need to remain open too: What can we learn about service learning? It
is premature to denigrate a perspective and method that connects
multicultural education with the communities it is intended to serve.

REFERENCES

Boyle-Baise, M. (1997). Crossing borders to rethink multicultural teacher education. *Curriculum and Teaching, 12*(1), 15–30.

Boyle-Baise, M. (1998). Community service learning for multicultural education: An exploratory study with preservice teachers. *Equity & Excellence in Education, 31*(2), 52–60.

Boyle-Baise, M., & Sleeter, C. E. (2000). *Community service learning for multicul-tural education.* Educational Foundations, Spring, 1–18.

Cruz, N. (1990). A challenge to the notion of service. In J. C. Kendall & Associates (Eds.), *Combining service and learning: A resource book for community and pub-lic service* (pp. 321–323). Raleigh, NC: National Society for Internships and Experi-ential Education.

DeJong, L., & Groomes, F. (1996). A constructivist teacher education program that in-corporates community service to prepare students to work with children living in poverty. *Action in Teacher Education, 18*(2), 86–95.

Dunlap, M. (1998). Voices of students in multicultural service-learning settings. *Michi-gan Journal of Community Service Learning, 5*, 58–67.

Fuller, M. (1998, April). *Introducing multicultural preservice teachers to diversity through field experiences.* Paper presented at the annual meeting of the American Educational Research Association, San Diego, CA.

Glaser, B., & Strauss, A. (1967). *The discovery of grounded theory: Strategies for qualitative research.* Chicago: Aldine-Atherton.

Helms, J. (Ed.). (1990). *Black and White racial identity: Theory, research, and practice.* Westport, CT: Greenwood.

Hones, D. (1997, March). *Preparing teachers for diversity: A service learning approach.* Paper presented at the annual meeting for the American Educational Research Association, Chicago, IL.

O'Grady, C. (1997, March). *Service learning, educational reform, and the preparation of teachers: Program models and institutions.* Paper presented at the annual meeting of the American Educational Research Association, Chicago, IL.

O'Grady, C., & Chappell, B. (2000). With, not for: The politics of service learning in multicultural communities. In C. Ovando & P. McLaren (Eds.), *The politics of multiculturalism and bilingual education: Students and teachers caught in the cross-fire* (pp. 208–224). Boston: McGraw-Hill.

Palmer, P. (1990). Community, conflict, and ways of knowing: Ways to deepen our educational agenda. In J. C. Kendall & Associates (Eds.), *Combining service and learning: A resource book for community and public service* (pp. 106–113). Raleigh, NC: National Society for Internships and Experiential Education.

Radest, H. (1993). *Community service: Encounter with strangers.* Westport, CT: Praeger.

Rhoads, R. (1997). *Community service and higher learning: Explorations of the caring self.* New York: State University of New York Press.

Scheckley, B., & Keeton, M. (1997). Community service learning: A theoretical model. In J. Schine (Ed.), *Community service learning: Ninety-sixth yearbook for the National Society for the Study of Education* (pp. 32–55). Chicago: National Society for the Study of Education.

Sleeter, C. E. (1995). Reflections on my use of multicultural and critical pedagogy when students are White. In C. E. Sleeter & P. McLaren (Eds.), *Multicultural education, critical pedagogy, and the politics of difference* (pp. 415–437). New York: State University of New York Press.

Tellez, K., Hlebowitsh, P. S., Cohen, M., & Norwood, P. (1995). Social service field experiences and teacher education. In J. M. Larkin & C. E. Sleeter (Eds.), *Developing multicultural teacher education curricula* (pp. 65–78). New York: State University of New York Press.

Vadenboncoeur, J., Rahm, J., Aguilera, D., & LeCompte, M. D. (1996). Building democratic character through community experiences in teacher education. *Education and Urban Society, 28*(2), 189–207.

Varlotta, L. (1997). Confronting consensus: Investigating the philosophies that have informed service learning's communities. *Educational Theory, 47*(4), 453–476.

Wade, R. (1998, November). *Service-learning in multicultural education: A review of the literature.* Paper presented at the annual meeting of the National Council for the Social Studies, Anaheim, CA.

13

The Empowering Role of Service Learning in the Preparation of Teachers

Irma Guadarrama
University of Houston

It is a hot, summer morning in Tetiz, Yucatán, México where 17 university students engage in a service learning and research project. I walk from our field house to the nearby *primaria* to check on its availability where the students will hold their English classes. The warm breeze sends gentle ripples through the tropical foliage characteristic of a Mayan town with a few modernlike houses amidst the multiplicity of round, clay or cement, thatch-roof homes. The two rows of block-cement classrooms near the *zócalo*, or the center of town are used by children in this 5,000 Mayan/Spanish-speaking community just 35 miles from the capital city of Mérida. The university-based students, most of them students of bilingual education or English as second language, serve as *maestros de inglés* to over 400 students of all ages. At the school, early-bird students carefully make their way to the classrooms and wait patiently for their classmates and their teachers. Many of the girls wear their traditional smock or *huipil*, with beautifully embroidered edges. The boys wear American-influenced pants and T-shirts, but just about everyone wears plastic or leather sandals, the practical shoe for the hot, humid weather. When the maestros arrive, the entire school seems to awaken as eager students pour into the classrooms.

Even though English classes are the order of the day, the focus of the program is based on an exchange of English for Maya. Mayan lessons for the maestros, dispersed throughout the day, are usually less formal and more spontaneous. In the classroom, the teachers integrate

227

Mayan language and culture into the English lessons while conveying to their students that they are equally as anxious to learn a second language. Armed with a solid belief that effective pedagogy emerges in response to the contextual structures as defined by the students and their families, indeed their community, teachers teach by engaging their students in constructive dialogue and other student-oriented activities in a culture-focused language exchange project.

Most of the participants in this project were aspiring teachers (Guadarrama, 1998). Their interest in teaching and service along with a propensity for travel and exploration of the unfamiliar attracted them to this project. Their role was broadly defined as teacher and anthropologist. Besides teaching, they assumed research tasks that required them to construct an ethnographic profile of the community. The premise for learning about their students and community was based on a knowledge-application paradigm, that is, the more knowledge they had about their students, the better they were able to respond to students' needs, culture, and experiences and to incorporate them into the curriculum. The anthropological perspective played a major focus in our discussions on the rationale and procedures for learning about students and their families. The stark contrasts and similarities in cultures between themselves and the community helped the participants sharpen their observation of the many unique and profound ways that students' cultures impact their learning at school. About a half dozen of the participants were Hispanic students in their final stage of their university degree program and had intentions of teaching in bilingual education classrooms.

The goal and context of the project, now in its third year, serve as an important function in the development of both a teaching philosophy and a teacher education model that prepare teachers to work with diverse student populations. In this chapter, I focus on this teaching philosophy and corresponding teacher education paradigms that include the service learning project in Mexico and the 5-year-old, field-based teacher education program at our university. The roles that participants play as both students and teachers point to the uniqueness of these participatory, empowering models and offer a strong rationale for integrating service learning as an established component in teacher education. Not every teacher education program can implement a service learning project such as the one in Yucatán. However, I argue that teacher education can and should promote service learning by systematically incorporating service learning activities into all of the community or field-based components. Without this community component and its emphasis on service learning in particular, teacher education lacks the capability of effectively educating teacher candidates in the richness and complexity of the community and its integral relationship to the inconsistencies in quality in the schooling practices of students.

RATIONALE FOR A PARADIGM SHIFT

The need for preparing teachers to work with diverse student populations in the public schools has been well documented, underscoring both the need for improved teacher education and the recruitment of minority teachers. Some reports have documented that the public schools will consist of up to a third minority students (Banks & Banks, 1989), most of them African Americans and Hispanics, although there exists a fast-growing Asian American group. Overall, most of the teacher education candidates in university programs are White, lower and middle-class females, English monolingual speaking, and prefer to teach in middle-class communities or ones similar to those in which they grew up (Avery & Walker, 1993; Zimpher & Ashburn, 1992).

Issues involved in the recruitment and retention of teachers are critical, especially for urban schools, where proportionately large numbers of minority students are schooled and tend to have fewer qualified teachers (Pflaum & Abramson, 1990). Reports indicate that approximately 50% of the new teachers across the country will leave the teaching field within an average of 6 years, whereas teachers in urban schools will leave in 5 years (Haberman & Rickards, 1990). Yet, the prospects for recruiting many more minority teachers are dimmed by recent reports that many qualified candidates choose nonteaching careers because of negative experiences in their schooling (Wideen, Mayer-Smith, & Moon, 1998).

Several studies focusing on the education of first-year teachers have revealed the difficulty in preparing teachers for schools with high minority student populations (Wideen et al., 1998). Many of the efforts seem to concentrate on the addition of a multicultural component but the results have not been as productive as expected. Indeed, the call for minority teacher candidates becomes more pronounced in light of the research that strongly points to the futility of attempting to conceptually change first-year teachers who are not well prepared to work with minority students because by this stage of teacher development, teachers have formulated a fixed view of how they will teach (Goodwin, 1997). Such views are not always congruent with an empowering philosophy of educating underrepresented students. However, the recruitment of minority teacher candidates will not guarantee an improvement in teaching, just as attaching a cultural component offers no such assurances either. Even so, there are a few studies that hold promise for recruiting and educating minority students as teachers who seem to have the motivation for using their negative experiences to produce positive ones for their students. In one study, the researchers found that Latino teacher candidates were particularly innovative in their desire to create learning experiences with their own classroom of Latino students (Cabello & Eckmier, as cited in Wideen et al., 1998). In my work with Latino candidates, I have discovered that many choose to pursue a career in teaching because of their experiences in negative or inadequate schooling (Martínez, 1996).

The consensus among teacher educators converges on the need for a teacher education program that is comprehensive, that is, one that recruits quality teacher candidates, especially in the content areas of critical shortages and among minority groups, and offers a contextually or culturally responsive, ecological design (Artiles, 1996; Wideen et al., 1998). Particularly important are the opportunities made available to teacher candidates for working with students in meaningful contexts. The results of studies that focus on teacher candidates that have rich, personal experiences in schools with minority students in ways that help them connect their own views with the conceptualization of teaching as science and art demonstrate that these "real" and contextualized, firsthand settings are very productive (Bollin, 1996; Valli, 1996). Thus, a teacher education program with a focused service learning component offers teacher candidates, and even experienced teachers, an opportunity to engage in meaningful interactions with students in real contexts that encourage reflection and conceptualization, which is especially important in working with minority students.

DEVELOPING A TEACHING PHILOSOPHY THAT EMPOWERS

An empowering teaching philosophy is anchored in the focal knowledge of the current, present, and past unequal educational practices of underrepresented students. It is also engendered within the context of resistance toward the biased and unfair, often discriminatory, schooling policies. Teachers who understand the educational system's biases and how students' failure experiences are a direct result of these and other socially based discrepancies, are more likely to resist the status quo in favor of advocating for the just treatment of students and changing the structural inequalities throughout the curriculum (Guadarrama, Patterson, & DeVoogd, 1997).

Many descriptions of empowering syllabi related to teacher education follow the multicultural education framework expounded by James Banks (1999). This author is highly regarded as the key expert in the field whose work has implications for operationalizing every facet of multicultural education in the public schools and in teacher education. Banks' ideas on the four levels or approaches to multicultural education reform have formed the foundation for many educational programs. The first level, the contribution approach, narrowly focuses on the heroes, holidays, and other cultural items. The second level, the additive approach, deals with content and concepts that have been simply added on to the curriculum. The third level, the transformation approach, describes a structural change in the curriculum that systematically enables students to acquire multiple perspectives on critical issues in their everyday lives. The fourth level, the social action approach, uses the transformation base as a springboard for helping students identify critical, relevant problems and then take social action to resolve them. Banks' framework includes a social inquiry model by which to direct students toward problem solving, a curriculum development system for developing thematic units on social protest, for instance, and a systemwide model for operationalizing a multicultural education program throughout the school.

The work of Paulo Freire as a teacher, philosopher, and writer, has been interpreted as the vanguard of critical pedagogy (McLaren & Lankshear, 1994; Shor & Freire, 1987). His lessons have had such a profound effect on teachers who work with minority students that he is often upheld as the emblem that epitomizes the power of human struggle within the democratization of education for the poor, oppressed, or exploited. Along with Freire's, the work of others has also been applied to develop a paradigm for educating minority or underrepresented students, as well as within the context of working with gender-related inequalities. For instance, Vygotsky's social-historical analysis of education and its implications for contextually based schooling practices has generated a dynamic dialogue that has resulted in a greater understanding of the role of context and mediation in schooling practices, much of which is lodged in critical pedagogy (Cazden, 1993; Dixon-Krauss, 1996; Vygotsky, 1978). The historical and transformative nature of critical pedagogy have been stressed by Giroux (1992), whose work is illustrative of the postmodern efforts by many who speak on behalf of the oppressed, marginalized, and exploited in a democratic society.

Cummins (1991), an advocate of bilingual education, wrote recently about the social and political influences of education and how students' empowerment is a product of a total community's effort of which the school is an integral part. Empowerment, according to Cummins, is the result of the institutionalization of structures in the curriculum that allow students to unequivocally succeed in their schooling efforts. The disabling nature of certain currently existing school structures and practices such as English-only policies, the exclusive or primary use of norm-referenced tests for gate-keeping purposes, and the tracking systems that adversely pigeon-hole students throughout their schooling experiences serve to systematically preclude academic success for underrepresented students.

In university classrooms across the country, the story and teachings of Nobel Peace Prize winner Rigoberta Menchú,[1] have been used to develop a genre called testimonio, or experiential narrative, that serves as a powerful vehicle for educating and sensitizing individuals about the injustices perpetrated against oppressed people (Carey-Webb & Benz, 1996). Courses are designed around the autobiography of Menchú (1987) that chronicled her life, political struggles, and philosophy borne from her experiences as an indigenous, Guatemalan woman. Pratt (1996), a professor who has developed an interdisciplinary syllabus using Menchú's autobiography, emphasized the importance of North American students not simply studying the text and suspending their stereotypes momentarily just to resume them after the course has terminated. The course, she argued, must be developed using notions of consciousness raising to help students overcome their stereotypes and misconceptions permanently, thus acquiring new and profound understandings of the realities within the political borders of Guatemala as well as in other societies that systematically oppress its citizens. Menchú's concern that North Americans cannot distinguish between knowledge that comes from life experiences and that which is attained through academic study is echoed by Pratt in her own admission that universities tend to overlook this epistemological distinction. Within this discourse, the argument in favor of service learning is well substantiated.

Citizenship education, described as well-defined, structured, authentic, and community-based service learning, is a likely goal of a democratic, participatory effort in learning (Guarasci & Cornwell, 1997). Certainly, a course based on Menchú's experience is likely to conjure a "rediscovery of social empathy" among the students, and the "demystification of the 'other' becomes a possibility" (Guarasci &

---

[1]While I'm aware of Menchú's embroiled controversy over the authenticity of her autobiographical text (1987), this does not distract from her contributions as a political emissary. I've included Menchú's work because of its relevancy to the theme of this chapter.

Cornwell, 1997, p. 25). But it is the field or experiential component of service learning in citizenship education that provides the most transformative impact for students.

A teaching philosophy that is empowering is individually constructed through active participation within a complex educational system that begins with a conscientious and systematic effort to know students and their families. The ethnographic perspective in this process generates an "ethnography for empowerment" that Delgado-Gaitan (1991) discussed as essential in acquiring an understanding of the framework that constitutes the lives of underrepresented youth and their families. A knowledge-application paradigm emerges and teachers who understand students, that is, their lives, struggles, aspirations, and experiences, are better able to address the immediate needs of their students in the classroom in broad, enduring terms.

A MODEL OF EDUCATION THAT EMPOWERS

Integral to an empowering teaching philosophy is a model of education that has a foundation focused on the imperative for schools to address the needs of students in markedly different ways rather than on maintaining the status quo. An empowering model is based on the economic, political, and social reality minority students tend to encounter who, as a group, represent our society's disenfranchised, marginalized, and exploited faction of the nation's population. Thus, whereas high standards are often articulated and regarded as priority in schools' mission statements of the status quo model, the subject-matter curriculum is generally designed around the traditional outcomes-based learning by rewarding academic performance that is primarily assessed by a standardized, norm-referenced system.

In contrast, an empowering curriculum is negotiated in terms of how it is made meaningful to the students. The assessment strategies are designed to enhance rather than disrupt learning, or even devalue a certain kind of culturally specific learning, often privileging the dominant European orientation based on a hierarchically determined power perspective. Students are guided to assume responsibility for their own learning and as a consequence, are poised to succeed rather than programmed to fail. Eminently important in this design is the integral role of the students' cultural experiences and the teacher's knowledge of how to genuinely incorporate them in the curriculum. Students who are schooled within a context of an empowering curriculum develop a healthy view of their culture and language and are prepared to aptly adapt to the exigencies of the dominant or mainstream society, socially, culturally, and cognitively.

Teachers Are Key to Empowerment

Teachers play a pivotal role in the development of programs that serve to promote active student and family involvement that result in academic success. The way that teachers become involved in working with students and their families has a direct bearing on the extent to which they both engage the active, long-term participation of parents and negotiate the curriculum. The lessons learned from exemplary models or strategies for teacher involvement have paved the way for strengthening the service component of our professional training programs in teacher education at the University of Houston. In our work with teachers, we have identified certain key roles that are emblematic of the changing educational paradigms. For example, teachers who serve as "supervisors" to their student teachers are encouraged instead to be their mentors who actively seek out issues, concerns, or problems that neophyte teachers should know about. Through their problem-solving strategies, the student teachers are also engaged in solving problems, becoming at once the observer and the participant. Teacher candidates are guided to experience the value of cooperative learning and peer coaching among their colleagues and are engaging in leadership roles in their schools and communities.

Helping teachers recognize alternative yet powerful roles that can result in empowerment for themselves and their students is one of our most important functions as university teacher educators. Described later are some of the programs in which we have engaged teachers in an effort to promote transformative role changes among themselves and their colleagues. These are the kind of community-based activities that lead teachers to understand the community—the families, their struggles, views, frustrations, values, goals, and so forth. When implemented within a context of consistency and sincere engagement, these programs are apt to effectively promote service learning among teachers and the student teachers that they mentor.

Funds of Knowledge for Teaching. This project was developed by a team of teachers and anthropologists in Arizona for the purpose of learning about their students and their families, using a framework of techniques and perspectives commonly employed by field anthropologists (Gonzales et al., 1993). Anthropologists helped teachers collect ethnographic data by visiting their students' homes and communities in an area populated by mostly Mexican Americans from modest to low income levels. The data, or funds of knowledge, enlightened teachers about the families' wealth of experiences and knowledge, most of them from practical rather than formal sources.

The regular debriefing sessions, scheduled as part of the project, engaged teachers and anthropologists in discussions that enhanced their understandings of the families in different and unique ways. One of the important goals was for teachers to incorporate the data into the curriculum, thus strengthening the program by making it more relevant for students.

In an attempt to help teachers learn about their immigrant students, we developed a research collaborative with similar goals as the Arizona teachers' project. Four university faculty members from two campuses solicited the involvement of two public school teachers each for a total of eight teachers who taught in elementary, middle, and high schools. Our research funds, awarded for this purpose from a university-based center for immigration research, allowed us to compensate the participating teachers for their work, albeit in a small way. They each made several home visits with two of their students throughout a period of 8 months. To facilitate them in honing their techniques for data collection and interpretation thereof, we held monthly Saturday meetings. Our dialogue sessions were lively, intriguing, and informative, according to the comments from the participating teachers.

The implications from this project pointed to the importance of teachers relating to parents in ways that permit them to exchange information about each other, unlike the most commonly used one-way model where teachers assume that their knowledge and voice are more valuable than the parents. The project also strengthened the role of the teacher as a researcher who uses field-based investigative strategies to collect or build information that will help him or her make informed decisions about the curriculum. The philosophy underlying the Funds of Knowledge for Teaching project was used as a foundation to orient students in service learning projects that add to the students' understanding that, in order to empower their students, they must first know the students and their families well and must be able to help them realize how their actions can have a direct impact on their children's success in school.

The Fable Writing Project.   The university educator (UE) introduced the idea of publishing children's original fables to a group of elementary school teachers in a professional development school (PDS) site. The UE is the coordinator of the student interns (or more traditionally called student teachers) and two of the four teachers have been mentors, or to use the term by the teacher education program, site-based teacher educators (SBTEs). The UE has experience and expertise in bilingual education, multicultural education, and desktop publishing. The purposes of the writing project were (a) to encourage writing and publishing by children; (b) to foster pride in the students whose native language was one other than English (most had Spanish as their first language, a few had English, but all children were bilingual and so were the SBTEs); and (c) to demonstrate through children's performances the richness of fables, especially when written by the children, and how they can be used as an empowering vehicle. Throughout the course of the project, both the UE and the SBTEs were pleasantly surprised with the students' creative powers, how they could take a traditional genre and integrate it into their lives, and how through their original fables they revealed so much of themselves. The fact that children created a story around a "lesson" that they could share with their peers and others gave them an opportunity to experience self-control and autonomy that had an empowering effect on their lives. Although the UE initiated the project with a predetermined plan that included reading and acting out published fables as well as an original one, the SBTEs provided support and assistance throughout this process. Also included in the project were the student teachers who had just completed their practicum with these teachers and who volunteered to transfer the children's fables onto diskette, using careful editing to make only minor corrections. The UE completed the publishing phase of the project by using a desktop publishing software to publish the fables, including a group photograph of each of the four classrooms with the use of a digital camera. The product was a booklet entitled, *Cuéntame más fábulas* (*Tell Me More Fables*), that was a second volume of published children's fables. The children received a copy of the booklet on the day that the UE brought a class of university students taking a course on teaching reading and language arts in bilingual education. During this visit, some of the children read or performed their fables. Two classrooms had videotaped the performances of children who had written the fables, directed them, and acted in them. This videotape was shown to the university students after their visit to the school, giving them an opportunity to learn about the project and the benefits for the children.

In a parental involvement activity, the monthly family night event featuring the language arts, SBTEs included a discussion on how parents could contribute to their children's academic progress by helping them read and write fables. Following the discussion, the SBTEs allowed some of their students to read their original fables to the parent audience.

In working alongside the SBTEs in the Fable Writing project, the UE established a position of collegiality that is essential in becoming an integral member of the school community. The UE and SBTE collaboration melded a combination of resources and expertise that had a positive effect on the instructional component of the school, and the parameters of the community broadened, not only for the UE and the SBTEs, but to a certain extent the entire school and university communities.

I include the Fable Writing project as an example of an activity that incorporated culture, parental involvement, and teacher research (a public and university teacher collaborative) into the curriculum and, in effect, allowed children to express themselves in their own terms using personal experiences to help them reap the benefits of thinking about how they can assume control over their lives. Unlike the subject-matter curriculum, this kind of activity was hinged on the teacher's acceptance of a philosophy that embraces the importance of knowing and valuing the culture and life experiences of their students. A service learning component in the preparation of teachers served as a vehicle for teacher candidates to connect with the community and to explore ways to include their knowledge as an integral, rather than peripheral, part of the core curriculum. Our attempt to include service learning in the teacher education program resulted in a more focused and effective field-based approach as described in the next section.

Service Learning Promoted in Field-Based Experiences. One of the most valuable professional experiences for the education student is the clinical field-based practicum in which they are guided through their internship in the schools and classrooms. As pointed out in a previous section, many professional colleges and universities have changed their traditional student teaching programs so that students receive a greater amount of guided clinical experiences prior to their student teaching. This program design, the professional development school (PDS), is relatively new in our state as it is across the country, and many programs are still in the developmental stages. There are many advantages to the PDS design. First, because students spend more time observing and teaching in the schools, they have a better opportunity to learn more about the students and the school community apart from effective teaching techniques. Second, because the students have an opportunity to complete their clinical component for an entire year, they have a better opportunity to become integral members of the school community. This allows principals to recruit students they wish to hire upon their completion of all the requirements. Conversely, the students will be able to make an informed decision on whether to accept the teaching assignment based on their year-long experience at the school. Thus, the PDS design also serves as a recruitment tool, a necessity for inner-city schools that have difficulty hiring qualified teachers. In two of our schools in a PDS site, nine former interns are now teaching as full-time teachers.

The PDS component of our university program, called the Pedagogy of Urban and Multicultural Action (PUMA), consists of several clusters or teams of two or more schools in 33 different school districts across the metroplex. Every cluster has at least two schools and up to 25 education students in their last year of their professional and undergraduate degree program. The two elementary schools assigned to our cluster have mostly Hispanic student enrollments in a mostly Hispanic working-class community. Only a mile away from each other, the schools have over 60% of the students classified as students who are immigrants and learning English as a second language; many of them are children of immigrant parents.

As a faculty member and on-site school coordinator, I consider my role as an advocate or mentor first, then, as a field experience manager and critical pedagogue. In a recent semester, I had 18 education students in my charge; 7 were Hispanics, 8 were African Americans, 1 was Asian American, and 2 were European Americans. Two days out of the week, the students worked with students and their teacher in classrooms assigned to them by a site coordinator from each school. Site coordinators were classroom teachers from each school who doubled in this role; one was a computer or technology teacher and the other a reading specialist. On two other days of the week, the students attended four classes regarded as methodology courses in the teaching of language arts and reading, science, social studies, and mathematics. Every Friday morning with the exception of once a month, students attended a 3-hour long seminar, which I facilitated for the purpose of helping students make conceptual and experiential connections and generate understandings of the teaching and learning process and being advocate teachers for their students. My syllabus was centered around the "learner-centered" competencies, a state-generated list of the professional content of the credentialing examination that students must take and pass before they receive their teaching certificate. However, my focus was on working with all students including the underrepresented, minority students. I organized the course objectives using a constructivistic perspective, balancing and negotiating the state guidelines with relevant, meaningful themes and objectives. The discussions on each competency were generally much more elaborate than at first glance. The competency on learning style, for example, became a discussion on how culture, language, and other experiences affect the way students learn, including an inquiry and reflection activity on how schools need to accommodate those differences. The seminars were most beneficial for students when discussions were centered around their experiences in the classrooms, their observations and interactions with teachers and students. Along with the inquiry/dialogue/reflection techniques, interns engaged in several assignments aimed at helping them collect ethnographic data inside and outside the school community that would subsequently aid them in their critical analysis activities.

One of the main projects required of the student interns was the development of a three-dimensional community map. The rationale for this poster-sized map of the school community was based on the premise that a meaningful curriculum emanates from a teacher's knowledge and understanding of the students' backgrounds and needs. The activity began with the interns' visit to a neighborhood center where an expert social worker described their services to the schools and how those activities, in collaboration or independent of the school efforts, helped the students and their families. The social worker, whose knowledge of the community was based on professional and personal experiences, articulated the description and needs of the community as interns pondered on how they could participate in the center. When asked to volunteer as tutors or mentors at the center, some interns accepted the challenge, whereas others, insisting on a problem of time constraints, contributed their services at another time. The point is that the experience allows for the planting of a seed that will eventually bear its fruits.

The students then worked in small groups to develop a community map that involved using several resources and taking numerous trips in their vehicles. The guidepost used in developing the map was based on a focus on the available resources in the community and the opportunities for recreation, education, and other socialization experiences. The emphasis was on using the students' community as a vital aspect of the empowerment process. As a result, the interns gained insight into the prevailing social and political inequities that were part of the students' lives, and began to understand their role in correcting these inequalities in the schools. Their realization of this difficult journey was the first step in perceiving themselves as potentially influential in their role as advocate teacher.

After each group of interns presented their community map models, a discussion ensued regarding their assessment of the community's strengths and needs in supporting the education and welfare of families residing in the communities. Sometimes interns shared a home-made video and photographs of the community as part of their presentation. We also discussed how the model could be used for instructional purposes. Interns have often suggested that the maps could be used to help teachers learn about the community because many reside outside the area and rarely take the time to visit their students. Other suggestions have included using the map as a game board to help students learn important social studies concepts and as a springboard for planning a thematic unit on the community. Afterward, the maps were placed in the schools, such as the library, office, hallways, and so forth, so that the school could become aware of the interns' products and their interest in learning about the community.

BUILDING BRIDGES BETWEEN
THE UNIVERSITY AND COMMUNITY

Clearly, one of the advantages of the professional development school model lies in the opportunity for universities and schools to develop collaborative working relationships. The partnerships are essential for many reasons; among these are (a) it allows faculty to work with teachers to construct effective teacher thinking and to develop practices that can be implemented by the practitioner and disseminated through university course work; (b) it opens and maintains communication lines that facilitate information dissemination and the development of ideas and innovations; (c) it facilitates positive and friendly relationships essential for maintaining productive public relations; and (d) it promotes service learning as an institutionalized component of higher education, particularly in preparing teachers. The premise that effective teachers are usually the products of school and university partnerships, particularly in the PDS sites, sets the stage for the construction of stronger bonds between the two parties. Equally important is the participation by the school communities in the university–school collaborative efforts. In this regard, the university must often initiate attempts to reach out to the minority community and must genuinely establish a productive working partnership. By promoting service learning within the teacher education program, the university communicates to the community its genuine desire to foster a relationship based on mutual understanding and trust.

CONCLUSION

As public school education continues to confront the issues of a growing minority student population and the lack of human resources to address the myriad of academic and social needs of these students, teacher education is faced with the challenge of not only producing competent and leadership-quality teachers, but also of creating a pedagogy that is aligned with social science themes inherent in teaching culturally and linguistically different students. In this chapter, I have attempted to describe the role of service learning in teacher education, especially as it relates to preparing minority and nonminority teacher candidates to work in predominantly minority school communities. The community-based, culturally integrated projects described herein are considered as venues that optimize the participants' opportunities to become knowledgeable of the community on a firsthand basis and challenges them to become involved independent of work or school requirements. Promoting service learning is the purview of teacher education programs. The seed of service learning can only germinate among teachers and their students when it has been planted within a context that values authentic experience, reflection, and participation in a democratic society.

Whether in a transnational context or urban, multicultural site, when students engage in service learning projects in which they play a dual role of teacher and learner, a dynamic interaction of empowerment emerges. As learners they participate in ways that help them acquire a fresh and profound perspective of contributing to a just cause, and as teachers they inspire their students to reach out to their community and thus, nurture a self-willingness to do the same.

REFERENCES

Artiles, A. J. (1996). Teacher thinking in urban schools: The need for a contextualized research agenda. In F. A. Rios (Ed.), *Teacher thinking in cultural contexts* (pp. 23–52). Albany, NY: State University of New York Press.

Avery, P. G., & Walker, C. (1993). Prospective teachers' perceptions of ethnic and gender differences in academic achievement. *Journal of Teacher Education, 44*, 27–37.

Banks, J. A. (1999). *An introduction to multicultural education*. Boston: Allyn & Bacon.

Banks, J. A., & Banks, C. A. M. (1989). *Multicultural education: Issues and perspectives*. Boston: Allyn & Bacon.

Bollin, G. G. (1996). Using multicultural tutoring to prepare preservice teachers for diverse classrooms. *The Educational Forum, 61*, 68–76.

Cabello, B., & Eckmier, J. (1995). Looking back: Teachers' reflections on an innovative teacher preparation program. *Action in Teacher Education, 27*(3), 33–42.

Carey-Webb, A., & Benz, S. (Eds.). (1996). *Teaching and testimony: Rigoberta Menchú and the North American classroom*. Albany, NY: State University of New York Press.

Cazden, C. (1993). Vygotsky, Hymes, and Bakhtin: From word to utterance and voice. In E. A. Forman, N. Minick, & C. A. Stone (Eds.), *Contexts for learning:*

Sociocultural dynamics in children's development (pp. 197–212). New York: Oxford University.

Cummins, J. (1991). Empowering minority students: A framework for intervention. In M. Minami & B. P. Kennedy (Eds.), *Language issues in literacy and bilingual/multicultural education* (pp. 372–390). Cambridge, MA: Harvard Educational Review.

Delgado-Gaitan, C., & Trueba, H. (1991). *Crossing cultural borders: Education for immigrant families in America.* London, New York: Falmer Press.

Dixon-Krauss, L. (1996). *Vygotsky in the classroom: Mediated literacy instruction & assessment.* White Plains, NY: Longman.

Giroux, H. A. (1992). *Border crossings: Cultural workers and the politics of education.* New York: Routledge.

Gonzales, N., Moll, L., Floyd-Tierney, M., Rivera, A., Rendon, P., Gonzales, R., & Amanti, C. (1993). *Teacher research on funds of knowledge: Learning from households.* Tucson, AZ: National Center for Research on Cultural Diversity and Second Language Learning.

Goodwin, L. A. (1997). Multicultural stories: Preservice teachers' conceptions of and responses to issues of diversity. *Urban Education, 32*(1), 117–145.

Guadarrama, I. N. (1998, April). *Educating bilingual/esl teachers in a language/culture exchange field school: A collaborative model in teacher education.* Paper presented at the Annual Meeting of the American Educational Research Association, San Diego.

Guadarrama, I. N., & Kirksey, L. (1996). *Discovering our experiences: Studies in bilingual/esl education, volume 3.* Houston: The University of Houston.

Guadarrama, I. N., Patterson, L., & DeVoogd, G. (1997). *Discovering our experiences: Studies in bilingual/esl education* (Vol. 4). Houston: The University of Houston.

Guarasci, R., & Cornwell, G. H. (1997). *Democratic education in an age of difference: Redefining citizenship in higher education.* San Francisco: Jossey-Bass.

Haberman, M., & Rickards, W. H. (1990). Urban teachers who quit. *Urban Education, 25,* 297–303.

Martínez, E. S. (1996). Reflecting on ideological baggage: Latino pre-service teachers and their experiences as students. In I. N. Guadarrama & L. Kirksey (Eds.), *Discovering our experiences: Studies in bilingual/ESL education, volume 3* (pp. 19–28). Houston: The University of Houston.

McLaren, P., & Lankshear, C. (Eds.). (1994). *Politics of liberation: Paths from Freire.* New York: Routledge.

Menchú, R. (1987). *I, Rigoberta Menchú: An Indian woman in Guatemala.* London: Verso.

Pflaum, S. W., & Abramson, T. (1990). Teacher assignment, hiring, and preparation: Minority teachers in New York City. *The Urban Review, 22,* 17–31.

Pratt, M. L. (1996). Me llamo Rigoberta Menchú: Autoethnography and the recoding of citizenship. In A. Carey-Webb & S. Benz (Eds.), *Teaching and testimony: Rigoberta Menchú and the North American classroom* (pp. 57–72). Albany, NY: State University of New York Press.

Shor, I., & Freire, P. (1987). *A pedagogy for liberation: Dialogues on transforming education.* South Hadley, MA: Bergin & Garvey.

Valli, L. (1996). Learning to teach in cross-cultural settings: The significance of trusting relations. In F. A. Rios (Ed.), *Teacher thinking in cultural contexts* (pp. 282–307). Albany, NY: State University of New York Press.

Vygotsky, L. (1978). *Mind in society: The development of higher psychological processes.* Cambridge, MA: MIT Press.

Wideen, M., Mayer-Smith, J., & Moon, B. (1998). A critical analysis of the research on learning to teach: Making the case for an ecological perspective on inquiry. *Review of Educational Research, 68*(2), 130–178.

Zimpher, N., & Ashburn, E. (1992). Countering parochialism in teacher candidates. In M. Dilworth (Ed.), *Diversity in teacher education: New expectations*. San Francisco: Jossey-Bass.

INTEGRATING SERVICE LEARNING AND MULTICULTURAL EDUCATION IN HIGHER EDUCATION: PROMISES AND POSSIBILITIES

14

Maximizing Impact, Minimizing Harm: Why Service-Learning Must More Fully Integrate Multicultural Education

Mark Langseth
Minnesota Campus Compact

As I argue here, relationships are fundamental to our work in both service-learning and multicultural education. And, of course, getting to know one another is fundamental to relationships. In this spirit, I want to begin with some brief comments about who I am, with particular attention to the perspective from which I approach the concepts and practices of service-learning and multicultural education.

I write from a number of perspectives:

- I am a White, middle-class, heterosexual male.

- I am a husband and father who is deeply concerned about the formal education my daughters will receive, both at the K–12 and higher education level.

- I am someone who spent half his life in a small rural town and has since resided in the inner core of a large metropolitan area.

- I am someone who has been involved in service-learning and campus-community collaboration work at the local, state, and national level for more than 15 years.

- I am someone who has created and led a variety of programs that integrate service-learning with multicultural education, including very deliberately involving diverse groups of K–12 and college students in service-learning experiences and, with some documented success, helping break down cross-cultural barriers and misunderstandings in the process.

- I am someone who believes that the "isms"—racism, classism, sexism, heterosexism, and related -isms—lie at the fundamental core of many social, economic, and environmental problems in the United States and around the world—that there is simply nothing more central for us to address if we are serious about bringing about social change.
- I am someone who believes that experiential education must form the core, not the fringe, of our formal educational system.
- I am someone who believes that the field of service-learning has focused far too much on student impact and not nearly enough on community impact (although there are some promising signs that this is beginning to change).
- I am someone who is generally more knowledgeable about the field of service-learning than of multicultural education.

For the purposes of this chapter, I write explicitly from the service-learning side of this book and make an argument for why we, as campus service-learning leaders, must more fully integrate multicultural education into all of our work and why we must do it now. I also want to offer some suggestions for how we might go about this.

I have made a fundamental assumption that both service-learning leaders and multicultural educators are interested in transformative change—in students, in communities, and in institutions. Given this assumption about our collective interest in change, I work from three core premises:

1. Relationships, as I said earlier, are the fundamental building blocks for change;
2. Every service-learning program in the country operates within a complex multicultural environment; and
3. In such environments, relationships—and therefore change—cannot be achieved without significant knowledge, without respectful mind-, heart- and soul-"fullness," without strategic intentionality, and without courageous leadership.

RELATIONSHIPS AS BUILDING BLOCKS
FOR CHANGE

At face value, this idea about relationships as fundamental to change may not appear exceedingly difficult to grasp. But, in fact, given the breadth and depth of its implications, this can be a very challenging idea both to understand and to put into action.

From my perspective, the most important relationships in any service-learning program are the ones between campus representatives and those in the community with whom they work. Although I also believe that student-to-student and student-to-faculty relationships are important, I am most concerned that we focus our attention first on community partnerships and relationships between campus and community representatives.

Far too often, campus–community partnership efforts, like so many other efforts at community change, do not adequately focus on relationships first. Rather, the focus is on finding the "right" programmatic "fix" and on doing this with some haste. We are, I believe, obsessed with finding the right program for the right problem, applying outdated or inappropriate models to community issues; the medical model of disease/diagnoses/drug, the military model of conflict/strategy/deployment, or the business model of problem/analysis/ solution. We do this all the time in service-learning and we're not alone. Most social service agencies, government agencies, neighborhood organizations, and civic groups do the same thing. Unfortunately, we have all been enculturated to believe that if we just deploy the right programmatic weapon or take the right programmatic pill, we can solve anything. We cannot.

A related myth of the medical/military/business models of creating change is that, when approaching an issue, we must begin with a dispassionate, third-party analysis of the disease, the problem, or the deficit. But as Kretzmann and McKnight (1993) documented via extensive research on troubled communities throughout the United States, community challenges are most successfully addressed when we focus first on assets rather than on deficits, and specifically on the perspectives, gifts, and talents of ordinary people, not experts. Similarly, public relationships—at least healthy ones—are built primarily by focusing on and interacting around each others' assets, not deficits.

Over the past 5 years, I have studied a variety of highly successful approaches to community change, including Kretzmann and Mc-Knight's "asset-based" approach, the Industrial Areas Foundation's building relationships/building citizen power approach (1990), the Highlander Education and Research Center's learning circle approach (see Horton, 1990) and many others. The one absolutely clear commonality in all of these approaches is that high-trust relationships and high-investment relationship building are the most important and most fundamental elements in creating lasting community change.

I hasten to add, however, that approaching the development of such relationships solely as a means to a programmatic end is counter-productive. That is, building high-trust, high-investment relationships—founded on understanding across differences—also requires us to approach each relationship as an end in itself. It is in this spirit that truly transformative relationships and truly transformative programs are forged.

Many service-learning programs have been developed without deep collaboration with the community. But, as more and more of us are discovering, these programs are very limited without the fundamental ingredient of high-investment, high-trust relationships. Designing a program without the building blocks of such relationships is like building a house without the foundation—looks fine, at least initially, from the outside, but will not stand the test of time.

In the context of service-learning partnerships, putting relationships and the assets of ordinary people first comes with a number of challenges:

1. It takes much more time and personal/emotional investment;
2. It is initially much more process oriented than task oriented, thus running the risk of seeming "unproductive, unscientific, subjective and/or touchy-feely";
3. It often "messes up" even the most well-conceived programs or plans;
4. It may mean that we need to seek different partners who share our beliefs about the importance of relationships and assets; and
5. It takes the college or university out of the "expert" role.

In high-trust, high-investment relationships, campus and community partners are cocreators, cocoordinators, coowners, and coevaluators of their joint efforts. They work together in a variety of highly strategic ways to effect longer range change in their communities. Their relationships often have a very "personal" closeness to them and involve a spirit of commitment to each other's continuous growth and development. And they work together strategically to build relationships among numerous individuals to ensure that the partnership outlasts changes in leadership.

In contrast, "lower trust" and "lower investment" relationships are characterized by a significant degree of professional distance between individuals and agencies who do not feel a strong stake in each others' development, and they tend to be much less creative and less jointly strategic about making longer range community change. This is not to say that lower trust, lower investment relationships are entirely without merit. It may well be that a campus and community-based organization desire exactly this kind of relationship and that productive community work occurs. But clearly, if our intention is to effect longer range community change and to create opportunities for multicultural education for students, these opportunities will be more available and much richer in the context of high-trust, high-investment relationships.

It is also interesting to note that a meta-analysis of several "principles of best practice" lists for service-learning, completed by Mintz and Hesser (1996), resulted in three themes—reciprocity, collaboration, and diversity. All of these themes are deeply rooted in this concept of relationships as fundamental to our work in service-learning, and they reinforce the importance of integrating multicultural education into service-learning as well.

Finally, some thoughts on student relationships and student impact. As I mentioned earlier, I believe that the greatest opportunities for positive student impact in general lie in the context of high-trust, high-investment campus–community partnerships. A growing body of research on service-learning at the K–12 and collegiate level also suggests that the presence of intentional, well-designed opportunities for reflection and education is the key factor in determining whether or not students exhibit academic, civic, and multicultural development via their service-learning experiences (Conrad & Hedin, 1991; Eyler & Giles, 1994; Search Institute, 1999; Waterman, 1997). Although the research is not quite as explicit in its assertion that relationships play a key role in the success of these reflection or education opportunities, it has been my experience that the quality of communication and relationships nurtured by faculty and program leaders in these educational sessions correlates directly with the richness of student learning and development. Certainly, multicultural educators have known for some time that the quality of communication and the degree of trust and connectedness that one creates among students are absolutely essential to effective practice in multicultural education.

COMPLEX, MULTICULTURAL ENVIRONMENTS

More than once I have heard colleagues from rural communities in Minnesota comment that there is no "diversity" in their town and lament that this limits their ability to do multicultural education via service-learning. What they usually mean is that there is not a tremendous amount of racial diversity in their community.

But, as more and more multicultural educators and service-learning leaders understand, there are many different kinds of diversity—along commonly recognized lines of race, class, gender, ethnicity, nationality, religion and sexual orientation, as well as the less-recognized diversity that exists within and between higher education cultures and grassroots community cultures. Certainly, all of these types of diversity can provide rich opportunities for multicultural education.

With such understanding in mind, it is clear that every service-learning program in the country operates within a complex, multicultural environment. We must recognize that, unfortunately, in such environments, we have a very real capacity to do harm. As Gugerty and Swezey (1996) pointed out, "although most institutions of higher education have the best intentions when they embark on service-learning programs, their lack of attention to power differentials and to ethnocentric values creates harm and distrust in many communities" (p. 95). Mulling (1995) articulated three myths related to campus–community collaboration that must be addressed to avoid doing harm:

- There exist superior and deficient cultures;
- There is a superior knowledge and experience in higher education as compared to their communities; and
- There is a hierarchy of wisdom, with faculty wiser than students and students wiser than the community.

Sadly, many of us in the field have borne witness to the negative effects these myths can have, both on student and community. Personally, I have read journals or heard students say such things as "what's wrong with these people?" or "just like I thought, they're a bunch of drunk old men who ought to get a job" and a variety of related generalizations that indicate their lack of understanding of people different from themselves and of related social issues. I shudder to think of the attitudes of superiority that some program leaders, faculty, and students bring to their community interactions. Clearly, these concerns point directly to the importance—the imperative—of service-learning leaders and participants possessing exceptionally strong multicultural knowledge, experience, and perspectives.

I must also hasten to note here that we ought not place the blame for such student attitudes at the feet of students only. In a culture where the old tradition of "noblesse oblige" is alive and well and where discourse on community and political issues remains at a frighteningly thin level, it should be no surprise that many students' understanding of these and related issues is equally thin.

Beyond doing no harm, I believe that one of our most important responsibilities is to ensure that we harvest the positive possibilities for multicultural education available to us via service-learning. Service-learning provides an ideal environment for student development in this area, because it is experiential and because it is located in a specific and shared, but external context to campus. In my experience, many traditional efforts at multicultural education are limited because they are exclusively on-campus discussions, which, although productive in some cases, often flounder in a mire of personal feelings and world-as-it-is versus world-as-it-should-be confusion, without a specific context or adequate set of relevant, shared experiences from which to draw. Service-learning can be an extremely effective means of addressing these limitations in traditional multicultural education efforts.

One final point to emphasize the critical place of multicultural education in service-learning: As we all know from our personal and professional lives, relationships are difficult to manage in any context, but they are particularly difficult to form and maintain in multicultural contexts. As wiger (1995) and others have pointed out, there are major obstacles to building campus–community relationships in addition to the myths previously cited. These include significant histories of individual or organizational dominance; current power dynamics that often perpetuate injustices and oppression; genuine cultural differences around definitions, values, or norms that can lead to misunderstanding and conflict; and a general climate of mistrust in intergroup relations. And just as campuses can view communities inaccurately, so can communities view campuses with undue cynicism. Communities might view colleges and universities as elitist, out-of-touch, White, or wealthy institutions that have little to offer them. There may be resentment of a "research subject" relationship between the university and the community or land, housing, admissions, employment, or parking conflicts, further complicating efforts to partner. Add to this the public's rising mistrust of institutions in general and the inherent problem of "service" language (implying a "have/ have not" framework) and we have a very complicated context in which to operate and an equally strong case for integrating multicultural education more fully and effectively into our service-learning efforts.

NEED FOR KNOWLEDGE,
RESPECT/"FULLNESS," INTENTIONALITY,
AND LEADERSHIP

In such complicated environments, it is critical that campus and community partners develop in all program leaders and participants the tools and perspectives of multiculturalism, including:

• Significant knowledge about the people we are working with, about the historical and current state of intergroup relations related to our context, about the larger social issues and power dynamics in which we are operating, and about our own personal and institutional biases, stereotypes, and prejudices.

If we are working in a particular neighborhood, for example, we need to know the history of that neighborhood, particularly as it relates to oppression or injustices that are commonly understood by people in the neighborhood. We need to be familiar with the current concerns of neighborhood residents. We need to know how our particular partnership fits in the larger scheme of efforts at neighborhood improvement and what the history of campus–community relations has been. We need to know about the larger social, economic, and political context. And we need to have significant knowledge about our own personal biases (often requiring both hard work and skilled guidance) and about our institution's policies and priorities as they relate to working within a particular community.

• A sense of respect and fullness: Building on this base of knowledge, we must nurture in ourselves and others a deep sense of respect and the heart-, mind-, and soul-fullness necessary to operate effectively in complicated multicultural environments. Granted, such attitudes and states of being, along with their commensurate behaviors, do not develop overnight. Nor are they easy to teach—for example, helping students distinguish between "respect" and absolute moral relativism is a very complicated endeavor. But we must pursue this important work in much greater earnest if we are serious about minimizing harm and maximizing positive impact of service-learning and campus–community collaboration efforts.

• A commitment to strategic intentionality: That is, as we approach both our community impact and student impact goals via service-learning, we must be very intentional and highly strategic about the programmatic choices we make. Too often, although we say we have the best intentions in mind, our actions do not reflect much intentionality or strategic thinking at all. For example, have we chosen community partners based more on convenience (i.e., they have a user-friendly volunteer program) than on what kind of partnership both the residents of that community and we believe will reap the most long-term impact? If we do not approach our community partnerships with such strategic intentionality, we are open to criticism that we are more interested in using the community as a learning laboratory or as research subjects than we are in serving as an ally for change.

Similarly, on the student impact side, we are often much less intentional than we ought to be in regard to integrating multicultural education into our programs or courses. Far too often, our efforts are relatively thin attempts to address very general issues about "difference" and "diversity," absent deeper theoretical understandings of multiculturalism and with little accompanying knowledge and analysis of the specific historical and current local context in which we operate. Moreover, even our efforts at understanding difference and diversity in more depth can be limited by our own capacity to facilitate truly meaningful discussion and learning in these areas.

• Courageous leadership: Finally, I believe that we, as service-learning leaders, must be well prepared to exercise courageous leadership in our community partnerships and with our students, faculty, and administration. One of the most common criticisms I have heard from communities of color and from low-income communities about campus partnerships—and partnerships with institutions in general—is that when the going gets tough and allies are needed to advocate for change in, for example, city policy or funding priorities, the campus is not there for them and therefore is not really serious about helping them.

That is not to say that a college or university should always stand with a particular community on a public issue. What it does suggest is that, with thoughtful, courageous leadership, we ought to be willing to explore creative ways to manage, not shy away from, potential political consequences and to welcome, not avoid, conflicts as "teachable moments." Regardless, we should be clear with our community partners up front about how we will approach such issues as they arise and what options might be available. For example, although the institution itself may not be willing put its weight behind a particular issue, perhaps a group of faculty or students might do so or might help mobilize others on campus or in the community to do so. Anticipating these situations can help tremendously in creating the kind of lasting relationship with a community that maximizes the opportunity for positive community and student impact.

MAKING IT HAPPEN

My organization, Minnesota Campus Compact, has begun research on campus service-learning programs that are committed to more effectively integrating multicultural education. From this initial research and from my experience consulting with campuses over the past 12 years, I would suggest several courses of action for readers interested in more fully and more effectively integrating multicultural education into your service-learning efforts. Please note that the "cross-cutting theme" for all of these areas is a commitment to building better and better relationships:

Make Multicultural Education a High Priority. I hope I have made a compelling case in this chapter that, for service-learning leaders, there is simply no way to reach our most desired outcomes for communities or students without a very strong commitment to multicultural education. Multicultural education is not just another aspect of our programming. In my opinion, it is the most important aspect to our programming, given that "-isms" and cross-cultural relations lie at the core of so many of our social, economic, and environmental challenges and at the very heart of our service-learning and campus–community collaboration efforts; and given the high potential to do harm if we do not focus our attention in this area.

Multicultural education is also one of the few issue areas that is relevant across all of our service-learning program activities, from recruitment of participants to community partnerships to reflective/education components. As a result, multicultural education can be a wonderful issue around which individual and collective campus efforts can coalesce, giving them a greater sense of coherence and purpose.

Relatedly, although most campuses have made multicultural education a priority, very few are satisfied with their efforts to integrate multicultural education into their overall educational experiences. Adopting an increased focus on multicultural education in service-learning, then, also affords us another avenue to demonstrate our direct relevance to larger campus priorities.

Finally, I want to suggest that a participatory process for making decisions about how to further integrate multicultural education can itself serve as a relationship-building tool—bringing leaders in service-learning together with others on campus and with community partners. Often, issues related to multiculturalism and diversity are foremost on the minds of grassroots community leaders and, for example, multicultural affairs offices on campus. Seeking input from a specific community partner or from your multicultural affairs office on how you might go about integrating multicultural education more effectively into your efforts can both help you improve your efforts and strengthen relationships with these groups.

Commit to Ongoing Personal and Professional Development. Given the enormous complexity of issues related to multiculturalism, no one, no matter how experienced, knowledgeable, and wise, is exempt from the need for continuous development in this area. For most of us, such development must be both internal (e.g., consistently uncovering our own backgrounds and biases, pains and passions) and external (e.g., educating ourselves about historical, theoretical, factual, and other perspectives on multiculturalism and change). In order to lead effective efforts at multicultural education, we must invest in ourselves. I simply cannot overemphasize this point.

Analyze and Revise Your Community Partnerships. As I argued earlier, multicultural education efforts are more effective when implemented in the context of high-trust, high-investment relationships with community partners. If a campus wishes to step up its multicultural education efforts within its service-learning initiatives, then it is advisable to review current community partnerships to determine what steps need to be taken toward this end. This may result in deepening relationships with existing partners or in creating altogether new partnerships.

The other key point here is that we will likely need to rely on our community partners to assist us in our efforts at more effectively integrating multicultural education. Although many community partners already help orient students for their role in their organizations, assisting with multicultural education efforts can require much more investment. If our relationships with them are relatively thin, the likelihood of their participation is diminished.

Analyze and Revise the Learning Component(s) of Your Efforts. Although many service-learning programs include some form of "diversity training" or "appreciation of differences" sessions, many of these efforts are weak in substance and brief in duration. Given the highly complex nature of multicultural education and the need to address a wide range of both personal development and broader social issues, much more rigor in these efforts is needed. We must make multicultural education a major priority of our reflection/education efforts if we hope to make a difference in the lives of our students. Combating -isms and developing strong multicultural attitudes, perspectives, and skills requires highly thoughtful, highly strategic efforts over significant periods of time.

This brings up a related point: Given the complexity of multicultural issues and the need for development and learning over time, it is important that we consider ways in which multicultural education can be woven into as many service-learning venues as possible. Cocurricular programs, service-learning courses and internships, community-based work-study programs, action research efforts, and other efforts should all include a strong emphasis on multicultural education. Similarly, multicultural education at its best would be woven into every aspect of each of these programs, from orientation and training to recruitment and celebration. Only then will most of our participating students be given the opportunity to explore multicultural issues in adequate depth over a significant period of time.

Connect With Larger Campus Agendas vis-à-vis Multicultural Education. As I said earlier, most colleges and universities have identified diversity or multicultural education as a significant priority in their overall strategic plan. It is important that we are familiar with past and current attempts at addressing these priorities at an institutional level. Do they focus mostly on recruiting and retention of students or faculty of color? Do they focus on creating a climate of respect and dignity on campus across a wide range of differences? Is there a concentrated effort to address some of these issues in, for example, an office of multicultural affairs? Are these the only efforts being pursued on campus? Who else is concerned about these issues?

To my knowledge, there are very few examples of collaboration between service-learning programs and multicultural affairs offices around multicultural education. This might be where service-learning leaders look first to collaborate and there may very well be possibilities for such collaboration. But often, as in any potential collaborative effort, barriers to collaboration are significant, ranging from little time for partnerships to lack of trust or competition between offices. Although I would strongly recommend exploring collaboration with your multicultural affairs office or its equivalent on campus, I would not advise staking your whole effort on this exploration. Regardless, however, you should keep that office informed of your intentions to more fully and effectively integrate multicultural education into your service-learning efforts and not let petty or competitive tensions interfere with the potential for further collaboration.

On a broader scale, I would strongly urge that you gain support from key institutional leaders for your particular effort, and position your efforts in such a way that they are seen (as much as possible) as complementary to, not competitive with, other institutional initiatives aimed at multicultural education.

Integrate Knowledge, Respect, Intentionality, and Leadership Throughout. See the previous paragraphs for further discussion of each of these areas. The key point to keep in mind is that multicultural education efforts in the context of service-learning ought to combine both personal development and theoretical and factual educational opportunities.

Choose (Wisely) Others to Help You. The pool of campus and community consultants, presenters and facilitators who might assist us in our own personal/professional development or in designing or implementing more effective multicultural education components in our programs has expanded significantly. As in any other field, the quality of help provided by these people varies significantly. At the same time, there are very few service-learning leaders who have the capacity to completely self-direct their personal/professional development or to design and implement multicultural education efforts without significant assistance. One of your key tasks, then, as a service-learning leader is to choose wisely people who can assist you in these efforts.

People I have found most helpful toward this end are visionary and hopeful, but understand the world as it is; believe in the importance of both deep internal work and the need for theoretical and factual information; are highly skilled at group process and can both support and challenge people; are highly knowledgeable about -isms and their impact on larger social challenges; and truly understand the specific context in which they are working. Experience working with students and in community change endeavors is also helpful.

Certainly, you will have other criteria by which you choose people to assist you in your efforts. Whatever they are, be very clear about them and be highly deliberate in your choices. It's worth the time to find the right partners.

Be Prepared to Receive Feedback. Because issues related to multicultural education are both highly complex and critically important to so many people, opinions about effective practice are often strong. I fully expect that I will receive feedback, both positive and negative, on this chapter. In order to keep growing and learning in this richly complicated area, I must be prepared to receive this feedback, particularly any negative feedback I may not wish to hear. Likewise, as you move forward with your efforts to integrate multicultural education, you will receive feedback, some of it negative. Rather than retreating from this feedback, I suggest you "lean into it," inquire further from those who criticize, put this feedback into your continuous reflection and revision loop and adjust as you see fit. The point is that you should expect feedback and be prepared to receive it, no matter what its content or tone.

As we implement strategies for "making it happen," we must also remember that weaving through all of these efforts is the challenge of creating high-trust, high investment relationships with all of our campus and community stakeholders. How exactly we accomplish this is highly dependent on our personal style and our particular campus and community contexts, but at every opportunity, we must pursue the development of such relationships.

A FINAL CHALLENGE

How can the service[-learning] movement influence itself to move beyond surface level needs and symptoms to contribute to problem solving and resolution of deeper institutional and systemic root causes? (Massengale, 1998, p. 11).

Service-learning in higher education is at a crossroads. For several years now, we have been building a critical mass of people interested in and committed to this innovative educational and community development strategy. The question now before us is: Are we really accomplishing what we say we wish to accomplish, in the community, with students, within our institutions? Clearly, issues related to the quality and impact of our efforts must now take center stage if the movement is to continue with the same momentum built so carefully by so many for so long.

Toward this end, I believe there are three highly interrelated investments we must make and must make now:

1. a renewed focus on longer-term community impact and deeper community relationships. Perhaps the most fundamental issue here is learning to cross cultural boundaries and to build cross-cultural bridges—strong. lasting bridges that stand the test of time and result in sustainable change.

2. highly strategic efforts to increase faculty/institutional investment in service-learning. Such support is absolutely critical to sustain our efforts and build more infrastructure, so we can pursue deeper, more lasting change in communities and in students. Although this topic is beyond the scope of this chapter, this is a critical piece of our work over the next several years. We simply cannot both operate on a shoestring and deliver the kind of community partnerships and student reflective/education components needed to really make a difference.

3. weaving multicultural education more fully and effectively into everything we do.

Significant state and national efforts are beginning to mount on the first two strategies. But building a collective momentum to weave multicultural education more fully and effectively into our philosophy and practice in service-learning remains undone. For the good of our communities, our students, our institutions, and the service-learning movement, let us begin now with this critical work.

REFERENCES

Conrad, D., & Hedin, D. (1991). School-based community service: What we know from research and theory. *Phi Delta Kappan, 72,* 743–749.

Eyler, J., & Giles, D., Jr. (1994). The impact of a college community service laboratory on students' personal, social and cognitive development. *The Journal of Adolescence, 17*(37), 327–329.

Gugerty, C. R., & Swezey, E. D. (1996). *Developing campus–community relationships.* In B. Jacoby & Associates (Eds.), *Service learning in higher education: Concepts and practices.* San Francisco: Jossey-Bass.

Horton, M., with Kohl, J., & Kohl, H. (1990). *The long haul: An autobiography.* New York: Doubleday.

Industrial Areas Foundation. (1990). *Standing for the whole.* Chicago, IL: Author.

Kretzmann, J. P., & McKnight, J. L. (1993). *Building communities from the inside out: A path toward finding and mobilizing a community's assets.* Evanston, IL: Northwestern University Center for Urban Affairs and Policy Research.

Massengale, T. (1998). *Report on a statewide dialogue on service and volunteerism in California* (p. 11). California: James Irvine Foundation.

Mintz, S. D., & Hesser, G. W. (1996). Principles of good practice in service-learning. In B. Jacoby & Associates (Eds.), *Service-learning in higher education: Concepts and practices.* San Francisco: Jossey-Bass.

Mulling, C. (1995, May). *Do no harm.* Paper presented in a panel discussion at the National Gathering, College Educators and Service-Learning, Providence, R.I.

Search Institute. (1999, January). Does service-learning make a difference? *Source, 15*(1), 1–3.

Waterman, A. (1997). *Service-learning: Applications from the research.* Mahwah, NJ: Lawrence Erlbaum Associates.

Wiger, F. (1995, May). *Do no harm.* Paper presented in a panel discussion at the National Gathering, College Educators and Service-Learning, Providence, R.I.

RELATED RESOURCES

Alinsky, S. D. (1971). *Rules for radicals: A pragmatic primer for realistic radicals.* New York: Vintage Books.

Cruz, N. (1996). *Diversity principles of good practice in combining service and learning.* Stanford University: Haas Center for Public Service.

Eyler, J., Giles, D. E., Jr., & Schmiede, A. (1996). *A practitioner's guide to reflection in service-learning: Student voices and reflections.* Nashville: Vanderbilt University.

Hollander, E. (1998). Picturing the engaged campus. Providence, RI: Campus Compact.

Jacoby, B., & Associates. (Eds.). (1996). *Service-learning in higher education: Concepts and practices.* San Francisco: Jossey-Bass.

Kendall, J. C. & Associates (1990). *Combining service with learning: A resource book for community and public service* (Vols. 1–3). Raleigh, NC: National Society for Internships and Experiential Education. (See especially Ivan Illich, "To hell with good intentions," and Nadinne Cruz, "A challenge to the notion of service," in Vol. 1.)

Langseth, M., Plaut, J., & Berger, J. (1999). *From charity to change: Model campus–community collaborations from Minnesota and the nation.* Minneapolis, MN: Minnesota Campus Compact.

Langseth, M., & Troppe, M. (1997, Spring). So what? Does service-learning really foster social change? *Expanding boundaries: Building civic responsibility within higher education, 2,* 37–42.

Magolda, M. B. B. (1997, November/December). Facilitating meaningful dialogues about race. *About Campus,* 14–18.

McKnight, J. (1989, January/February). Why servanthood is bad. *The Other Side, 25,* 38–41.

McKnight, J. (1995). *The careless society: Community and its counterfeits.* New York: Basic Books.

Morton, K. (1995). The irony of service: Charity, project and social change in service-learning. *Michigan Journal of Community Service-Learning, 2,* 19–32.

Schneider, J. A. (1996, Fall). Intergroup relations in the United States: Some basic concepts. *NSEE Quarterly, 4–5,* 28–29.

Schneider, J. A. (1996, Winter). Intergroup relations in the United States: Components of interaction. *NSEE Quarterly, 8–9,* 26–27.

15

Strengthening Multicultural Education With Community-Based Service Learning

Christine E. Sleeter
California State University Monterey Bay

The following examples of poor attempts at multicultural teaching may be familiar to multicultural teacher educators.

- A second-grade teacher laments the lack of interest parents of her students seem to have in education. "They just won't help out at home," she says, "They have this belief that education is only the school's job and that they don't have to help out. They don't come in for conferences, they don't read to their kids at home—they just don't seem to care!"
- The principal of an elementary school is struggling with community desires that the school's curriculum be more multicultural. He decides to respond by organizing a cultural fair in conjunction with Cinco de Mayo. He is puzzled when an African-American teacher comments that having a fair might be fun, but doing so is pretty irrelevant.
- A White preservice teacher grumbles that course work in multicultural education is a waste of time. Her mother is a teacher, and has told her that teachers don't need that kind of course work. One of her assignments is to develop a set of multicultural lesson plans. She wants to pass the course, so she turns in lesson plans she developed for a science methods course, sprinkling the word "culture" here and

there (for example, Discuss how different cultures use water), without addressing the idea of culture in any substantive way.

Most educators find it quite hard to acknowledge that we rarely understand a community to which we do not belong as well as we might believe that we do. At the same time, many teachers assume they know their students well because they see them in the classroom everyday. Further, many teachers assume they can create multicultural curriculum simply by adding in what they believe to be true and relevant about "other" cultures.

Multicultural education means reforming schools to address culture, difference, and power. A problem in doing this is getting adults to realize that, well educated as they might be, what they know about culture, difference, and power probably incorporates stereotypes and ignorance to a far greater degree than they are aware. And for preservice teacher education students, these are not simply concepts one can learn from a book or from sitting in a class. Although texts help immensely in making sense of experiential learning, texts alone do not provide the real-world grounding for multicultural education. I was certified to teach in a program that required us to live in the community and spend some time getting to know it. I ended up taking that very seriously, living in an inner-city, racially mixed, working-class neighborhood through most of my public school teaching career. In the process, I spent a good deal of time relearning culture, community, and race relations through African-American friends.

As a teacher educator, having worked with teacher education students for about 15 years, the most profound course-based learning experiences my students have told me about have involved them working in community centers as part of a course. Not all students have had profound learning experiences in the community, but a great many have, and they have learned more in the community than in any other experience I have ever engaged them in.

It is the combined experiences of my students and myself that have led me to see community-based learning as an essential part of multicultural teacher education. In this chapter, I argue that community-based learning is essential to multicultural education. When it is guided carefully, such learning can provide the experiential basis for constructing a view of children and their families that recognizes their strengths, and that situates community problems within a larger network of power relations. This view affirms the worth of diverse communities and cultures, and directs us toward challenging institutional discrimination in schools and local communities.

SERVICE LEARNING, COMMUNITY-BASED
LEARNING, AND CONCEPTIONS OF POWER

Community-based learning experiences are increasingly being considered for inclusion in teacher preparation programs as a part of preparation for cultural diversity (e.g., Kahne & Westheimer, 1996; Tellez, Hlebowitsh, Cohen, & Norwood, 1995; Wade, 1995). Service learning, which is becoming more popular in schools and on university campuses, can be viewed as a form of community-based learning. Service learning is

> a credit-bearing educational experience in which students participate in an organized service activity that meets identified community needs and reflect on the service activity in such a way as to gain further understanding of course content, a broader appreciation of the discipline, and an enhanced sense of civic responsibility (Bringle & Hatcher, 1996, p. 222).

I began using service learning without knowing it had a name and a body of practice and literature. In an effort to help my preservice students become acquainted with the communities children come from, years ago I began to organize field placements in community centers that were culturally different from the preservice student. I favored grassroots community centers, because working there as a volunteer gave the student a role and a reason for being in the community; I knew several community center directors who were trying to develop working relationships with schools and welcomed volunteers who were training to be teachers; and community centers staffed by people from the community being served were excellent sites for learning "insider" perspectives on the community, its needs and assets. Through this form of community-based learning, I attempted to construct for my students, on a small scale, the kind of learning that had affected me very deeply.

Multicultural education must rest on an assets model of children and their communities, rather than on a deficit model. Preparing teachers for multicultural education means challenging the worldview that a great number of them bring. Table 15.1 illustrates this challenge.

From a mainstream perspective, the social system is open to anyone who has ability and tries. Although people do not always get what they work for, those who adhere to a mainstream perspective believe that most of the time our efforts pay off, and membership in ascribed groups no longer structures opportunity significantly. This is the per-

TABLE 15.1
Two Worldviews

	Mainstream Perspective	Multicultural Perspective
Nature of Society	fair, open, best system, works reasonably well for everyone	rigged in favor of "haves," Whites, people with money
Nature of "have not" groups	lack education, morals, values, organized communities, supportive families, language, interest in working hard, etc.	strong, resourceful, culture is source of strength and resilience

spective that schools teach, and one that resonates with the life experiences of most people who are White, middle class, and/or whose families have gained social mobility. If one believes that society is open and fair, how does one understand the nature of "have nots"? The mainstream perspective tends to frame those who are not succeeding in terms of what they lack. When applied to historically marginalized ethnic and racial groups and to people who are poor, this framing fits common stereotypes. If one adheres to a mainstream perspective, one might try to see diversity positively, but one still needs a way of understanding the social stratification system that is evident and obvious. The deficiency perspective, supported by stereotypes, provides an understanding. Well-meaning people who adhere to this perspective believe that what needs to be changed is the culture of "disadvantaged" groups.

A multicultural perspective makes a different set of assumptions. The social system, rather than being fair and open, is run by those with power, who have rigged the system in their favor, historically as well as today. Institutional discrimination is the result, and this is what needs to be changed. Oppressed groups should be understood in terms of cultural and community strengths and resources. This does not mean that there are no problems within the group that may also need to be addressed. But the community and its culture have served the group as a source of memory, strength, and resilience, and need to be understood as assets on which to build rather than as problems to fix.

Community-based learning, when carefully structured, can provide a context for learning a multicultural perspective. Service learning provides pedagogical guidance that facilitates community-based learning. The concept of "service," however, is problematic. On the one hand, engaging in service to one's own community can be regarded as a form of community empowerment. Youth and adults in many communities of color learn to "give back" to the community by helping out in various ways, such as tutoring children or volunteering in church. Community center directors often depend on volunteers to help make things possible for youth (McLaughlin, Irby, & Langman, 1994).

On the other hand, the notion of service fits within the mainstream perspective, and can reinforce the idea that a subordinate culture needs to be fixed rather than understood as a source of strength. Service can also mean performing charity work, and in that regard, can be quite paternalistic.

> Do-gooders who come to an inner-city youth organization intending to "fix" or change the youth who gather there send all too familiar negative messages to youth about their worth. . . . Volunteers who consciously or unconsciously belittle youth's families, personal circumstances, and cultural backgrounds demean the very youth they intend to benefit. (McLaughlin et al., 1994, p. 156)

Whether one calls community-based learning "service learning" or not, the problem of outsiders trying to fix the community in a paternalistic manner is very real. I usually do not use the term service for this reason, although whether one uses that term or not, the problem of looking at other people's communities from a deficit perspective is still there. For those going into teaching, this problem is very widespread; community-based learning does not cause this problem, but is only a context in which it is manifest. But community-based service learning has the potential to challenge the deficit perspective more powerfully than school field placements. The remainder of this chapter explains why.

CULTURALLY RELEVANT TEACHING

Successful teachers know how to make their teaching culturally and linguistically relevant to their students, and in order to do that, they are familiar with the cultural and linguistic backgrounds of their students. They can "read" students' behavior correctly, adapt to students appropriately, and connect instruction effectively with what students know and can do. There is wide agreement about this idea among educators who have worked successfully with, or conducted research on, children of color and language minority children (e.g., Au, 1980; Garcia, 1988; Gay, 1994; Hollins, 1996; Ladson-Billings, 1995; May, 1994; Shade, 1989; Trueba, 1989).

For example, Trueba (1989) explained that learning is a highly social process, and teachers who teach effectively are able to engage children in their "zone of proximal development," which refers to the range of knowledge and experiences that connect to what students already know, but merge into what students do not know. This is the range where students are learning, understanding, and remembering. Based on a study of Asian immigrant children, Kiang (1995) identified several important strengths the children brought to school. They included

> homeland reference points, critical thinking skills, well-tested survival strategies, resilience, maturity, discipline, motivation to succeed based on family duty, deep desires for peace and healing, bilingual and bicultural skills, recognition of the importance of voice, dynamic views of identity and changing gender roles, and collectively minority group awareness. Schools cannot afford to let these strengths go untapped and unrecognized. (p. 220)

Although teachers can get a sense of what their students do not know by working with them in the classroom, the classroom is not necessarily the best place to get a sense of what they do know. In classrooms, teachers see children reacting to a context that was organized by professional educators who may or may not be familiar with the community from which the children come. For example, teachers have images of the proper way children should convey respect and enthusiasm in the classroom. Children that respond too assertively come to be defined as behavior problems; children who respond too passively are often ignored.

Language minority students often have much better language and reading skills in their own language than they do in English, and teachers who are only able to judge their skills on school tasks in English may severely misjudge their academic skills and abilities. In a study of elementary Spanish-speaking children in English-speaking classrooms, Diaz, Moll, and Mehan (1992) found that the teachers underestimated students' cognitive and literacy skills by as much as three grade levels when focusing only on what the students were able to do in English. Students in impoverished communities sometimes have aspirations and academic resources of which teachers are unaware. For example, Taylor and Dorsey-Gaines (1988) found that children with whom they worked, who lived in a very poor neighborhood, used literacy in their everyday lives to a far greater degree than their teachers were aware. Further, some of their parents had much higher academic aspirations for their children than teachers realized. As a result, classroom work was boring and "dumbed down," but teachers were unaware that children's uninspired class performance was due to the dullness of the class work more than to the literacy abilities of the children.

When children enter classrooms, most teachers think of them as individuals, entering with complex psychologies that comprise their individual make-up (their interests, capabilities, temperaments, aptitudes). A good many teachers simply do not think of them as bringing cultural resources from their communities, or as having community-based identities that serve as sources of strength and power. When children behave and learn as we intend, teachers often attribute this to children's individual aptitude or to their parents' capability or interest in schooling. When they do not learn, or behave in ways that we do not intend, teachers attribute this to lack of aptitude, an unruly temperament, and/or their parents' failure to cultivate "proper" behavior. If one is learning multicultural teaching only in classrooms, one may never understand the cultural context within which the children's classroom behavior makes sense. Instead, one commonly learns to interpret their behavior through lenses of the dominant society.

In community settings, teachers and preservice students see children in culturally relevant contexts. For example, several of my students had field placements in a local Boys and Girls Club. There, they worked with children who had an amazing ability to attend to multiple conversations simultaneously. My students, accustomed to listening to just one speaker at a time, were surprised. We discussed this interaction pattern in terms of how it is manifested in classrooms. My students came to realize that they had assumed that the classroom rule of one speaker at a time always helps everyone. At the Boys and Girls Club, however, they realized that this rule did not necessarily always fit. It might help the teacher, but it may also lead the teacher to become frustrated with students' talking, and to refer children for disciplinary action on the assumption that they are being rude when they may simply be engaging in familiar interaction patterns.

Another student, working in a different community center, interacted with parents who came with their children while they received help on homework after school. This student was surprised to hear the African-American low-income parents talk repeatedly about school. The parents were clearly interested in how their children were doing in school, and were often critical of poor teaching they thought might be occurring. Over the semester, her understanding of the parents' aspirations for their children was revised significantly upward, and her inclination to work with parents grew.

Some of my students have discovered skills and abilities children use in church, in community centers, or at home that suggest a higher level of responsibility, as well as cognitive knowledge and/or linguistic skills, than the children display in classrooms. By building academic material on what children do know and can do, teachers can engage children much more effectively in academic learning.

Further, community-based learning is a full-bodied, emotional learning experience. In schools and universities, we think that we attend to the mind and our bodies are irrelevant; but that idea only obscures feelings and reactions that are connected with our physical selves. Feelings about people we encounter in the flesh, whether acknowledged or not, shape much of how we interpret and deal with each other. As Ng (1998) argued, unequal power relations are inscribed in our bodies.

> All intellectual encounters are exercised through confrontations of bodies, which are differently inscribed. . . . Each time I stand in front of a classroom I embody the historical sexualization and racialization of an oriental female, even as my class privilege, formal authority and qualification ameliorate some of the effects of this signification. (p. 2)

When a preservice student becomes a minority in the context of adults from a background different from hers or his, the student must contend with a range of emotions. Commonly these emotions initially are fear and apprehension; they may also include disrespect and paternalism. If the student stays in the setting long enough to get beyond the fear, and long enough to get to know people, there is a chance that the student will be able to learn from them, and to develop a willingness to work with them in the future, when he or she becomes a classroom teacher.

COMMUNITY STRENGTHS AND RESOURCES

Successful teachers are able to recognize and work with strengths and resources of the community. Doing this requires an ability to see other people's communities in terms of their strengths and assets rather than their problems.

Haymes (1995), for example, analyzed how Whites tend to think about urban life. For many Whites, the city is a racialized metaphor that defines blackness as "the urban Other, the disordered and the dangerous" (p. 4). If one views the community from which one's students come as other, as disordered, as dangerous, then one views one's role as a teacher either as hopeless, or as attempting to save the children from the effects of their neighborhood and its culture. Policies of suburbanization and urban renewal (i.e., ridding a neighborhood of its poorest residents) stem from this view. As an alternative, Haymes argued that the city can be seen as a "homeplace" in which "blacks have been able to construct alternative identities and relationships based on ties of friendship, family, history, and place" (p. 112). African-American neighborhoods can be understood as places where people care for each other, give each other strength, share historical memories, and develop survival strategies. When one sees a community in terms of its strengths, one is able to identify children's roots and the soil in which they will flourish.

Several years ago, a community center director recommended developing a "community day" for teachers with whom I was working, to orient them to community resources. He was concerned that he and his staff work with the same children the teachers taught, and that they could provide various forms of help and support of which the teachers seemed unaware. The day included visits to two community centers, and discussions with several community center and organization directors. We focused primarily on organizations serving low-income African-American and Latino children and youth.

In a discussion, it became evident that most of the teachers did not know who these community leaders were, or how much impact they had on kids. When the teachers were asked to name the leaders of a particular Latino neighborhood, for example, their guesses were incorrect. We realized that many of them had never talked with adults in the community other than parents of children in their classes. Most of them had no idea there were adults who wanted to collaborate with them; most assumed that these communities, being poor, lacked helpful human resources.

Viewing communities in terms of strengths and resources is fundamental to community development, and to working constructively with families and other support systems. Kretzman and McKnight (1993) contrasted the "needs-driven" view of communities with the "capacity-focused" view. In the needs-driven view, communities are seen in term of their problems, and the assumption is made that outsiders must intervene in order to meet community needs that insiders are incapable of meeting. In contrast, the capacity-focused view identifies strengths from the inside.

> For it is clear that even the poorest neighborhood is a place where individuals and organizations represent resources upon which to rebuild. The key to neighborhood regeneration, then, is to locate all of the available local assets, to begin connecting them with one another in ways that multiply their powers and effectiveness, and to begin harnessing those local institutions that are not yet available for local development purposes. (Kretzman & McKnight, 1993, p. 5–6)

The assets of a neighborhood can be categorized as individuals, associations, and institutions.

Community agencies are one of those institutions, and are usually staffed with individuals who are strong community assets. This is why I favor having my students spend time there. McLaughlin et al. (1994), in their study of six successful inner-city community organizations around the United States, described "wizards," who are the dedicated people who run such organizations. They wrote:

> The "it" that wizards know how to do is not a model program, but a community created by the adults associated with the program that respects the interests, attitudes, and needs of the youth themselves. Impatient with the time-worn debate about who is at fault for the plight of the inner cities and with policies based on fictions, contemptuous of perspectives rooted in culture-of-poverty assumptions that ghetto youth need to be "rehabilitated," the wizards seek autonomy and trust from the larger community so they can get on with the job of providing youth with the opportunities they need to learn a new view of the future and then move into that future. (p. 218)

When teacher education students work with wizards—and every community I have had contact with has them—learning can be profound. Students begin to learn the community from the inside, through the eyes of people who know its problems and who recognize and believe in the community's strengths and capacities.

POLITICAL AND ECONOMIC CONTEXT

Multicultural education should mean teaching for social justice—recognizing both interpersonal and institutional injustices, and addressing these through the process of education. As Greene (1998) put it:

> Opened . . . to what the suffering of others may mean, brought through active and collaborative learning to name the cause of it and the expanding consequences, students may come to see that each one's status really depends on a just order. It must be an order that extends further and further from small group to small group, from classroom to kitchen, from kitchen to a back room in a church or a hospital. . . . To teach for social justice is to teach for enhanced perception and imaginative explorations, for the recognition of social wrongs, of sufferings, of pestilences wherever and whenever they arise. (p. xlv)

Teachers of multicultural education and social justice are able to place the community in a larger political and economic context that locates many of the problems people experience in terms of lack of access to economic and political resources, rather than lack of ability or motivation. Resources for youth in poverty areas, for example, are in short supply, and this can be traced to many actions, policies, and attitudes of the dominant society, such as cutting public funding for social services and education, moving jobs out of inner cities, redlining, suburbanization, and so forth.

Teachers often use culture incorrectly to explain problems that have structural roots. For example, impoverished communities often experience high crime rates, as people attempt to survive in an absence of enough jobs to support people. But teachers often describe such communities in cultural terms, to the exclusion of economic terms. One hears about the culture of poverty, or culture of violence in inner cities, and think tanks are convened to develop solutions to these cultural problems. Missing from such discussions very often is a direct analysis of the loss of jobs. Whereas residents of impoverished communities may be well aware that their problems have an economic basis, people who live outside the community attribute problems to the cultures and lifestyles of inner-city dwellers.

Aronowitz (1997) argued that the United States has never had a significant discourse about social class, and as a result, we frame many class problems in ethnic and cultural terms. He argued:

> that there are fewer Black men working than are unemployed in the cities—Black male unemployment in the cities had reached 58% by 1996—is not primarily a function of the deficits of Black culture, such as the absence of a two-parent household, lack of skills, or the absence of cultural values such as adherence to family and work as desirable states of being. The "lack" is one of jobs. (p. 197)

Through spending time in community-based organizations, especially those that are grass-roots operated, teachers can gain a sense of how institutionalized racism and poverty work. For example, one of my White teacher education students was assigned to help an African-American organization with their computer systems. When this student began, he told me later, he assumed that African-American culture is not technologically oriented, which is why inner-city kids do not seem to have good computer skills. After working in the organization, he realized that the problem was lack of access to economic and technological resources. He discovered that the staff was very interested in technology and some staff were knowledgeable about what kinds of equipment the center should have, but the center simply could not afford to buy new equipment, and had to manage as best they could with the resources they had.

When power relations are considered, culture becomes not just something passed down from one generation to the next, but also everyday ways in which dominant groups impose or maintain their power, and subordinated groups cope with, survive, and resist subordination. In the example of computers in the community organization, the local African-American community culture did not include a high level of technological sophistication, but this was due to lack of economic resources rather than to a lack of interest. The dominant society builds structures such as the information superhighway that are well connected to some communities and that virtually ignore or bypass others. The people who live in these different communities create lives and cultures around the resources to which they have access. Access and power, then, become key issues that one can see, if one is in the community and is being helped to focus on structural roots of its problems.

CONCLUSION

Knowledge rests on both experience and interpretive frameworks. Universities specialize in providing students with interpretive frameworks, but not with experience off-campus. For multicultural teaching, experience in communities other than our own, and help in interpreting that experience from an "insider's" point of view and from a critical point of view, is essential. Service learning, when connected with multicultural education course work, can provide such a learning experience.

As a multicultural education teacher, I have found service learning to be an essential part of teacher education for multicultural education. This volume attempts to show why multicultural education and service learning should be connected, and how to connect them in ways that work. In this chapter, I have explained why this makes sense. I must conclude, however, by acknowledging that many people do not see the connection. I have yet to work in a teacher education program in which community-based service learning is institutionalized as a part of the teacher education program, and explicitly connected with multicultural education. Teacher educators see value in classroom field experiences, but far less value in community placements. Yet, it is teachers' perceptions of the communities children come from that shape a good deal of what happens in the classroom. Perhaps service learning could be of as much benefit to teacher educators as it is to teacher education students.

REFERENCES

Aronowitz, S. (1997). Between nationality and class. *Harvard Educational Review*, 67(2), 188–207.

Au, K. H. (1980). Participation structures in a reading lesson with Hawaiian children: Analysis of a culturally appropriate instructional event. *Anthropology and Education*, 11(2), 91–115.

Bringle, R. B., & Hatcher, J. A. (1996). Implementing service learning in higher education. *Journal of Higher Education*, 67(2), 221–239.

Diaz, S., Moll, L. C., & Mehan, H. (1992). Sociocultural resources in instruction: A context-specific approach. In Bilingual Education Office, California State Department of Education (Ed.), *Beyond language: Social and cultural factors in schooling language minority students* (pp. 187–230). Los Angeles, CA: CSU Los Angeles.

Garcia, E. (1988). Effective schooling for Hispanics. *Urban Education Review*, 67(2), 462–473.

Gay, G. (1994). *At the essence of learning: Multicultural education*. West Lafayette, IN: Kapp(a De)lta Pi, Inc.

Greene, M. (1998). Introduction: Teaching for social justice. In W. Ayres, J. A. Hunt, & T. Quinn (Eds.), *Teaching for social justice* (pp. xxvii–xlvi). New York: Teachers College Press.

Haymes, S. N. (1995). *Race, culture and the city*. Albany, NY: State University of New York Press.

Hollins, E. R. (1996). *Culture in school learning: Revealing the deep meaning*. Mahwah, NJ: Lawrence Erlbaum Associates.

Kahne, J., & Westheimer, J. (1996). In service of what? The politics of service learning. *Phi Delta Kappan*, 77(9), 592–598.

Kiang, P. N. (1995). Bicultural strengths and struggles of Southeast Asian Americans in school. In A. Darder (Ed.), *Culture and difference* (pp. 201–226). Westport, CT: Bergin & Garvey.

Kretzman, J. P., & McKnight, J. L. (1993). *Building communities from the inside out*. Evanston, IL: Center for Urban Affairs and Policy Research, Neighborhood Innovations Network, Northwestern University.

Ladson-Billings, G. (1995). Toward a theory of culturally relevant pedagogy. *American Educational Research Journal*, 32(3), 465–492.

McLaughlin, M. W., Irby, M. A., & Langman, J. (1994). *Urban sanctuaries: Neighborhood organizations in the lives and futures of inner-city youth*. San Francisco: Jossey-Bass.

May, S. (1994). *Making multicultural education work*. Philadelphia: Multilingual Matters, Ltd.

Ng, R. (1998, April). *Is embodied teaching and learning critical pedagogy?* Paper presented at the American Educational Research Association, San Diego, CA.

Shade, B. J. R. (1989). *Culture, style, and the educative process*. Springfield, IL: Thomas.

Taylor, D., & Dorsey-Gaines, C. (1988). *Growing up literate: Learning from inner-city families*. Portsmouth, NH: Heinemann.

Tellez, K., Hlebowitsh, P. S., Cohen, M., & Norwood, P. (1995). Social service field experiences and teacher education. In J. Larkin & C. E. Sleeter (Eds.), *Developing multicultural teacher education curricula* (pp. 65–78). Albany, NY: State University of New York Press.

Trueba, H. T. (1989). *Raising silent voices: Educating the linguistic minorities for the 21st century.* San Francisco: Newbury House.

Wade, R. (1995). Developing active citizens: Community service learning in social studies teacher education. *Social Studies, 86,* 122–129

Afterword

Carolyn R. O'Grady
Gustavus Adolphus College

Can higher education successfully incorporate and integrate multicultural education and service learning? The authors in this book share an optimism that it may be possible, while understanding the obstacles that reinforce the status quo in colleges and universities. The academy is an essentially conservative institution, and it is easy for those who work within it to become cautious and even disillusioned. Institutional norms, including the faculty review and reward system, the hierarchical nature of power between professor and student, and the emphasis on cognitive knowledge as preeminent, may limit the kinds of risks faculty are willing to take in their teaching or advocacy for educational change. The traditional distance the academy has had from the larger community of which it is a part can reinforce the isolation faculty may feel from the real-world context of their work. As Rob Shumer noted, the institutional framework of higher education places the academy, not the community, at the center, and consequently reinforces the notion that power is held only by the academy. Shumer said, "The curriculum does not reflect reality. We need to understand better that we're all part of the community. The old notion that universities should be separate, that the definition of academic is theoretical, not practical, value—we need to challenge those notions" (as quoted in Stanton, Giles, & Cruz, 1999, pp. 224–225).

We must not forget Palmer's (1990) reminder that community is essentially about relatedness. It is this belief in our connectedness to

277

others that enables us to develop meaningful relationships across sociocultural barriers and to feel that we share a common value and a common destiny. Holding to this belief is not always easy; indeed, it demands courage to move beyond our fears and our engrained assumptions about others. Often, it is an act of will to hold to a relational perspective when much of the world around us seems determined to reinforce individualism. But it is the high value we place on our connectedness with others that prompts us to take action for social justice. As LeSourd (1997) said:

> To suffuse a service ethic in a pluralistic nation, relationships must have the power to teach people to place genuine value upon the worth of each human being, extend moral consideration to all groups, and determine to act in the interest of others. (p. 158)

We may not always be successful in this work, but we must hold a long-term view of change. Dwight Giles described it as "transcendent hope" against all odds (as cited in Stanton et al., 1999, p. 179), and Helen Smith reminded us not to expect victories. She said, "Victories come, but they build on little things. You're just adding to it. Somebody else will push it further along. You do what you can under the circumstances where you are, and you don't give up" (as cited in Stanton et al., 1999, p. 180).

Those who are committed to service learning and multicultural education must take leadership in challenging the primacy of the theoretical over the experiential. Each is incomplete without the other if we wish our students to learn to be responsive to the demands of community in a diverse and democratic nation. We must advocate actively for this integration, strengthen our expertise in its practice, and continue to build a foundation for education as a vehicle for social justice. If we can imagine an integration of service learning and multicultural education that is responsive and reciprocal, then we can work to put our vision into action. As Crowell, Caine, and Caine (1998) described it, responsive learning

> is that which draws upon the interests and expressive qualities of the student; it is also that learning which takes action in the world around us. Responsive learning draws us inward to tap the originality and creativity of thought and understanding. It also draws us outward, asking us what the responsibility of our knowing is, what kind of people we will be. (p. xiii)

As responsive and committed educators, we must ask ourselves not only what kind of people *we* will be, but also what kind of people we want our *students* to become.

REFERENCES

Crowell, S., Caine, R. N., & Caine, G. (1998). *The re-enchantment of learning: A manual for teacher renewal and classroom transformation.* Tucson, AZ: Zephyr Press.

LeSourd, S. J. (1997). Community service in a multicultural nation. *Theory Into Practice, 36,* 157–163.

Palmer, P. (1990). Community, conflict and ways of knowing: Ways to deepen our educational agenda. In J. C. Kendall & Associates (Eds.), *Combining service and learning: A resource book for community and public service* (Vol. 1, pp. 105–113). Raleigh, NC: National Society for Internships and Experiential Education.

Stanton, T. K., Giles, D. E., Jr., & Cruz, N. I. (1999). *Service-learning: A movement's pioneers reflect on its origins, practice and future.* San Francisco: Jossey-Bass.

Author Index

A

Abramson, T., 229, *242*
Adams, M., 3, *16*, 116, 123, 125, 126, *133*
Addams, J., 71, *90*
Aguilera, D., 209, *226*
Albom, M., 160, *166*
Alexander, Z., 115, *134*
Allport, G., 63, *68*
Amanti, C., 234, *242*
Amir, Y., 63, 65, *68*
Anaya, R., 136, *150*
Andersen, M., 165, *166*
Anderson, J. A., 99, *111*
Anderson, J. B., 12, *16*
Aparicio, F. R., 10, *16*
Arias, A. A., 117, *134*
Aronowitz, S., *275*
Artiles, A. J., 230, *241*
Ashburn, E., 229, *243*
Astin, A., 77, *90*, 195, 196, 197, *206*
Astin, H. S., 190, 195, 196, 197, *206*
Au, K. H., 267, *275*
Avery, P. G., 229, *241*

B

Banks, C. A. M., 229, *241*
Banks, J. A., 4, *16*, 53, *57*, 229, 231, *241*
Barber, B., 8, *16*, 47, 49, *57*, 186, *187*
Bell, L.A., 3, *16*, 116, 123, 125, 126, *133*
Bellah, R., 48, *57*
Bennett, C. I., 190, *206*
Benz, S., 232, *241*
Berman, S., 9, 10, *16*
Berry, H. A., 12, *16*
Billingsley, R., 47, *57*
Biting, P. F., 50, *58*
Bollin, G. G., 230, *241*
Boyer, E., 8, *16*, 84, *90*
Boyle-Baise, M., 209, 211, 212, 213, 215, 218, 224, *225*
Boyte, H. C., 48, *57*
Brewer, M., 63, 64, *68*

Bringle, R. B., 265, *275*
Broker, I., 137, *150*
Brown, J., 123, *134*
Brown, M. Y., 102, 103, 104, *111*, 111, 123
Bruchac, J., 137, *150*
Bulosan, C., 154, *166*
Burgos-Debray, E., 232, *242*

C

Caine, G., 278, *279*
Caine, R. N., 278, *279*
Callan, M. J., 10, *17*, 154, *167*
Carey-Webb, A., 232, *241*
Carnoy, M., 53, *57*
Castro, V., 115, *134*
Cazden, C., 231, *242*
Chance, W., 117, *134*
Chappell, B., 2, *18*, 210, *226*
Chesler, M., 153, *167*, 201, *206*
Cohen, M., 12, *19*, 71, *91*, 209, *226*, 265, *275*
Collins, P., 165, *166*
Connolly, W. E., 116, *134*
Conrad, D., 8, *16*, 251, *261*
Cook, S., 63, 65, *69*
Cordova, F., 154, *167*
Cornwell, G. H., 10, *17*, 232, 233, *242*
Counts, G., 51, *57*
Couturie, B., *150*
Covey, M., 60, *69*
Crowell, S., 278, *279*
Cruz, N., 6, 10, *16*, 210, 225, 277, 278, *279*
Cummins, J., 231, *242*

D

Dahms, A. M., 15, *16*
Daloz, L. A., 104, 105, 110, *111*
Darling-Hammond, L., 74, *90*
de Niro, R., *150*
DeJong, L., 209, *225*

Delgado-Gaitan, C., 233, *242*
Delve, C., 8, 10, *16*, 60, *69*
Densmore, K., 5, 15, *16*
DeVoogd, G., 230, *242*
Dewey, J., 49, 51, *57*, 59, *69*, 172, *187*, 202, *206*
Diaz, S., 268, *275*
Dixon-Krauss, L., 231, *242*
Dorsey-Gaines, C., 268, *275*
Dunlap, M., 209, 224, *225*
Dunn, S. J., 127, *134*

E

Eads, S. E., 47, *57*
Edelman, M. W., 101, *111*
Eisler, R., 147, *150*
Elstain, Jean Bethke, 179, *187*
Erickson, J. B., 99, *111*
Etzioni, A., 47, 48, *58*
Eyler, J., 6, 8, 10, 14, *17*, 61, *69*, 124, *134*, 203, 204, 251, *261*

F

Floyd-Tierney, M., 234, *242*
Fox, H., 10
Fox, M., 148, *151*
Franklin, W., 119, *134*
Freire, P., 24, 28, 30, 31, 32, 33, 34, 35, 36, 37, 38, 39, *43*, 148, *151*, 153, 159, 166, *167*, *187*, 231, *242*
Fuller, M., 209, *226*
Fusco, J., *150*

G

Galura, J., 7, 10, *17*, 154, *167*
Garcia, E., *275*
Garcia, J., 6, *18*, 267
Gardner, J. W., 189, *206*
Garrison, T. C., 115, *134*
Garza, C. L., 139, *151*
Gay, G., 2, 14, *17*, 53, *58*, 267, *275*
Gere, A. R., 76, *91*
Giles, D. E., Jr., 6, 8, 14, *17*, 60, 61, *69*, 124, *134*, 203, 204, 251, *261*, 277, 278, *279*
Gillese, E., 80, 81, *91*
Giroux, H. A., 231, *242*
Glaser, B., 211, *226*
Gonzales, N., 234, *242*

Gonzales, R., 234, *242*
Goodlad, J. I., 80, *90*
Goodwin, L. A., 229, *242*
Grant, C. A., 4, 5, 6, 11, *17*, *19*, 53, *58*, 118, *134*, 148, *151*, 190, *207*
Greene, M., 272, *275*
Greenleaf, R., 204, *207*
Greenwald, A., 65, 66, *69*
Griffin, P., 3, *16*, 116, 123, 125, 126, *133*
Grillo, M., *151*
Groomes, F., 209, *225*
Guadarrama, I. N., 230, *242*
Guarasci, R., 9, 10, *17*, *187*, 187, 232, *242*
Guest, K., 12, *16*
Gugerty, C. R., 252, *261*
Gundara, J., 55, *58*

H

Haberman, M., 229, *242*
Hall, M., 10, *17*
Hammond, C., 8, *17*
Harris, V., 137, *151*
Hatcher, J. A., 265, *275*
Haymes, S. N., 270, *275*
Hedin, D., 8, *16*, 251, *261*
Helms, J., 224, *226*
Herzberg, B., 76, *90*
Hesser, G. W., 10, *18*, 60, 61, 62, 65, *69*, *261*
Hlebowitsh, P. S., 12, *19*, 71, *91*, 209, *226*, 265, *275*
Hollins, E. R., 267, *275*
Hones, D., *207*, 209, *226*
Honnet, E., 60, *69*
hooks, b., 162, *167*
Hoppe, M. H., 193, *207*
Horton, M., 9, *17*, 153, *167*, 249, *261*
Hovland, C., 65, *69*
Howard, J., 7, 10, *17*, 154, *167*
Humphreys, H. C., 78, *90*

I

Irby, M. A., 267, 272, *275*

J

Jacoby, B., 10, 11, *17*, 24, 27, *43*
Johnson, D., 64, *69*
Johnson, R., 64, *69*
Jose-Kampfner, C., 10, *16*

K

Kaestle, C. F., 52, *58*
Kahan, D., 85, *90*
Kahne, J., 51, 52, *58*, 97, *111*, 265, *275*
Kasdan, L., *151*
Katz, W. L., 144, *151*
Katznelson, I., 52, *58*
Keen, C. H., 104, 105, 110, *111*
Keen, J. P., 104, 105, 110, *111*
Keeton, M., 212, *226*
Kendall, J. C., 7, 8, 10, 14, *17*, 24, 25, 26, 43, 62, *69*
Kiang, P. N., 268, *275*
Kilpatrick, W. H., 49, 51, *58*
Kinsley, C. W., 6, 7, 12, *17*, 24, 27, *43*
Kitano, H., 147, *151*
Kohl, H., 249, *261*
Kohl, J., 249, *261*
Kolb, D., 60, *69*, *134*
Koppelman, D. J., 88, *91*
Kottack, C., 164, *167*
Koulish, R., 169, 171, 182, *187*
Kouzes, J. M., 199, *207*
Kraft, R. J., 10, *17*
Kretzmann, J. P., 12, 13, *17*, 249, *261*, 271, *275*
Kromer, T., 99, *111*

L

La Belle, T. J., 45, 53, *58*
Ladson-Billings, G., 267, *275*
Langman, J., 267, 272, *275*
Lankshear, C., 231, *242*
Lazerson, M., 52, *58*
LeCompte, M. D., 209, *226*
Lennon, M., 80, 81, *91*
LeSourd, S. J., 278, *279*
Levin, H. M., 53, *57*
Levison, L. M., 12, *18*, 61, *69*
Limerick, P., 147, *151*
Lipka, R. P., 81, *91*
London-Vargas, N., 197, *207*
Lott, C. E., 77, *91*
Lucas, C. J., 171, *187*

M

Macy, J., 102, 103, 104, *111*, 111
Madsen, R., 48, *57*
Mahan, J. M., 105, *111*
Martínez, E. S., 230, *242*

Massengale, T., 260, *261*
May, S., 54, *58*, 267, *275*
Mayer-Smith, J., 229, 230, *243*
McCarthy, C., 53, *58*
McIntosh, P., 146, *151*
McIntyre, A., 130, *134*
McKnight, J. L., 12, 13, *17*, 249, *261*, 271, *275*
McLaren, P., 231, *242*
McLaughlin, M. W., 267, 272, *275*
McPherson, K., 6, 7, 12, *17*, 24, 27, *43*Mehan, H., 268, *275*

Meiland, R., 10, *17*, 154, *167*
Menchú, R., 232, *242*
Mercer, J., *150*
Mercer, P., 80, 81, *91*
Michalec, P., 6, *18*
Michelmore, C. W., 77, *91*
Miller, J., 8, *18*
Miller, N., 63, *68*
Mintz, S., 8, 10, *16*, 60, 61, 62, 65, *69*, *261*
Moll, L., 234, *242*, 268, *275*
Montero-Sieburth, M., 5, *18*
Moon, B., 229, 230, *243*
Morgan, G., 3, 4, 11, *18*
Morton, K., 24, 26, 27, *43*
Mulling, C., 252, *261*
Mun Wah, L., 146, *151*
Murray, H., 80, 81, 83, *91*

N

Napier, A., 165, *167*
Newman, F., 189, *207*
Ng, R., 270, *275*
Nieto, S., 2, 5, *18*
Norwood, P., 12, *19*, 71, *91*, 209, *226*, 265, *275*

O

O'Connell, W. R., Jr., 6, *18*
O'Grady, C. R., 1, 2, *18*, 209, 210, *226*
Okun, C., *151*

P

Pacheco, S., 115, *134*
Palmer, P., 9, *18*, 166, *167*, 212, *226*, 277, *279*
Parks, S. D., 105, 110, *111*
Patterson, L., 230, *242*

Peck, M., 160, *167*
Pettigrew, T., 63, *69*
Pflaum, S. W., 229, *242*
Pickeral, T., 99, *111*
Pitnick, R., 119, *134*
Pollack, S., 115, 116, *134*
Porter Honnet, E., 196, *207*
Posner, B. Z., 199, *207*
Poulsen, S., 60, *69*, 196, *207*
Powell, R. R., 6, *18*
Pratt, M. L., 232, *242*
Putnam, R. D., 186, *187*

R

Radest, H., 209, 212, *226*
Rahm, J., 209, *226*
Reardon, K. M., 11, 12, *18*
Rendon, P., 234, *242*
Rhoads, R. A., 9, 10, 11, *18*, 24, 25, 26, 27, *43*, 209, 212, *226*
Rice, K., 115, 123, *134*
Rickards, W. H., 229, *242*
Rifkin, J., 48, *58*
Rimmerman, C., 179, *187*
Rivera, A., 234, *242*
Roberts-Weah, W., 10, *18*
Robinson, M., 80, 81, *91*
Rockwood, V., 49, *58*
Root, M., 154, *167*
Rosenthal, J., *150*
Ross, R., 7, 10, *17*, 154, *167*
Rothbart, M., 63, 65, *69*
Rushdie, S., 170, *187*

S

Salinas, M. C., 115, *134*
Sanford, N., 163, *167*
Satir, V., 165, *167*
Scales, P. C., 88, *91*
Scheckley, B., 212, *226*
Schmidt, S. L., 127, *134*
Schmiede, A., 124, *134*, 203, 204
Schorr, L. B., 203, *207*
Schutz, A., 76, *91*
Seigel, S., 49, *58*
Serow, R. C., 50, *58*
Shade, B. J. R., 267, *275*
Shaver, K., 65, *69*
Shirts, R. G., 125, *134*
Shor, I., 231, *242*
Sigmon, R. L., 24, 26, *43*, 60, 65, *69*
Silcox, H., 8, *18*

Sirotnik, K., 80, *90*
Slade, A. M., 115, *134*
Sleeter, C., 3, 4, 5, 6, 11, 12, 15, *19*, 53, 58, 118, *134*, 148, *151*, 190, 207, 209, 212, 215, 218, 220, 225, 226
Smith, M. W., 8, 10, *19*
Smith, R., 10, *17*, 154, *167*
Soder, R., 80, *90*
Soltis, J., 80, *91*
Some, M., 158, 159, *167*
Spring, J., 6, *19*, 52, 53, *58*
Stanton, T., 6, 8, 10, *19*, 61, *70*, 204, *207*, 277, 278, *279*
Stephens, L. S., 7, 10, *19*
Stewart, G., 8, 10, *16*, 60, *69*
Strauss, A., 211, *226*
Strike, K., 80, *91*
Sullivan-Cosetti, M., 77, *91*
Sullivan, W., 48, *57*
Swadener, M., 10, *17*
Swezey, E. D., 252, *261*
Swidler, A., 48, *57*

T

Takaki, R., 52, *58*, 154, 157, 160, *167*
Tate, W. F., 6, *17*
Taylor, D., 268, *275*
Taylor, M., 137, *151*, 268
Téllez, K., 12, *19*, 71, *91*, 209, *226*, 265, 275
Thich Nhat Hanh, 93, *111*
Thurow, L., 171, *187*
Tipton, S., 48, *57*
Trueba, H., *242*, 267, *276*
Tyack, D., 52, 53, *58*

V

Vadenboncoeur, J., 209, *226*
Valli, L., 230, *242*
Varlotta, L., 209, *226*
Vygotsky, L., 231, *243*

W

Wade, R., 6, 7, 8, 10, *19*, 24, 25, 27, *43*, 97, 99, 105, *111*, 209, *226*, 265, 276
Waldock, J. M., 10, 12, *19*
Walker, C., 229, *241*
Ward, C., 45, 53, *58*, 81

Waterhouse, D., 7, *17*, 154, *167*
Waterman, A. S., 8, *19*, 251, *261*
Weir, M., 52, *58*
West, C., 48, *58*
Westheimer, J., 51, 52, *58*, 97, *111*, 265, *275*
Whitaker, C., 165, *167*
Wideen, M., 229, 230, *243*
wiger, f., 253, *261*
Will, G., 119, *134*
Wister, J. A., 77, *91*
Woo, M., 126, *134*
Woodridge, B., 115, *134*
Wright, A., 232, *242*

Y

Yarbrough, D. B., 99, *111*
Yolen, J., 137, *151*

Z

Zehn, S., 6, *18*
Zimpher, N., 229, *243*
Zinn, H., 160, *167*

Subject Index

A

Ableism, 130, 133
Action, as component of change, 4, 7, 26, 30–31, 52
Active learning, 8
Activism, 3, 31
Additive approach, 231
Advocacy, 98, 107, 108
Agents of change, 35–37, 41, 100
Alliance for Service-Learning in Education Reform (ASLER), 7, 27, 43, 60, 62
Ally building, 125–126
Altruism, 49, 51
American Dream, 149, 177
Anthropological perspective, 228
Anthropologists, 234–235
Antioppression ideology, 10, 16
Antiracist ideology, 10, 16
ASLER, 7, 27, 43, 60, 62
Asset-based approach, 249
Assets
    as focus of successful teachers, 270
    model of communities, 249, 265, 272
Assimilationist educational policies, 54
Assumptions. *see also* Bias; Prejudice; Stereotypes
    examination of, 121, 123, 132–133, 269
    in needs-driven view of communities, 271
    perpetuation of, 12–13, 124
Attitude change, 59–68, 81
Awareness. *see also* Reflection
    about cultural diversity, 209, 212
    of democratic citizenship, 189
    of differences between groups, 123–124, 130, 146

B

Behavior, cultural context of, 269
Benefaction, 209

Beneffectance, 66
Bentley College service learning projects, 169–187
Bentley Immigrant Assistance Program. *see* BIAP
Bentley Service Learning Center (BSLC), 169–173
Best practices of service learning, 27, 59–60, 62, 63, 251
BIAP (Bentley Immigrant Assistance Program), 169–187
    course contexts, 178–181
    literature used in curriculum, 180–181
    student enrichment through, 177, 181–184
Bias. *see also* Assumptions; Prejudice; Stereotypes
    antiworking class, 156
    cognitive, 66
    gender, 158
Bilingual. *see also* ESL
    education, 227–228, 231–232, 235–236, 268
    issues, 140, 141
BSLC (Bentley Service Learning Center), 169–173
Building relationships approach, 249

C

C-Day (Citizenship Day), 174–185
California State University Monterey Bay. *see* CSUMB
Campus Outreach Opportunity League (COOL), 60
Capacity-focused view of communities, 271
Change. *see also* Reflection; Social change agents, 35–37, 41, 100
    approaches to, 249
    in attitude, 59–68, 81
    leaders as advocates of, 255
    relationships as foundation for, 248–251

287

social, 5–7, 55–56
students feeling empowered to create, 15, 41
Charity, 25–26, 50, 51, 177, 267
Children's literature, multicultural, 136–144
Citizenship, 8, 10–11. *see also* Civic responsibility
    acquiring, 180
    active, 24, 54, 100, 186, 190, 199
    education, 232–233
    exclusion from, 52
Citizenship Day (C-Day), 174–185
Civic
    awareness, 7
    education, 49, 178–180
    engagement, 179, 180, 186
    responsibility, 7–14, 29, 47, 196, 265
Civil rights, 2–3, 149, 155
Civilian Conservation Corps (CCC), 6, 50
Class, social, 12, 164–166, 273
Classism, 116, 130, 248
Classroom
    activities, 142
    as democratic, 162–163
    Cognitive
    bias, 66
    conservatism, 66
    refencing, 65
Colearner, 63–64, 240
Collaboration, 182, 252, 258
    as advantage of PDS model, 240
    in service learning, 7–8, 12, 66, 185, 250
    as best practice, 62, 251
Commission on Community Service, 96
Common school, 52. *see also* Public school
Community, 14. *see also* Relationships between school and community
    agencies as placement site, 272
    development, 28
    education, as component of change, 106–107
    elders, service learning with, 156–166

    members, identifying needs, 37–38, 41
    needs-driven view of, 271
    partnerships, 131–132, 249, 257
    sense of, 9–12
    service, 6, 26–31, 54, 169
    strengths of, 239, 270–272
Community-based service learning, 211, 265. *see also* Service learning

Connectedness, 15, 251, 277–278. *see also* Interdependence; Relatedness
Conscientization
    definition of, 35
    of oppressed people, 29
    and problem-posing, 40–42
    in service learners, 39
Consciousness
    critical, 27–29, 166
    ethnic, rise in, 53
    raising, 232
Constructivistic perspective, 238
Contact theory (CT), 63–68
Contribution approach, 231
Coteachers, student, 128
Council for the Advancement of Standards in Higher Education for Student Leadership Programs, 198, 206
Course meta-question, 148
Critical multiculturalism, 118–119
CSUMB (California State University Monterey Bay)
    relationship with community, 117, 119
    service learning curriculum, 121–129
    challenges of, 129–132
    as graduation requirement, 115, 120
    integrated with multicultural education, 115, 132
    outcomes-based format of, 120–121
    vision statement, 117–118, 129, 132, 136
CT (Contact Theory), 63–68
Cultural
    action, 29, 31, 33
    associations, 145
    differences, as obstacle to relationships, 253
    diversity
        increased acceptance of, 54, 171–172, 212, 265
        intolerance of, 53
        service learning as first exposure to, 212, 224
    identity, 119
    lenses, 146
    screening, 212
    "Zeitgeist", 67–68
Culture. *see also* Dominant culture
    mainstream, 265–267
    subordinate, 267, 274
Curriculum
    conventional, 136, 144

cultural experiences included in,
233–235, 237
development, 202, 230
gender-balanced, 147–148
New West, 145, 147–148
social-justice oriented, 135
Cycle of socialization model, 123–124

D

Deficit model, 265–267
Democracy, 8, 28–29, 52–54
complete, 55
definition of, 45
enhanced by service learning, 9–12,
49, 77
and volunteerism, 51
Dialogic encounters (conversations), 164
Dialogue
about worldviews, 164
between faculty and student, 128
groups, 127
as requirement of engagement, 61
and service learning pedagogy, 30,
37–39, 42
between students and stakeholders,
40–41
Differences, cultural, 56, 253, 257
Disadvantaged groups, 55, 66, 266
Discrimination, 4, 124, 212
institutional, 264, 266
in literature, 108
racial, 11–12
in schooling policies, 230
Diverse
classroom, 135
communities, 136, 149, 189, 264
faculties used in BIAP, 178
groups, social interaction among, 56
Diversity
acceptance of, 209
appreciation of, 181
as best practice of service learning,
62, 171, 181, 251
and classroom dynamics, 127
cultural, 53–54, 171–172, 212, 265
reflection about, 198
Dominant
culture
interpreting behavior through
lense of, 269
reality as defined by, 163
responsible for inaccessibility of
resources, 54, 273
students prepared to adapt to,
233

tactics of prejudice and discrimination, 147
elite, 33–34
groups, 52, 123–124, 127, 133, 274
Domination, 28, 30–33, 123, 253. see
also Oppression

E

Economic resources, access to, 53–54,
272–273
Education. see also Teacher education
banking model of, 159, 163
bilingual, 227–228, 231, 235–236,
268
citizenship, 232–233
as contested territory, 2–3, 5, 11
equity in, 57
experiential nature of, 7, 51, 59–60,
205, 248
outcomes-based, 120–121
problem-posing, 38–39
traditional, 253
as vehicle for social justice, 278
vocational, 53
Education, higher. see also Public
schools; Schools
expectations for, 189
public disillusionment with, 170, 171

role of student action organizations
in, 205
vision for, 202–205
Educational
reform, 55–56, 136, 142
reformers, 54
theorists, 7, 54
Ego-defensive strategies, 65–66, 68
Egocentricity, 66
Elders and service learning, 156–166
Elitism, 45
Emic worldview, 163–164
Empowerment
community, 266–267
to create change, 15
linked with cognitive growth, 204
of student, 145, 198, 232
through service learning, 97,
227–240
English as Second Language. see ESL
Equal status contact, 64–65
ESL (English as Second Language),
174–176, 227–228, 236, 238,
268
Ethnocentrism, 144–146, 177, 181, 252
Ethnographic

data, 239
perspective, 233
research, 157, 160, 228, 234
Etic worldview, 163
Eurocentric teaching, 136, 144
Experiential
    activities, 125–126
    education, 7, 51, 59–60, 205, 248
    learning, 59–60, 264
    narrative, 232
Exploitation, 45, 116. *see also* Domination; Oppression

F

Fable Writing Project, 235–237
Faith, 37–39, 42
False generosity, 33
Family mapping, 164–166
Federal National and Community Service
    Act, 7
Feminine perspective, 147–148
Field experiences in teacher education,
    6–7, 210, 237–240, 263–274
Films used in service learning
    The Color of Fear, 146
    Earth and the American Dream, 149
    Grand Canyon, 145
    Thunderheart, 145
Freirean perspective of service learning,
    24, 28–42
    conceptual issues in, 30–37
    pedagogical
        approaches to, 37–39
        implications for, 40–42

G

Gender issues, 12, 76, 147–148, 158
Grassroots community
    culture, 252
    leaders, 256
    organizations, 265, 273

H

Helping
    call for revival of, 47
    as doing good, 16, 24, 25, 267
    need for service learning to go be-
        yond, 42, 55, 97, 199, 206
Heterosexism, 130, 248
Higher Education Research Institute,
    195–196

Historicity, 166
Holistic
    curriculum, 147–148, 205
    thinking, 171
Homogenous culture, 56
Homophobia, 133
Hull House, 47, 50
Human rights, 169–170
Humility, 37–39, 42

I

Immigrant assistance program (BIAP),
    169–187
    application of service learning in,
        173–178
    integration of literature with,
        180–181
    obstacles in, 184–186
    student outcomes, 182–184
Immigration and Naturalization Service
    (INS), 174
Individualism, 9, 51, 278
Information. *see* Knowledge
Information-control strategies, 65–66, 68
Injustice. *see also* Social justice
    institutionalized, 51
    perpetuation of, 33, 253
    structural, 132
    students adapting to, 54
    teachers and students addressing, 55
Insider's view, 136–137, 156, 274
Interdependence, 64, 118, 205. *see also*
        Connectedness; Relatedness
Interethnic racism, 146
Internalized oppression, 125–126, 130
Interviews with community elders, 157,
    160

J

Journal writing, 128, 139–142, 182
    as requirement for service learning,
        157, 174, 180, 198
Justice. *see* Social justice

K

Knowledge
    about multiculturalism, 234–235,
        254
    control of, 45
    as dynamic, 171–172
    prior, 71

as required for change, 248
source of, 186, 274
Knowledge-application paradigm, 228, 233

L

Leadership
among educators, 278
courageous, 255
development, 199–202
social change model of, 195–196
effective, 192–195, 199, 241
from a multicultural perspective, 191–199, 202
opportunities in service learning, 189–206
positions occupied by men, 131
social reconstructivist, 205–206
societal views of, 199–202
Learner-centered competencies, 238
Learning
active, 8
cultural contexts of, 267–270
outcomes-based, 233
passive, 60
reciprocity of, 27
responsive, 278
as a social process, 267–268
and zone of proximal development, 268
Learning circle approach, 249
Liberation, 30, 148
Literacy, 268–269
Literature
about different ethnic groups, 160
discrimination in, 108
multicultural children's, 136–144
required in "New West" curriculum, 147–148
used in BIAP, 180–181
viewed more critically, 186
Love, 37–39, 42

M

Mainstream perspective, 265–267
Marginalized groups, 55, 231, 233
Meaning, constructions of, 209–225
Mental constructs, 38–39, 41
Meta-question, course, 148
Metaprinciples, 61–62
Migrant's eye view of the world, 170, 186
Minority groups, 52–53, 55
Minority students
language skills misjudged, 268

as recipients of empowering teaching, 230–240
working together, 197
Moral
dilemmas for professors, 72, 77, 80–84
imperative for teacher educators, 75
responsibility to be familiar with service learning, 81–82, 86–87
Multicultural
affairs offices, 258
children's literature, 136–144
leaders, 156–166, 202
Multicultural education
approaches to, 4–6
based on an assets model, 265
complemented by service learning, 13–15, 256–260, 258, 263–274
conflicting definitions of, 53–54
criticisms of, 6, 13–14
examples of poor attempts at, 263–264
experiential nature of, 1–2, 15
factors contributing to, 53
integrated into teaching, 202
as political movement, 2–3, 13–15
and reform, 46, 54–57, 231
requires changes in teaching, 55
viewed as radical, 13–14
Multiculturalism
authentic understanding of, 199
CSUMBs commitment to, 116–121
tools and perspectives of, 254–255
Mutuality, 27, 34, 212

N

National Association for Multicultural Education, 14
National Community Service Trust Act, 50

National Service-Learning Conference, 96
National Society for Internships and Experiential Education, 14
National Youth Administration (NYA), 50
National Youth Leadership Council, 14, 158, 205
Needs-driven view of communities, 271
New West curriculum, 145, 147–148
Noblesse oblige, 209, 225, 253

O

Objectivism, 166
Opportunity costs, 72, 78–80, 87

Oppressed groups
  education for, 231
  history of, 144
  liberation of, 148
  strengths and resources of, 266
Oppression
  awareness of own role in, 126, 130
  blindness to one's own, 35–36
  definition of, 116
  forms of, 28
  Freirean perspective on, 28–37
  and multicultural education, 3–6, 14,
    118, 121
  perpetuation of, 24, 124–125, 128,
    133

P

Parent mentor, 211, 221–223
Parental involvement, 236–237, 269
Passive (rote) learning, 60
Paternalism, 12, 25, 27, 267, 270
Patronizing behavior, 25, 209, 223. see
    also Superiority, mentality of
PDS (Professional Development School),
    237–238
Peace Corps, 6
Pedagogical
  approaches, 37–39
  competence, 81–82
  implications, 40–42
  reasons for service learning, 171–172

  support for instructors, 128–129
Pedagogy
  constructed by Freire, 28–42, 29
  effective, 190
  service learning as, 118, 132, 157
Pedagogy of Urban and Multicultural Ac-
    tion (PUMA), 238
Pluralism, 4, 147–148, 224, 278
Political
  activism, 5, 98, 196–197
  multicultural education as, 2–3,
    15–16
  policies, 33
  resources, access to, 53–54, 272–273
Poverty
  and community size, 77–78
  institutionalized, 273
  understanding dynamics of, 11–12
Power, 41, 118, 121, 128, 194–195. see
    also Privilege
  access to, 4, 54
  balance of, 27, 33–35, 33–35, 61

communities providing source of,
    269
  dynamics, 123, 253
  issues, better understanding of, 14
  need to equalize, 39
  relations, 54, 119, 264, 270, 274
Powerlessness, 179, 182
Practicum. see Teacher education field ex-
    periences
Praxis, 5, 13, 34, 42
  definition of, 30–31
Preexisting ego formulations, 65–66
Prejudice. see also Assumptions; Bias;
    Stereotypes
  necessary conditions to reduce,
    63–68
  reinforcement of, 65–66
  service learning as tool to reduce,
    59–68
  targets of, 124
Preservice teacher, 197
  education students, 264–265
  perceptions of, 209, 223
  and placement issues, 73–74
  race issues for, 213, 221
Principles of best practice, 27, 59–60, 62,
    63, 251
Prior knowledge, 71
Privilege, 41, 118, 121, 124. see also
    Power
  access to, 4
  as basis of service relationship, 209
  definition of, 116
  in leadership positions, 193
  perpetuation of, 30
  of students and teachers, 30, 34, 36,
    127–128, 199, 201
  in United States society, 28
  of volunteers, 50
  white, 130, 146, 163, 194–195
Problem-posing, 38–39, 41–42
Professional development school (PDS),
    235, 237–238, 240
Professor, obligations of, 71–90. see also
    Teacher
  to engage in service learning, 84–87
  and principles affecting service learn-
    ing, 80–84
Project Community, 153
Public schools. see also Education;
    Schools
  minority
    student population increasing in,
      240–241
    teachers needed in, 229
  participating in social reform, 55–56

quality of service learning projects in, 93, 96–97, 98
as uninformed about multicultural education, 141

Q

Quantitative assessment tools, 182

R

Racial
discrimination, 11–12
identity, 145
minorities, 55
Racism
institutionalized, 53, 273
interethnic, 146
as social problem, 127, 133, 156, 248
student awareness of, 45, 116, 130
Reality. see also View
creating new, 36
as dynamic, 42
problematizing of, 32
views of, 31–33
Reciprocity
as best practice of service learning, 62, 251
description of, 34, 60–61
as important component of service learning, 27, 198, 212
in relationship with service recipient, 123, 125, 132
"R"eflection, 124
Reflection, 128, 148, 161, 257
as best practice of service learning, 251
in BIAP service project, 181
collaborative, 39
as component of change, 5, 30–31
as component of engagement, 61
as component of service learning, 24, 26–27, 133, 218–221
ethical, 116, 118, 120–121
importance of, in service learning, 8
in-class, 211
leading to action and change, 5
necessary component for service learning to be transformational, 199
papers, 137–138, 149
as process with positive learning outcomes, 60

required for conscientization of privileged, 36
stereotypes perpetuated without, 11
and student growth, 100, 127, 132, 198, 251
as transformative, 33, 133, 199
Relatedness, 9, 199, 277–278. see also Connectedness; Interdependence
Relationships, 277–278
as foundation for change, 248–251
fundamental to service learning, 251
important for integrating service learning and multicultural education, 256
nonhierarchical, 39
between school and community, 55–56, 62, 141
as equal partners in service learning, 119
as essential in service learning, 12, 15, 150, 158–159, 240, 249
as high in investment and trust, 249–251, 257, 260
strengthen over time, 225
Resources, access to, 53–54
Responsibility. see also Social responsibility
as best practice of service learning, 62
for others, 181
student sense of, 206

S

Schools. see also Public schools; Relationships
as microcosms of society, 41
with minority students, difficulty of preparing teachers for, 229–230
policies as barriers to success, 232
professional development (PDS), 235, 237–238, 240
as reinforcing social inequity, 46
Search Institute, 251, 261
Self-help, ideology of, 51
Self-reflection. see Reflection
Servant-leaders, 204
Service, 97–98, 121, 266–267
as a contested term, 116
descriptions of, 25–26
distinguished from charity, 25
implications of, 161
learners, 35, 64, 139

as way to effect social reform, 51–52
without learning component, 73
Service learning
   as academic requirement, 80–84
   as answer to social problems, 13,
      49–52, 77, 260–261
   as antiprejudice tool, 59–68
   benefits of, 11–12, 57, 274
   best practices of, 27, 59–60, 62, 63,
      251
   collaborative nature of, 177–178
   context of, 74–77
   definition of, 24–25, 73, 265
   effectiveness of
      as an antiprejudice tool, 59–68
      research on, 8, 47, 81, 90
   expectations of, 213, 224–225
   experiential nature of, 7, 25, 86, 121,
      212, 253
   as first exposure to cultural diversity
      and poverty, 212, 224
   as form of community-based learning,
      211, 265
   fundamental weakness of, 56–57
   funding for, 13, 109
   harm, potential to do, 62, 252, 256
      by increasing prejudice, 65–66, 68

      by perpetuating stereotypes, 209
   integrated with academic curriculum,
      24–25, 87–90, 202
   multicultural education, compared
      to, 13–14
   origins of, 6, 14
   pedagogical
      assumptions of, 48–49
      reasons for, 171–172
   pedagogy, 30, 33, 59, 160
   as requirement for professors, 84–87
   in rural communities, 77
   student resistance in, 86–87, 107,
      130
   time commitment
      long-term as ideal, 40, 98. see
         also CT
      for professors, 85–86
      for student's field placement, 100,
         137–138, 148–149, 162
      when integrated into student
         teaching, 90
Service Learning Institute, 115, 116, 128,
   129, 134, 136
Sexism, 45, 116, 130, 133, 156, 248
Simulation as educational activity,
   125–126
Site-based teacher educators (SBTEs),
   235–237

Social
   action, 76–77, 190, 199, 231
   change, 26, 46, 54–57, 190, 202
      model of leadership, 195–196
   hierarchies, 197
   inequality, 55, 118, 190, 198, 204
   inquiry model, 231
   reform, 51–52, 54, 136
Social justice, 9, 12–16, 98, 148
   curriculum, 135–136, 149
   historical contributors to, 147
   and multicultural education, 3–6,
      150, 272–273
Social reconstructionist multicultural ed-
      ucation, 4–6, 16, 118, 190
   connected with service learning and
      leadership, 195–199,
      202–206
Social responsibility, 190, 196, 202. see
      also Responsibility
   and service learning students, 9, 49,
      118, 121
Society for Field Experience Education,
   14
Solution models, 249
Southern Regional Education Board, 6
Stakeholders, 35, 39, 40, 42, 56–57, 260
Status quo
   going beyond the, 24, 233
   perpetuation of, 30, 33, 52
   teacher's questioning of, 98
Stereotypes. see also Assumptions; Bias;
      Prejudice
   awareness of, 97, 116, 123, 130, 264
   characteristic of Eurocentric teach-
      ing, 136
   decrease in, through BIAP experience,
      186
   deficiency perspective supported by,
      266
   reinforcement of, 12, 65–66, 100,
      209
Strategic intentionality, 254–255
Student
   as agent of change, 190, 198
   attitudes toward social problems, 48
   coteachers, 128–129
   cultural experience incorporated into
      curriculum, 233
   empowerment, 145, 198, 232
   minority population, growing, 240
   preparation
      to be proactive citizens, 171,
         182–184, 186, 196
      for service learning, 132
   resistance, 86–87, 107, 130

as responsive community participant, 121
as servant-leader, 204
as social advocate, 200
teachers, 198, 237–238
teaching, 71, 87–90, 198, 237–240
Subordinate culture, 267, 274
Superiority, mentality of, 3–4, 12, 209, 225, 252

T

Target groups, 127, 133
Teach for America, 74–76
Teacher. see also Professor
    as colearner with students, 39
    familiarity with students' cultural
        backgrounds, 228, 267, 274

    successful, 267–268, 270
Teacher education, 71–78, 224–225, 227–241
    field experiences, 6–7, 210, 237–240, 263–274
Teaching
    Eurocentric, 136
    minority students, 229–230
    moral dimensions of, 80–84
    need for changes in, 202–205
    philosophy, 230–233, 237
    principles that impact service learning, 80–84
    recruitment of, 229–230, 237–238
    as a service profession, 74
    strategies, 7, 190, 202
Testimonio, 232
Totalitarian ego theory, 65–66, 68
Transformation
    approach, 231
    of experience into learning, 133
    from object to subject, 163–164
    in service learning, 39, 146, 150, 164

    of society, 36, 132
Transformational leadership, 193, 199

U

Underrepresented groups
    insider's view of, 136–137
    lack of literature about, 142

need to remove obstacles of, 55
understanding perspective of, 144–146
Unitary view of society, 4, 11
United Nations Declaration on Human Rights, 169
University educator (UE), 235–237
University of Michigan, service learning at, 153, 156–166
University Service Advocate (USA), 138, 140

V

View
    activist, 217–218
    capacity-focused, 271
    deficit, 214–215, 224, 225
    insider's, 136–137, 156, 274
    mainstream, 266
    migrant's, 170, 186
    multicultural, 266
    needs-driven, 271
    pragmatic, 215–216, 224
    self-exploratory, 216–217
    of student and role as teacher, 270–271
    supremacy, 225
    unitary, 4, 11
Vista programs, 6
Vocational education, 53. see also Education
Volunteerism, 7, 29, 47–48, 50–52, 80, 130

W

Wingspread Declaration, 196
Wingspread principles (ASLER), 27, 60, 62

Y

Youth Conservation Corps, 6
Youth Fellows Project, 205

Z

Zone of proximal development, 268

About the Contributors

Marilynne Boyle-Baise is an assistant professor in the department of Curriculum and Instruction at Indiana University-Bloomington. She teaches and writes about multicultural education, social studies, and curriculum theory.

Kathleen Densmore is an associate professor in the College of Education at San José State University in California. Her teaching and research address issues of multicultural education, school–community relations, and the relationship between educational and social change. She is currently working to establish community learning centers in three urban public schools. She is co-author of *Just Schooling: Teachers' Cultural Practices*.

Patricia Efiom is the mother of four children, ages 3 to 17. All are students in the Bloomington, Indiana school district. Patricia oversees student life issues in an undergraduate residence center. Originally from New York, Patricia and Nigerian-born husband, Patrick Efiom, have lived in Bloomington for 10 years.

Joseph A. Erickson is an associate professor in the education department at Augsburg College in Minneapolis, Minnesota. Since 1991, he has studied and promoted service-learning in K through 12 and postsecondary schools, focusing on various ways to integrate service-learning into teacher education programs. He is co-editor (with Jeffrey B. Anderson) of the monograph, *Learning With the Community: Concepts and Models for Service-Learning in Teacher Education*, published in 1997 by the American Association for Higher Education.

Joe Galura is the director of Project Community, an innovative partnership between the School of Education, the Department of Sociology, and the Division of Student Affairs at the University of Michigan. Project Community is one of the nation's oldest and largest service-learning courses, placing nearly 500 students with criminal justice, education, health, and social change agencies each academic year. Joe founded the OCSL Press, which publishes *The Michigan Journal of Community Service Learning*. He edited the three-volume Praxis series with Jeff Howard and is currently working on Praxis 2000.

Irma Guadarrama is an associate professor at the University of Houston specializing in teacher education, bilingual and second language education, social themes in literacy and writing, and program development. A 30-year veteran in education, her roles include teaching in elementary education as a Teacher Corps intern and bilingual educator, consulting and training, developing courses and programs at the university level including the Yucatán/UH Exchange Project, and is currently a coordinator in the field-based teacher education program for preservice and inservice teachers. Her current research interests include service-learning, teacher research and development, literacy and writing in bilingual education, improving educational programs for second-language learners, and developing effective partnerships between universities and schools.

Robert E. Koulish (PhD, University of Wisconsin, Madison) is director of the Bentley Service Learning Center, and assistant professor of government. He teaches immigration politics, public policy, and American government, and integrates service-learning and dialogic modes of teaching and learning into each course. Robert has conducted research and published several articles on such topics as human rights on the U.S./Mexico Border, immigration, citizenship, and service-learning.

Mark N. Langseth is executive director of Minnesota Campus Compact, a coalition of 45 college and university presidents and hundreds of community and campus leaders committed to expanding higher education's role in community and public service statewide. Mark is also a Group XVI Kellogg Fellow, through which he is pursuing personal/professional development in grass-roots organizing, community and economic development, and cultural competence.

Herbert L. Martin is assistant professor of Cross-Cultural Competency at California State University at Monterey Bay. His specialty is world mythologies and how to work with them in elementary school. He has won teaching awards in teaching excellence at Louisiana State University in Baton Rouge as well as at CSU, Sacramento.

Susan E. O'Connor is an assistant professor of education at Augsburg College in Minneapolis, Minnesota. Her main area of study is in special education and community support for people with disabilities and broader issues of diversity and multicultural education. She has worked to incorporate service-learning in her courses. She has also co-authored a chapter in Erickson and Anderson's *Learning With the Community: Concepts and Models for Service-Learning in Teacher Education.*

Carolyn R. O'Grady is associate professor of education at Gustavus Adolphus College in Minnesota, and a frequent workshop facilitator for schools and small organizations on issues of diversity, including race, gender, and sexual orientation. Her research interests include education as social change, spirituality in education, and the intersection of multicultural education and service learning. She has an Ed.D from the Division of Cultural Diversity & Curriculum Reform at the University of Massachusetts/Amherst.

Seth S. Pollack received his PhD in international development education from Stanford University. As an organizational sociologist, he has conducted research and written about the history of higher education's "service" mission and the contemporary service learning field. He is currently director of the Service Learning Institute at CSU Monterey Bay, where he teaches courses and leads campuswide faculty development efforts in service learning. In the community he works with local neighborhood groups in developing grass-roots neighborhood improvement efforts.

Stella Raudenbush is the director of the Michigan K–12 Service-Learning Center and the Great Lakes regional partner for the National Service-Learning initiative. She oversees the Center, whose mission is to promote excellent education for all children through service-learning methodology in K–12 schools and community settings. Stella also teaches courses at the University of Michigan School of Education on service-learning, schools, curriculum, and communities, while collaborating with other faculty in the development of service-learning approaches in teacher preparation courses.

Kathleen Rice   received her PhD in college student personnel from the University of Maryland. Kathleen teaches the course, Introduction to Service in Multicultural Communities, develops training materials, and provides ongoing faculty development for instructors of all sections of the course. She is involved in the local community by reading weekly to a first-grade class, serving as a bilingual literacy tutor, and assisting a family advocate at Alisal Community Healthy Start in Salinas, California.

Cynthia Rosenberger is a lecturer in the early childhood education and development program in the Teacher Education and Curriculum Studies department at the School of Education, University of Massachusetts, Amherst. She teaches courses in contemporary issues, social studies, service learning, and integrated curriculum methods. In 1997–1998 she received a University Service Learning Fellowship to integrate service learning into a teacher education course.

Verna Cornelia Simmons began her career as a preschool teacher in Minneapolis, Minnesota and is currently the director of First Year Experience and Leadership Programs and a lecturer and researcher at the University of Minnesota, Twin Cities. She works with a number of organizations and schools to improve the quality of education for children of color, particularly urban African Americans, and is a consultant for the National Youth Leadership Council and the W. K. Kellogg Foundation. She received her PhD in Education Policy and Administration from the University of Minnesota.

Christine E. Sleeter is a professor in the Center for Collaborative Education and Professional Studies at California State University, Monterey Bay, where she coordinates the Master of Arts in Education program. Previously, she was a professor of teacher education at the University of Wisconsin-Parkside. She consults nationally in multicultural education and multicultural teacher education. Dr. Sleeter has received several awards for her work including the National Association for Multicultural Education Research Award, the AERA Committee on the Role and Status of Minorities in Education Distinguished Scholar Award, and the University of Wisconsin-Parkside Research Award. She has published numerous books and articles in multicultural education; her most recent books include *Multicultural Education as Social Activism*, (SUNY Press), *Keepers of the American Dream* (Falmer Press), *Developing Multicultural Teacher Education Curricula*, with Joseph Larkin (SUNY Press), *Multicultural Education, Critical Pedagogy, and the Politics of Difference*, with Peter McLaren (SUNY Press), and *Making Choices for Multicultural Education*, with Carl A. Grant (Merrill). In addition, she edits the book series entitled *The Social Context of Education* for SUNY Press.

Kip Téllez is associate professor in the College of Education at the University of Houston where he serves as the coordinator of the Bilingual/English-as-a-Second Language program area. His research interests include teacher education, language learning schools, the educational experiences of children of color, and program evaluation.

Rahima C. Wade is associate professor of elementary social studies at the University of Iowa. She is the author of numerous publications on community service-learning and is project director of the National Service-Learning in Teacher Education Partnership.

Wokie Roberts-Weah is vice president for Programs for the National Youth Leadership Council (NYLC), coordinating the development and administration of service learning and youth leadership programs in school districts across the United States. Before joining NYLC in 1991, she served as principal of the B. W. Harris School in Monrovia, Liberia, West Africa. She conducts professional development seminars and lectures on the integration of service-learning and multicultural education. Weah holds a Bachelor's Degree in English and secondary education and a Master's of Science in education administration and supervision.

Terri Wheeler is a part-time instructor at California State University at Monterey Bay. Her teaching and research interests focus on multicultural children's literature, service learning, American Indian studies, Celtic studies, and multicultural education. She holds a Master's of Arts in education.

Please remember that this is a library book,
and that it belongs only temporarily to each
person who uses it. Be considerate. Do
not write in this, or any, library book.